DON'T WORRY
GOD
I got this...
until I didn't

DON'T WORRY GOD I got this...

until I didn't

Conversations in the dark

CATHERINE RAMSHAW

For information about this title contact the publisher:

Rooftop Messages
CatherineRamshaw.com
Rooftopmessages@gmail.com

Library of Congress Control Number: 2024903295

ISBNs:
979-8-9889558-2-5 (hardcover)
979-8-9889558-0-1 (softcover)
979-8-9889558-1-8 (eBook)

Printed in the United States of America

Cover and Interior design: 1106 Design

Dedication

*To God be the Glory. Thank You Heavenly Father
for faithfully whispering in my ear, reassuring me
that You are always right here with me.*

And . . .

*To my husband, Richard, without whose love and support
these pages would not be bound together, and to my
kids, thank you for allowing me to share our story.*

Acknowledgment

*Thank you to all those who spurred me on to write this book.
You will never know how important your words were
in this process. Thank you for the shot of courage!*

"What comes into our minds when we think about God is the most important thing about us."
—A.W. Tozer

Contents

The Lessons

The Story

The Lessons

The Story

The Lessons

The Story

2017

The Lessons

The Story

2018

The Lessons

The Big Lessons

Prologue

Twisted metal, torched, and flipped upside-down, no longer motoring down the road. Flashing lights surround the rubble. We lean forward in our seats for a closer look, cricking our necks backward as the flashing lights fade. A wreck on the side of the road is a magnetic object, pulling our curious eyes to it. It's the wreck that captures our attention but only for moment. Someone's phone beeps, or we see a "Food and Gas Next Exit" sign, and the tragedy disappears from our minds as quickly as it had appeared.

We were that wreck on the side of the road.

No—we had not been involved in an *actual* car crash. It was the kind of tragedy that catches everyone's attention and makes you sick to your stomach. We heard words we never wanted to hear. Our life crashed, twisted into a scene of heartbreak and disbelief, taking the breath from our lungs and strength from our knees.

Life had been torn from our grasp, flung into a far-off place, out of reach and out of sight. Life skidded to a halt.

This book shares the conversations I had with God in the dark and what I learned about who God is, surviving my walk through the valley of the shadow of death and a desert that seemed to have no end. I share the doubts most don't want to admit and the questions you ask God only when you are walking in a darkness you never imagined possible. *"Why did you let this happen?" "What did I do wrong?" "Are you really good all the time?"*

I hope that sharing the journey I never thought God would allow and the lessons I learned along the way will help others survive their own overwhelming journey and honestly proclaim that God is good and worthy of praise, even when life is nothing like you imagined it was going to be like.

> *"What I tell you in the dark, speak in the daylight;*
> *what is whispered in your ear, proclaim from the rooftops."*
> —MATTHEW 10:27

Are My Truths True?

"Even when it seems that things are not going my way,
I know that they are going Your way and that,
in the end, Your way is the best for me."
—Henri J. M. Nouwen

"The act of obedience is trusting God."
—Unknown

S*o, it was the middle of the night*, and I was fighting with my brain to believe what I had said I believed my whole life—that "God's plan is better than mine. He loves me more than I can fathom. I trust in Him." The truths I have built my entire life on, I am now fighting to reconcile as true.

When we discovered that Ryan had a mass on his spine, multiple people sent me the song "Just Be Held" by Casting Crowns. Many nights I have played it over and over until sleep came, filling my mind with the words, willing myself to believe that God was still on the throne and to just allow Him to hold me.

He's on the throne. I believe *that*. I know where Jesus is. Even now that we know Ryan has Ewing's Sarcoma, and we are getting a vision of how much life is changing for him and the suffering that lies ahead for him, I must trust Him. Tonight, I searched through the scriptures, looking for words that would bring me peace. I came upon this note I had written in my Bible: "The act of obedience was *trusting God*, not the *walking around the wall*."

> *The Lord said, "See, I have delivered Jericho into your*
> *hands . . . On the seventh time around, Joshua commanded*
> *the army, 'Shout for the Lord has given you the city!'"*
> —JOSH CHAPTER 6

When the Israelites were instructed to march around Jericho seven times, it wasn't "the walking" that God wanted from them; it was the act of *trusting*. I imagine there were more than a few women, just like me, thinking *This doesn't make sense*, questioning the plan of the march. "How can walking around the wall surrounding Jericho do anything?" I can hear the doubt in my own head.

The act of obedience is trusting God, even when it appears your world is falling apart, and nothing makes sense. I'm putting this in writing as an act of obedience. I will trust you, Lord.

> *"Trust is not a passive state of mind. It is a vigorous act of the soul*
> *whereby we choose to lay hold on the promises of God and cling to*
> *them despite the adversity that at times seeks to overwhelm us."*
> —JERRY BRIDGES—*Trusting God*

Equilibrium

December 5, 2015, was a Saturday; I woke thinking about my grocery list and all I had to do that day, looking forward to a family dinner with our three sons. "Be still and know that I am God" was not the first thing on my mind. It wasn't anywhere on my list. What a difference a day makes. On December 5, it was groceries. On December 6, I awoke confused, as my mind tried to catch up with my racing heart and make sense of the hospital bed I had slept in.

It's not like life had been easy before the words "Mass on your spine" were spoken to Ryan. Just five weeks before, we'd admitted our eleven-year-old daughter to a program for children with complex trauma and Reactive Attachment Disorder. At age three, she had been left at our home and subsequently became our adopted daughter. How could a little strawberry-blond girl turn our peaceful home into her war zone, complete with grenades erupting daily from the depths of her pain? Before arriving at our house, she had spent her first three years surviving abuse, neglect, and the kind of trauma that taught her to battle with guerrilla warfare-like skills. It had been eight years of struggle trying to help a wounded child heal—with little success.

Our adopted daughter suffered from Reactive Attachment Disorder, RAD, a name that does not begin to explain the complexity of the condition and all the behaviors that come with it. To a child who lives in a constant state of fight, flight, or freeze, living in a safe and loving family, in her mind, is like living behind enemy lines. A nurturing mother is the most dangerous enemy of all. She is afraid, not because I am the mother to be feared, but because, in her mind, I am all the mothers who had abused, neglected, or abandoned her. In her mind, I am *them*. I am not safe. I am to be feared. She must fight for her life!

After eight years of grueling attempts, we could look back and say that, while we did all we could, we were not gaining enough ground with Caelen, and we needed to try a full-time, professional treatment program. In October 2015, God performed a miracle and provided a way for us to get her treatment at the best place we could find for kids who share the same issues as Caelen. We had learned that it didn't matter if you were abused and neglected in Russia or Oklahoma—the symptoms were the same; they were complex and hard to heal. She was admitted to an out-of-state Attachment Therapy program, where she would be cared for and treated for the next four to six months. In truth, we winced as we drove away, wondering if they would call us in a few weeks and tell us, "This is all your fault. *She's* fine. *You* are the ones who need help." When you try to help a child and seemingly make little progress, you wonder if you are the problem. Maybe it's you who needs fixing.

Hard times make you lose your perspective; it's hard to know what's true anymore, especially when those hard times isolate you from the life you knew and the people you love. We operated in the dark for the first couple of years, with very little information on her history. We knew that, at the age of three, she came to us—now her fifth family—and that was about it. After much investigative work, we discovered she had been severely neglected for the first three years of her life. She had been left in her car seat unattended or cared for, for the first year of her life. By the age of one, she did not sit up on her own, crawl, or walk, and she no longer wanted to be touched by another human. She no longer cried when she was hurting. Her behaviors indicated she had spent more time with dogs than humans.

Even with some history and understanding that she had endured abuse, neglect, multiple abandonments, poverty, and even homelessness, I still questioned myself and wondered what I could have done better. Surely, there was something we could have done. Children couldn't be that broken by age three—could they?

Within a few weeks after we left her with the treatment professionals, we received an update from the team telling us that she had significant mental illness. She was one of the most difficult RAD children they had ever treated. They concluded that she was a child who required so much attention and effort that a group home was all they could recommend. One family could not raise her alone.

Later, it was determined that she had been exposed to alcohol *in utero* and, most likely, had been shaken as a baby or thrown. There was evidence of damage to the frontal lobe, which operates executive functioning, language, cause-and-effect thinking, and impulse control. Years later, intellectual disabilities were added to her diagnosis, something no professional had mentioned until her maturation revealed that her peers were progressing, and she was not.

Caelen's complex diagnosis proved to be impossible to decipher on a daily basis. Determining if it was the lower intellect or the trauma driving the behavioral outbursts was like trying to untangle a necklace chain knotted into a ball. Such attempts instilled a particular form of madness and exhaustion in me. For years, I blamed myself for not being able to "fix" her, "love" her better. I felt the judgment of that failure from some of my closest relationships; this was the most heartbreaking of all.

"When you finally learn that a person's behavior has more to do with their own internal struggle than you, you learn grace." (Allison Aars)

Wow! That's a difficult lesson.

Before we left her at the treatment program, we sat at a large conference table with the staff that would be helping Caelen. Of all the words said that day, these were the ones that stuck: "Go home and find your equilibrium."

Equilibrium? The word echoed in my mind. I didn't know what that was anymore. I wasn't one to carelessly lose things, but apparently, our "equilibrium" was AWOL, and we were sent to go find it. The immediate weeks after leaving Caelen set me on a quest for something I wasn't sure I would recognize upon discovering it. I didn't know where to start.

It had been about five weeks since we'd been given the assignment of finding our "equilibrium." For me, assignments come with a charge to immediately devise a plan of action to avoid failure. I'm not what you would call someone who can put things on a shelf to think about them later, yet this quest for equilibrium was a more significant challenge than I had expected.

The immediate weeks after leaving Caelen set me on a quest for something I wasn't sure I would recognize upon discovering it.

I don't remember the day I lost it. Where *did* I put that equilibrium? Weeks had passed, a blur of fatigue and confusion. My focus had been so singular for so many years, it took me a while to get my bearings.

What did I do before Caelen? Who was I before Caelen? Nothing was the same. I was not the same.

A goal of this enormity requires a multistep plan. Step One: Food! The boys love good food. My game plan on December 5th: Make a nice dinner for the boys, and enjoy a peaceful family night together. I couldn't wait. I was so excited! I was on my way to "find our equilibrium."

December 5, 2015

"Go find your equilibrium." The assignment was stuck on "Repeat" in my mind, like a needle on a scratched record album. As we drove Ryan to the ER—he was experiencing unbearable pain—it repeated, "Go find your equilibrium." "Go find your equilibrium!" It was early Saturday morning, and my plan was already unraveling. I wasn't sure where I had misplaced my equilibrium, but I knew it wasn't in the ER.

"God, I'm supposed to be grocery shopping. I'm making dinner tonight, God. I am supposed to find my equilibrium, God. Can you hear me, God?" I realize my words sound ridiculous now. Who worries about dinner plans on the way to the ER? But you must understand: You don't take your twenty-year-old son, who is in college and the Air Force, to the ER and think, "We won't be coming home tonight." At this point in the story, the ER was an unforeseen delay, a detour. I was expecting pain meds and continued physical therapy; the doctors had determined, months earlier, that he was suffering from a bulging disk.

I wasn't sure where I had misplaced my equilibrium, but I knew it wasn't in the ER.

We sat for hours behind the cloth curtain of the examining room. My husband, Richard, and our oldest son, Ryan, watched football as I stewed and watched the clock tick away at my plans. Football was doing nothing to distract me from my frustration; then they finally grew tired of the sports channel, and we watched the last half of the movie *Erin Brockovich* as we waited for the MRI results. In the middle of all that, I secretly wondered if my life would ever impact people like Erin Brockovich's life had. She had helped people, and here I was, unable to finish my grocery list and find my equilibrium.

All the thoughts swarming in my mind that day would instantly disappear, never to return. My plan, my quest for equilibrium, would all be gone with the doctor's words, "You have a mass on your spine. We don't know what it is. You will be very sick for a very long time. We are referring you to a neurosurgeon, and you will be admitted today." The words hung in the air as I scanned the exam room for clues.

Wait! What? I couldn't have heard the white coat correctly. *What did he say?* And then I watched my son curl into a ball, drawing his legs to his chest, the same position he'd held as I carried him in my belly twenty years ago. It was that motion, that fetal position, that confirmed that I had heard the doctor correctly.

Our life exploded into pieces. My plan and our quest for equilibrium vanished, and our lives would never be the same.

Tennis Ball

A*fter hours of sitting in the ER*, contemplating my failure to execute step one of our quest for equilibrium—a peaceful family dinner—there was no quest at all. In my mind, I had prepared for the worst-case scenario. We can stop off at the pharmacy for pain meds and buy a couple of pizzas on the way home, ditching the grocery store and homemade dinner entirely. The distance between *my healthy son coming to the ER because of back pain* to *my son has a tumor and will be very sick for a very long time* was too far to travel in an afternoon; my brain could not make that leap.

The twenty-year-old son we drove here was healthy. We came here for back pain! In a fog, I walked behind the rattling metal bed through the white-basement tunnels of the hospital. I remember them wheeling the bed into the oversized elevator for patients, sick people.

Catapulted forward in time, now gathered around another conference table, much like the one we'd sat at for Caelen just five weeks earlier. It was now nighttime; friends, some we hadn't seen in years but who were the friends you call in a crisis, all gathered around the table for what looked like a medical briefing. I didn't sit. Attention was focused on the front of the room, where a good friend and doctor pointed to a plastic molding of the human spine. His familiar, quiet, and calm voice spoke. The only words I remembered were "a tumor the size of a tennis ball" as he pointed to the location on the plastic spine.

Tennis ball. I'm sure I must have made an audible gasp. Now, this mass that was going to make Ryan very sick had a size. Now I could see this nameless invader. I paced around the perimeter of the chairs, like the tiger trapped at the zoo, nervously pacing back and forth beside the bars that cage him. Tigers know they don't belong behind bars, and so did I. There was no escaping this cage.

"Take these. Drink this." I woke the following morning in crisp white sheets that were not mine. I was not in my bed. As I blinked, it all came back. It had not been a dream.

The Finnish Fling

Last night, a friend asked me how I was holding on. The Finnish Fling, which I had not thought of in 40 years, came to mind. Strange what the brain remembers. Worlds of Fun was a local amusement park; one summer, the "Finnish Fling" was all the buzz as the new thrill. You walk into a giant barrel and wait to be "finished" off—or at least that's how I saw it. As the riders stand around the perimeter, the barrel begins to spin fast enough that, when the floor drops out, it's just the centrifugal force holding you. I never rode that ride. I try to avoid green as a skin color.

Four days ago, our world had started spinning so fast that the bottom dropped out, and yet, at the same time, I find myself being held by a force so strong, I cannot fall. On this ride, full of friends and family coming from every corner of life to love and comfort us, God shows up with centrifugal force. "Just Be Held" by Casting Crowns eloquently says it all. Life felt like the "Finnish Fling"—my world was spinning, yet I knew that I was being held. It's a thrilling ride God allows, even if it's not one we want. Somehow in the middle of all this spinning, God was holding us tight.

... God shows up with centrifugal force.

Hard to Swallow

But he said to me, "My grace is sufficient for you, for my power is made perfect in weakness." Therefore, I will boast gladly about my weaknesses so that Christ's power may rest on me. That is why, for Christ's sake, I delight in weaknesses, in insults, in hardships, in persecutions, in difficulties. For when I am weak, then I am strong."
— 2 COR 12:9-10

Let's be honest; that word "delight" goes down crooked, like trying to swallow a stick sideways. We spent a week in the hospital doing tests, biopsies, and scans. Each day presented another possibility of what this mass was—names I couldn't pronounce. The days passed with good memories and a flood of friendships all at once, mixed in with disbelief and

I paced around the perimeter of the chairs, like the tiger trapped at the zoo, nervously pacing back and forth beside the bars that cage him.

overwhelming sadness. It was a week of *This Is Your Life, Ryan Ramshaw.*

The volunteer greeter at the hospital entrance asked me one day, "Are you Ryan's mom?"

"Yes," I answered.

"I have never seen so many visitors for one person in all my time volunteering. I told my friend, 'It must be someone very special and important, like a general or someone, because of all the people in uniform coming.'"

As I'm writing this, I cry as I recall this moment.

The greeter added, "I pray for everyone in the hospital, but I pray especially hard for Ryan." And with that, I stepped onto the elevator.

Haven't I commanded you? Be strong and courageous.
Don't be afraid. Don't be dismayed, for the LORD
your God is with you wherever you go.
—JOSH 1:9

"God has got this all figured out!"
— Ryan Ramshaw, 12-8-15

He Shelters Our Eyes

They *released Ryan from the hospital* a week after his admission. His biopsy had been sent to a national lab because the cells were not indicating any of the common cancers. Only a week had passed, and life was unrecognizable. On our way home, we stopped at the pharmacy and received a call from Ryan's oncologist. It is cancer, and it's called Ewing's Sarcoma. Now the mass had a name. On Monday, our journey of treatment would begin.

Early on, our ignorance of the cancer world sheltered us from the cruel realities we would face. We would later learn that the treatment would be much longer than we ever imagined, and that Ryan would miss two full semesters of college. Had the length of the journey been revealed immediately, I'm not sure we could have survived those early days.

> *"The shepherd always walked ahead of his sheep.*
> *He was always out in front. Any attack upon the sheep had*
> *to take him into account first. Now God is out front. He is*
> *in our tomorrows, and it is tomorrow that fills people with*
> *fear. Yet God is already there. All the tomorrows of our life*
> *have to pass through Him before they can get to us."*
> — F.B. MEYER, *Streams in the Desert*

Miraculous

> *He has shown you, O man, what is good. And what*
> *does the Lord require of you? To act justly and to love*
> *mercy and to walk humbly with your God.*
> — MIC 6:8

Let me provide some context for those who have never stepped foot into the cancer world—just as we hadn't. This is not a cancer book, but understanding that the rare and aggressive cancer called Ewing's Sarcoma is a deadly pediatric cancer provides perspective to our story.

A *sarcoma* is a solid cancer mass. Ewing's Sarcoma is very rare, with 200 cases in the U.S. each year. The U.S. sees about 255,000 breast-cancer diagnoses per year. Oncology doctors can go their entire careers without seeing a Ewing's Sarcoma patient.

A sarcoma the size of a tennis ball would typically indicate that the patient would be full of cancer that had metastasized throughout the body. Cancer metastasizing to other locations in the body drops the survival rates significantly. Ryan's PET scan showed no cancer anywhere else. Miraculous!

Sing the praises of the Lord, you His faithful
people; praise His holy name.
— Ps 30:4

This Isn't Nordstrom!

God's *attention to detail,* in even our most minor needs, amazes me. Today, we traveled at warp speed. We walked into the cancer-center lobby two days after being released from the hospital. Through double electric doors that belong in a "Big Box" retail store, there I was with my six-foot-tall, grown son. My "mom" brain flashed back to our trips to the doctor's office with Ryan as a baby for checkups, when my biggest worry was the shots the nurses would put into his little fat thighs. Nothing about this felt like we were at the pediatrician's. His hands were no longer small. His fingers no longer wrapped around mine. Nothing about this experience made sense. As I looked around, I saw the lobby was full of gray-skinned people with no hair. *We do not belong here!* reverberated through me. As we stood in line for the receptionist, I positioned myself where Ryan could not see my face. I couldn't let him see me cry. In the corner of the vaulted waiting area was a large grand piano, being played by a sweet soul donating her time, but I wanted to scream, *"This is not Nordstrom! Stop playing that music!"*

I texted a handful of friends for support and prayer. *We don't belong here!* Here we were, his first appointment, and I was breaking down. The music pelted my head with every note. I wanted to take Ryan by the hand, as I had so many times before, and lead him away, announcing to the waiting-room onlookers, "We've come to the wrong place. Excuse us, but we're leaving now." But it was like we were already on a roller-coaster ride. We couldn't get off; the straps were over our shoulders, the buckles were secured, and the bar was across our laps. I wanted to scream, *"We aren't supposed to be on this ride!"*

Once checked in and shuttled to see the adult oncologist he had in the hospital, we were shuttled into another room, to meet a pediatric oncologist. In a small room off the "Nordstrom" lobby, we met Dr. T. She was Dr. T because no one could pronounce her last name. You couldn't ignore her thick accent and commanding presence. Her movements were large and abrupt. There was nothing subtle about her.

Sometimes dirt-movers are what you need, especially when moving a lot of dirt at once.

One doctor, a fellow co-worker, later described her as ". . . a bulldozer. . . ." I don't think he meant that endearingly. I like bulldozers. Sometimes dirt-movers are what you need, especially when moving a lot of dirt at once. A shovel doesn't work when you need a bulldozer. Something in the pit of my stomach told me we did.

We had barely sat down before she was up again and opened the door to the lobby. Looking back at us, she firmly proclaimed, "I'm going to tell them to stop playing that obnoxious music!"

I couldn't believe it—*she hated the music more than I did!* It didn't fit. It wasn't helping. Yes, I like *bulldozers.*

As we sat across from Dr. T, she spared no words about the seriousness of Ryan's cancer, the treatment that would be required, and the fact that we had to start immediately. I could tell that Ryan and Richard were a bit taken aback by her demeanor, but when Dr. T stopped the music, it was like God said, *I know exactly where you are, and I know you want off this ride. I'm right here; you are not alone.*

At 10:30 that night, I received a text from my sister-in-law, who had been on my "emergency text group" earlier that day. Her text read, "I prayed that the music would stop." I gasped as I thought, *He is just showing off. He is taking both my tiny and giant requests.* I am begging that He heals Ryan miraculously, so miraculously, that it is evident that He was there all the time. To God be the glory.

> *My flesh and my heart may fail, but God is the strength of my heart and my portion forever.*
> — Ps 73:26

I Can't Feel Your Peace

Today, *the house was quiet;* I was alone for the first time in two weeks. Ryan felt well enough to go to the KU basketball game, and we were happy to see him do something that resembled normal. I attempted to catch up on the news I had recorded, but my mind could not focus. I would have to replay the stories repeatedly to get my brain to collect the details. About the time I had given up, I received a call that Ryan was in pain and could not stay at the KU game.

As I prepared to rush out of the house, with the crook of my arm, I scooped the multiple medications off the counter and into a grocery sack. My brain struggled to believe that all of these were Ryan's. *This doesn't make sense! How can Ryan be this sick?*

Thankfully, the medications helped, and we got him home and comfortable for the rest of the day. Tonight, as we all watched *The Office* on Netflix, Ryan would laugh out loud. All the boys laughed. Laughter—I wasn't sure we would ever laugh again. But there it was, and I savored that sound I had taken for granted.

As I sat in my chair watching with the boys, my soul was not at rest; my heart was racing. The feeling that *This is not how it should be* pulsated through my body with each heartbeat. The boys went to bed, and I attempted to watch a beautiful music video a friend had sent, "It Is Well with My Soul." I couldn't finish the song. *My soul wasn't well.* I was overcome with sadness and grief, begging God to change this reality for Ryan, for me. As I wept, I cried out to God, *Please stop this. Please don't make Ryan go through this pain!* I read Psalm 61:1-3:

> *Hear my cry, O God;*
> *listen to my prayer*
> *From the ends of the earth I call to you*
> *I call as my heart grows faint;*
> *lead me to the rock*
> *that is higher than I.*
> *For you have been my refuge,*
> *a strong tower against the foe.*

I wanted God to know my heart was faint. I couldn't take much more. Alone in the dark, I got down on my hands and knees. Face down, I rocked myself, crying out to Him, *"I can't feel your peace. I can't feel your peace."* My mind was saying, *"You promised me peace; where is it?"* And in an instant, the song "Step by Step," by Michael W. Smith, entered my head.

My voice quavered with each repeat. The peace He promised came when I sang His praises. I speak these words out loud because the enemy doesn't want us to share how painful life is and that we sometimes need to cry out and beg for peace. Writing this out helps me. Let this be a witness to who God is.

"There is power in worship and praise. It is like a weapon
against the greatest sorrow, and it is at the same time an act
of submission that you will praise Him even in the storm."
— CHARLES SPURGEON

When you pass through the waters,
I will be with you.
and when you pass through the rivers,
they will not sweep over you.
When you walk through the fire,
you will not be burned;
the flames will not set you ablaze.
— Is 43:2

Ferrari Doctor

Early into Ryan's diagnosis, we were on a crash course for everything—cancer, navigating extended hospital stays, insurance, and treatments. One of the more helpful pieces of advice was when a friend of ours, a physician—not one on Ryan's treatment team, but one who knew the seriousness of Ewing's Sarcoma—explained, "Ryan needs a Ferrari doctor. I am a Toyota doctor, a really good Toyota Doctor, but not a Ferrari Doctor." These words and this explanation were so helpful. Toyota Doctors aren't bad doctors; sometimes they are what you need. Ryan needed a Ferrari Doctor, which played a big part in our decision to seek treatment at MD Anderson Cancer Hospital in Houston, Texas.

Hurricane

I*t was December 21*, and I was in our bank lobby, when the Houston area code popped up on my phone. My heart raced as I answered. A very matter-of-fact voice began to tell me about our first appointment at MD Anderson on December 23rd. I dug for paper and a pen. I could barely breathe as I stood in the bank lobby, scribbling down directions from multiple doctors' offices on scrap paper from the bottom of my bag. How could something so important be scribbled onto a throwaway piece of paper? *Breathe. Breathe.* "You must be here Wednesday morning; prepare to stay three weeks for tests and treatment, and bring the biopsy slide." *Click.*

My entire mother-being went into overdrive; there was so much to do before we left—finding housing, obtaining the only biopsy slide from our local hospital to be hand carried to MDA, etc. In the middle of all of this would be Christmas, packing for our family, a twelve-hour drive that would need to start tomorrow to be there on the 23rd.

There was so much I didn't know about cancer. There is only one biopsy slide, because you don't want to cut into a cancer tumor, as cuts open it up to spreading cancer cells into the body. So, there is only one slide, with one sliver of Ryan's tumor, and it is the key to everything. MD Anderson wouldn't do anything until they confirm the type of cancer themselves.

Later that day, as I walked to my car from the same hospital where I delivered Ryan, my arms now wrapped around the padded envelope that held Ryan's biopsy slide, holding it to my chest like a newborn baby. Housing offers were pouring in; people, strangers, friends of a friend of a friend calling to offer a place to stay in Houston. There seemed to be no end in the abundance of people reaching out to provide help. *Breathe. Breathe.*

On top of the parking garage, the wind pushing against me, these words

There seemed to be no end in the abundance of people reaching out to provide help.

played in my mind, like a personal message from God. It's amazing how the words you listen to, sometimes for years, and even sing along with in the car, not fully grasping the meaning, until a moment in time arrives, and the picture painted by the artist that you once couldn't see is now reflected in your life. David Crowder sings a song called "How He Loves," and he describes God's love as being as big as a hurricane, and we are just trees. Truthfully, that comparison always felt out of place, awkward, until today, as I was walking to my car. The wind pushed against me. I wrapped my arms tighter around the precious package. Calls and offers from strangers wanting to help poured in *like hurricane winds, so powerful and overwhelming, His love and mercy, so much love and mercy I cannot stand.* I've sung that song so many times before, feeling like a hypocrite, because I had never felt the power of His love like I was right now. For a few moments driving home alone, His glory swallowed up all my fears until it was just Him. The words I'd never really comprehended were now my truth.

Tonight, I helped Ryan sort through all his clothes from college, the Air National Guard uniforms, KU basketball shirts, and jeans that were too big. We packed a bag for the hospital and new XL shirts that comfortably covered the port in his chest. We included two favorite hats for what was to come. It felt like we were packing away the life he had just two weeks ago, T-shirt by T-shirt. *Breathe. Breathe.*

> *"How happy we are if the hurricanes that blow across life's raging sea have the effect of making Jesus more precious to us! It is better to weather the storm with Christ, than to sail smooth waters without him."*
> —JR MACDUFF—"STREAMS IN THE DESERT"

Houston, We Have Liftoff!

T*he day before we left for Houston,* those few hours before we were on the road, I'm not sure how to describe, but it was more than I could take in. We didn't know anyone in Houston and had never been there. In less than 24 hours, five of us had to be packed with preferably clean clothes, the Christmas gifts we had bought before December 5th. Who has time to shop for Christmas when their equilibrium is missing? We had the frozen, fully prepared Christmas dinner that Jennifer's parents had sent us, complete with the Christmas ham.

It's time to introduce Jennifer, Ryan's girlfriend, and her family. We met Jennifer, as Ryan's official girlfriend, when he was admitted to the hospital. Their friendship was two years old, and their courtship was only five weeks, not exactly storybook writing. Jennifer's dad had a heart transplant her senior year in high school and a mechanical heart before that. (Coincidentally his transplant was on Ryan's birthday. I think God likes to show us He is in the details.) The summer following his transplant, she was his full-time caregiver. Jennifer knew more about the life we were walking into than we did, and so did her parents, hence the sending of the Christmas ham.

Once we had an appointment scheduled, I had put on Facebook that we were leaving the next day and needed to find housing for the five of us for three weeks. I don't know what I was expecting. It was four days before Christmas. People aren't looking to add unexpected houseguests on December 21st. I never imagined the early Christmas gifts we were about to receive. The first offer was seven nights, paid in full, at a hotel connected to the hospital; this came as a gift from a friend of a friend. I didn't even know there were hotels connected to hospitals. I had so much to learn.

The second offer came from a young single man, also a friend of a friend, who offered to move out of his apartment in Houston and let us live there for the next three weeks. That young man's mom knew what she was doing when she raised that boy!

The third was a friend of a friend of another friend, who called me on my appendage, aka my cell phone, which, in the last couple of weeks, had grown permanently attached to my hand and head. There were times I'd walk through the house with the phone up to my ear, and no one was on the line with me. I wasn't talking to anyone. Did my brain forget to tell my arm to remove the phone from my ear at the end of one call, or was I intending to call someone and forgot to dial?

Either way, my brain was overloaded and unable to complete the task. Jennifer was the only one who noticed me walking around with the phone to my ear, talking to *no one*. She had a way about her: she could laugh and smile during the hard times, finding humor in the humanity of it all. No one ever accused me of keeping things light, especially when things weren't going as planned. I liked Jennifer's quick smile and her honest laugh. I hoped she'd stick around.

I remember running through our house, probably doing laundry or in some stage of the process when I got "the call." I'm sure she told me her name, but the words I remembered were, "I heard about your story, and I think God wants you to live in our house. (No matter how many times I read this account, tears fill my eyes.) We have five kids the same ages as yours, and we are leaving for vacation. We want you to stay at our home while you are here." The generosity dumbfounded me.

As I recall as much as I can about the details of those crazy hours before we hit the road, I can't help but see the similarity between these great unexpected gifts from strangers and the gold, frankincense, and myrrh that the wise men brought to baby Jesus. We like to put God in a box. Make Him small. Maybe our "small" minds or small faith can't imagine how God will figure this all out. God used a star to guide wise men to the manger long before cell phones and Google Maps existed.

After listening to the king, they went on their way.
And behold, the star that they had seen when it rose went before
them until it came to rest over the place where the child was.
— MATT 2:9

Here we were, two thousand years later, wondering if God could figure out a place for us to live in Houston. We had a 2001 Suburban—yes, it had 247,000 miles on it, but it wasn't a donkey, and we weren't traveling across country on foot, and I knew we would not land in a manger. God was showering us with his provision in the middle of this hard journey. I think I've had a misunderstanding about God and His provision, His blessings. In my mind everything must be perfect, Pinterest perfect, for God to be involved. If it's messy, how could God be part of it, right? I don't know where I got this idea.

The Bible is full of stories—stories that would never be posted on Pinterest because they are too hard, too messy, and full of far-from-perfect people. Mary riding on a donkey wasn't captured in the soft sunset light, wearing a clean white linen gown and her hair falling around her shoulders perfectly as she cupped her round belly. The manger looked nothing like the nursery pictures posted on social media months before the baby arrives. Mary wasn't contemplating the hospital she would birth her child in, or whether it would be a private room. None of the Christmas story resembles our modern expectations of what God gives us. No, His stories are full of battles, long journeys, prisons, and fiery furnaces, and, in the middle of it all, He comes to the rescue. Sometimes He showers gifts, like gold, frankincense, and myrrh—or strangers wanting to help a family in need.

> *The Bible is full of stories—stories that would never be posted on Pinterest because they are too hard, too messy, and full of far-from-perfect people.*

By noon the next day, less than twenty-four hours after getting the call, our 15-year-old Suburban was packed to the roof with luggage, Christmas presents, and the Christmas ham. We were on the road for the next twelve hours. Houston, we have liftoff!

A Feast

We *arrived at the hotel at midnight.* We decided a hotel was the best place to start our three-week stay since it was connected to the hospital. We still couldn't quite believe that a stranger had paid for our first seven days. We had two adjoining rooms, and, when we checked in, the front desk said that room service had already been covered and they would be bringing it up momentarily. That's never happened when I checked into a hotel before!

As we were getting settled for the night, no one was feeling particularly upbeat. It was nothing like arriving at a hotel on vacation. The boys were too old and too tired to be excited, like a normal hotel stay. No one was looking for the pool. About then, room service arrived. Two large carts were rolled into our room stacked with food, and a message, "I wasn't sure what the boys would want so I ordered one of everything." Our friend, of a friend, a stranger, *ordered everything on the menu!*

It had been seventeen days since we walked into the ER. Fifteen of those days, Ryan and I had been in the hospital. It's hard to describe that level of tired, sad, and overwhelmed. Watching them wheel in the carts of food, it felt like we were royalty. It was over-the-top generosity from a stranger. Food can bring such pleasure and comfort. I doubt food is the first thing we see in Heaven, but I imagine there will be a feast when we get there. A feast so grand, with a table that stretches farther than you can see. God's abundant love!

This gift of generosity, this abundant feast, none of us will ever forget. I couldn't help but feel that God wanted us to know that He was right here with us, and that, although this journey was hard, He would be showering us with His abundance.

> *You prepare a table before me in the presence of my enemies;*
> *you anoint my head with oil; my cup overflows.*
> — Ps 23:5

Isn't this MD Anderson?

Our *appointment with the oncologist* was the following day. We had arrived in the middle of the night and couldn't have imagined the surroundings outside the hotel. The hotel was connected to the hospital, so how hard could it be? Ryan and I went to the front desk to get directions on how to walk to the hospital, and Richard went to get the Suburban and park it in the hospital parking garage. At this point in the story, it's critical to stress that we had absolutely no idea where we were, not just the surroundings but no concept of just how big this medical area was. What we knew was that we had an appointment at MD Anderson, the world's #1 Cancer hospital.

The front desk clerk gestured to an oversized stairway, and we were off. On the appointment sheet I printed before we left, we had the elevator letter and floor number for our appointment. How hard could this be? There was the pressure that it was December 23rd and that this would be the last day our doctor would be seeing patients before Christmas, so we couldn't miss our appointment.

We exited the hotel directly into a covered walkway, and everything connected seamlessly. We found the elevators, but they weren't labeled with a letter like our appointment sheet indicated. We went with it. All elevators go up, right? We looked for our floor and pushed the button. Upon reaching the floor, the room numbers didn't match at all. Nothing matched the information on our appointment sheet. We rode the elevator down, found another elevator, and rode it up, and again, we couldn't see where we were to go.

As time passed, my anxiety built. We entered a room and asked the receptionist for directions. We must not have mentioned we thought we were at MD Anderson, only the room and floor we were looking for. She stared blankly at us. I thought, *We can't be that far away.* How could she not help us with directions? At this point, I'm sick to my stomach. I'm sure Ryan was, too. You know that feeling you get in a dream when you're late for a test? That dream was playing out in real life, and the stakes were much higher than any bad dream I had ever had.

We eventually showed a security guard our appointment sheet. He quickly pointed out that our appointment was at MD Anderson, at which point I'm sure I responded with frustration, "Isn't that where we are?" No, we were at Houston Methodist Hospital. "What?" *There is more than one hospital connected to a hotel?* My heart was racing. How far away were we? The security guard, sensing my panic, walked us through a maze of hallways and out a side door of the hospital. It spit us out on a back alley, not a main thoroughfare. I looked up. Giant hospitals disguised as skyscrapers surrounded us. It could have been New York City!

I wanted to start running. I wanted to throw up, too. Ryan's tumor had been pressing on his nerves, making his leg numb and unstable; we could only go so fast. I'm sure my sweet and unflappable son wished for a better tour guide than me at this point. All I could think was, *We can't miss this appointment. We can't!*

Through a maze of buildings, we found MD Anderson. Inside were multiple elevator bays, housing 6-8 elevators each. This hunt for MD Anderson, the right elevator, the correct floor, in time for our only chance to see this doctor, had all the elements of "The Amazing Race" reality show, except this race was for life!

You Will Beg
Your Parents to Stop

T*here are moments in time* burned in my memory. Often, the words spoken by the white coats, that hang in space, like a star suspended in the sky. I can't remember what came before or was said after because that one phrase made time stand still; everything before or after is lost in space.

I don't remember if we were late or on time to that appointment. What I can recall next, was a small exam room; Ryan sat on the exam table. Richard was there. *How did he find us?* He and I sat in plastic chairs, and the doctor stood next to the light-bright machine that displayed Ryan's MRI scans. I had my spiral notebook in my lap opened to the pages where I had scrawled my questions.

I can't remember what came before or was said after because that one phrase made time stand still; everything before or after is lost in space.

When the white coat walked in, her presence startled me. She was a large woman with legs like oak trees. We would learn that she was an Orthopedic Surgical Oncologist. There are so many kinds of doctors of oncology; I had no concept of this cancer world. This doctor specialized in the hip and pelvis. Part of Ryan's tumor trailed down into his sacrum and Psoas muscle, close to the hip, so we were referred to her. She was the kind of doctor who could cut you open and remove your hip bones, strong and confident. I cannot imagine cutting open a person and removing their hip in a million years. I am sure more technical words are used to describe the process, but there is no reason for me to convince you I know them. We learned that Ewing's is an "amputation cancer"; if they could cut it off, they did. Arms and legs are the more common locations for a Ewing's tumor. Only 7% of Ewing's tumors are on the spine, and spine tumors have almost always metastasized (moved) to the lungs by the time they are discovered. Metastatic cancer changes *everything*.

The doctor pointed to the MRI image, and I tried to understand what was supposed to be there and what wasn't. She explained the protocol to Ryan:

1. Chemo regimen
2. Surgery
3. Recover from surgery
4. Chemo and radiation together
5. More chemo.

We learned a tumor is like a jelly donut. The doctors often explained things in simple terms. They could have explained the more technical details, too. I remember the jelly donuts. If a doctor goes in, you must have clean margins to remove a tumor surgically. Translation, you must be able to cut out the entire donut without any of the jelly coming out.

Ewing's is aggressive in that, even if there is a localized tumor, the body is essentially full of microscopic Ewing's cells. A Ewing's cell happens when chromosomes 11 and 22 mistakenly combine, forming a tumor that the body fails to see as cancer. I picture a dandelion that has gone to seed. You blow on that delicate sphere of tiny seeds, held together by what looks to be the thinnest of thread, and poof, seeds go everywhere. Rogue Ewing's cells were hiding throughout his body. To eradicate the cells, they use a recipe of five chemos—unbelievably toxic chemicals, one of which they call the *red devil*. The name fits—it is red, and it ruthlessly kills everything, even things it's not meant to kill.

I had a long list of questions. I know I was writing down as much as I could keep up with, until she said the words that hung in the air, making time stand still. "Ryan, you will beg your parents to stop. If you stop, you will die." I couldn't breathe. She might as well have punched me in the gut. My hands fell to my lap, and my throat swelled shut. I'm not sure how long it was before I could speak. I don't remember what I said, but as I type, recalling this moment so vividly, my body remembers it all. The only difference is this time, I can cry as loud as I want.

Chemo Is a Recipe

A*t some point, she told us that* because Ryan's biopsy was sent to a national lab for identification, they would not require us to go through the routine testing they had planned for the next three weeks. "Chemo is like a recipe. If your oncologist at home follows the same recipe we do, you can go home and take it there. We will see you in a few weeks to check on how much the tumor is shrinking from the chemo."

We called Jackson (18) and Cooper (16), who were exploring the area, I'm sure, trying to figure out what they would do for the next three weeks. We told them to pack up. We were going home!

I want to add this information to help with context and make me appear less clueless to the reader. I pulled this directly from the City of Houston government site.

"Houston is known internationally as the home of one of the best medical communities in the world. That's not surprising since the Texas Medical Center (TMC), the largest medical center in the world, is just 10 minutes from downtown Houston. TMC is housed on 675 acres, and is home to 42 nonprofit and government institutions, including 13 teaching hospitals, two medical schools, four colleges of nursing, a dental college, a college of pharmacy, and a college of optometry. Altogether 4.8 million patients visit them each year."

Later I would learn there is a navigation app for the MD Anderson hospital. A Google Map for a *hospital*. I had no idea where we were headed. I'm sure glad God did.

Welcome to Buc-ee's!

On *Monday afternoon, December 21st*, we received the call to come to Houston for an appointment on December 23rd and prepare to stay for three weeks. In 24 hours, we were packed and on the road for the next twelve, arriving at midnight to eat an abundant feast, sleep a few hours, and start our race to the hospital. Our time there was no more than a couple of hours before we were returning home, in time for Christmas Eve.

My memory recalls immediately falling asleep once outside the terrifying Houston traffic. About an hour down the road, Richard stopped at a highly advertised travel station, claiming the cleanest bathrooms in Texas! Buc-ee's, an oversized Beaver sporting a baseball cap. "Potty Like a Rock-Star."

I didn't even know we had stopped when Richard jostled me awake. *I wish he hadn't.* He had awakened me from a Rip Van Winkle sleep. My head throbbed like I had been crying for hours. I wanted nothing but to go back to sleep. I dragged myself out of the suburban to enter Buc-ee's two days before Christmas. It was packed with jolly travelers "on their way to grandmother's house." Upon crossing the threshold, a Texas-sized exuberant employee yelled, "Welcome to Buc-ee's! Welcome to Buc-ee's!" It felt like a scene from a low-budget comedy that wasn't funny.

I looked around, my head in a fog. Buc-ee's is a convenience store on steroids. They had more than 100 gas pumps and nearly as many bathroom stalls "The Cleanest in Texas. Guaran-peed." Every possible kind of food, hot, cold, breakfast, dinner, BBQ, boiled eggs, endless aisles of candy and snack food, and enough beverages to ensure you will need to stop at the next Buc-ee's down the road. Housewares, tea towels with cute country quotes, candles and hand lotion, jewelry, wall art with scripture and inspiring quips, and *Buc-ee was everywhere*, hats, shirts, cups, and he even had his signature Buc-ee nuggets.

We would grow to look forward to stopping at Buc-ee's on future trips. They did serve great frozen coke, and everyone likes a pristine bathroom. It was our first trip to Buc-ee's. I add this story to paint a realistic picture of our life during this arduous journey. There were days when it felt like we were on the show "The Amazing Race," doing all we could to survive to the next checkpoint and not be eliminated.

Home

O*n Christmas Eve,* we sat around our dining room table with the Christmas ham that had traveled cross country more than once. Nothing was Pinterest perfect. Our friends decorated our home sometime during the December chaos. They may have scrounged through a basement closet and found rogue Christmas decorations that never made it to the attic the year before. It is heartwarming how much people want to help. Many times, the challenge is knowing what to do.

At our rectangular table, I sat at the far end, my back to the big picture window. Ryan, a lefty, always sat to my right. He still had his hair, but the white coats told us it would fall out soon. He still looked like Ryan. I didn't know how much that was about to change.

Peace Pill

All this I have told you so that you will not fall away.
—Jn 16:1

I*t's Saturday morning, December 26th.* Usually, I would be resting in my chair, exhausted from the pre-Christmas-prep, the work it took to make it look as close to the Pinterest images as possible. I would be staring at the Christmas decorations that I now would immediately want to put away to avoid thinking about the dreaded task a moment longer.

Instead, I've been sitting in my chair for hours, perusing Facebook, all the joy-filled pictures posted of friends and family and listening to the year in review on TV. 2015 has been a year I never want to repeat. Richard is in his chair, reading a book about cancer that someone we don't even know sent us in the mail. It arrived on Christmas Eve. My breath struggles to make my chest rise under the heaviness of it all.

Last night I searched scripture, trying to paste together a "go-to" list of inspired words of God to get me through my crisis moments.

John, Chapter 16 starts,

All this I have told you so that you will not fall away. (Good start for a crisis.)

About midway through chapter 16, Jesus says,

> *Very truly I tell you, you will weep and mourn, while the world*
> *rejoices. You will grieve, but your grief will turn to joy.*
> —Jn 16:20

Jesus is speaking about when He leaves His disciples and ascends to heaven. It has nothing to do with December 26th. It's not the Christmas story, no mention of a manger or wise men. Watching the world rejoice when I could barely breathe, I felt no "comfort" *or* "joy."

Instead of the gifts from the three Wise Men, this story tells of the gift from Jesus, the courage and comfort of His Holy Spirit, that He leaves with us while He waits for us in Heaven. That is the *gift*, His Spirit, living in you. At the end of John 16, He leaves us with this message:

> *I have told you these things, so that in me you may*
> *have peace. In this world you will have trouble.*
> *But take heart! I have overcome the world.*
> — v. 33

My words aren't meant to make anyone feel guilty for rejoicing with family and friends. Christmas is a celebration of the ultimate gift God gives us, His Son. These words are for anyone searching for peace in a time of trouble. It's hard to find that peace sometimes and truly *feel* it.

I'm as guilty and lazy as anyone. I fill my brain with all sorts of easy distractions—TV, Facebook, and house-decorating shows. The world has done a number on us with all that we have at our fingertips, taunting us with a life of perfection. But sometimes life delivers a blow so big there is no distraction big enough to take our mind from our troubles. It takes work to focus on the truth of God's word and all He has given us.

> *Christmas is a celebration of the ultimate gift God gives us, His Son.*

I must cram these thoughts in. Sometimes the action is so heavy and laborious the fatigue overtakes me. I wish there was a peace-pill I could swallow or that it was as easy as placing a "Peace on Earth" pillow on the couch. I wish there were a show that would take my mind to another place, but there isn't a sufficient distraction anymore.

So, for anyone who needs peace and no worldly distraction big enough to numb your pain, I say these words to help you. I pray you don't give up seeking Him. Don't fall away! He has overcome the world.

> *I pray that God, the source of hope, will fill you completely with joy and peace because you trust in Him. Then you will overflow with confident hope through the power of the Holy Spirit.*
> — ROM 15:13

Let this be a witness to who He is.

No, Sha La La La's

W*hen I was little, my brothers called* me a "Worry Wart." So, as I think about it, I deeply consider the irony that my favorite verse starts with, "*Do not be anxious about anything,*" as if I had some command of it or had mastered not being anxious about anything. The verse was easily my most quoted verse. I mean it was quoted like a Karen Carpenter song that rolls off the tongue, smooth with lots of "Sha La La La's." I remember memorizing it while I exercised to my Cindy Crawford workout tape circa 1990-something. It had been in my head and on my tongue for a long time.

Today it doesn't matter if it's a waitress innocently asking, "How is everything?" or a friend texts, "How are you?" a lump appears in my throat so large I can't swallow, and my brain hurts from the strain of holding back tears.

> *Do not be anxious about anything* (Don't worry!), *but in*
> *everything, by prayer and petition, with thanksgiving,*
> *let your requests be made known to God. And the*
> *peace of God which surpasses all understanding, will*
> *guard your hearts and minds in Christ Jesus.*
> — PHIL 4:6-7

I battle to put that *truth*, the *truth* that God is in control, on the throne, has won the war and has overcome the world, into my mind.

There is a long list of *truths* I battle to put in my mind *every single day.* Why doesn't the "truth" stay there? I fought this same battle yesterday! Must I fight it again today?

> *We demolish arguments and every pretension that*
> *sets itself up against the knowledge of God, and we take*
> *captive every thought to make it obedient to Christ.*
> — 2 COR 10:5

That is not a verse that rolls off my tongue. Not a verse I have memorized. No, Sha La La La's! *"Take captive every thought to make it obedient to Christ." "Take captive!"* Them's fightin' words!

But here's the part that amazes me. Sometimes I wail and cry uncontrollably, but when I *"take captive"* my thoughts, *that peace* that surpasses all understanding *does come.* I know *that peace* is not from me, and it does *"surpass all understanding."* There is no worldly reason for me to have peace right now.

No Sha La La La's. It's a war! And it looks like it will be a battle every day.

> *"The beginning of anxiety is the end of faith,*
> *and the beginning of true faith is the end of anxiety."*
> — GEORGE MUELLER

I Will Trust in You

So, *this is a doozy,* but here goes putting it out there. Several people sent me the song "Trust in You" by Lauren Daigle. The topics or words of her songs are raw and honest. They touch my soul. If God is listening right now, I'd love for her to be my neighbor in Heaven. That sister can sing!

When I listen carefully to the words in "Trust in You," it's not a song that is easy to confess as your truth. It played on the radio as Ryan and I drove to the hospital for five days of chemo. Those were long, hard days. It was not a coincidence I heard the song as we drove to the hospital.

In the song she is proclaiming that when I ask and don't receive the answer I want, I will still trust in You. I don't do that well. I like my plan. Sometimes I don't even pray because I don't want to be disappointed if *He* chooses another plan or doesn't give the answer I asked Him for. *Just don't pray*; that way, you don't have to reconcile His silence and your disappointment in Him.

> *Sometimes I don't even pray because I don't want to be disappointed if* He *chooses another plan or doesn't give the answer.*

This verse came to me today as we walked across the hospital parking garage. God in His mysterious ways continues to message me in His perfect timing, even when my brain is mush.

> *And without faith, it is impossible to please God, because anyone who comes to Him must believe that He exists and that He rewards those who earnestly seek Him.*
> —HEB 11:6

So, out of my desperate desire to please God, I must have faith in Him. Trust! I will trust in Him, *even when. . .* He doesn't move the mountains or part the waters like I want Him to. The stakes are high right now, and I do a lot of begging at His feet. But I refuse to fall into the trap of *not* laying my requests before Him because *I'm afraid He might not answer the way I want.* I am not alone. There are others afraid to lay their heartbreak at His feet, fearing He won't answer the way they want.

My Part of the Bargain

W*e walked out of the hospital tonight. Five* more days of chemo done, at home once again, but nothing feels the same. I see pictures of Ryan all over the house, and I can't reconcile them with what I see in real life. "I can't fix this!" Nothing I say makes it better—not like a mom wants to make it better. How do we do this?

> *So do not fear, for I am with you;*
> *do not be dismayed, for I am your God.*
> *I will uphold you with my righteous right hand.*
> — Is 41:10

As I read this verse, it states *five things* God is or will do.

God's list:

- "I am with you"
- "I am your God"
- "I will strengthen you"
- "I will help you"
- "I will uphold you"

My list:

- "Do not fear"
- "Feel My strength."

Surrendering Ryan to God, I have no words for this. Until now, I wanted Him to do it *my* way. Write the ending I want! As I write, know that I will reread my words, reminding myself *who* I am trusting and what He promises. This doesn't mean He will heal Ryan here on Earth. God's word is absolute truth, and *the truth of His word is not dependent on life's circumstances.* No matter how this story ends, those words written in Isaiah 41:10 remain true.

Let this be a witness to who God is.

Know Your Enemy!

It *is incredible to receive a text* from someone I've never met saying, "Our whole family is praying." Friends touching base or passing along scripture and prayers; I read them all, and they encourage me. As I have shared, I am writing to myself as much as I am writing to anyone else struggling. Writing helps me corral my racing thoughts. I re-read my own words to stamp my belief firmly on my heart. *Declaring truth.*

The other day, I watched my two-year-old grandniece stomp her feet in protest over not getting her way. When Great-Grammy responded, "Let's go get a snack in the kitchen," her stomps ceased. She oozed, "I love it when I get my way." While I am not revealing the identity of said grandniece, we all know who she is. She came out of the womb stomping her feet. That vision has not stopped playing in my head, and with it comes the reality that *I am just like her.* I want to stomp my feet and say, "Stop this suffering!" "God, not my son," and scream, "It's not fair!"

> *I want to stomp my feet and say, "Stop this suffering!" "God, not my son," and scream, "It's not fair!"*

I've avoided the biblical topic of suffering all my life. I prefer to skip over words like famine, plague, and leprosy, and concentrate on peace, joy, and love. Maybe if I avoid the topic, I can prevent it—a "keep my head down and hope the teacher doesn't call on me" strategy.

Today I received an email from an old friend I hadn't spoken with in years. She shared her story, advising "Trusting in God is not something you just say; it is something you do." I am grappling with the *"How"* of that statement. Watching your child who can no longer walk up the stairs without the help of the railing collides with the directive "fear not." Watching his body shrink before my eyes is a head-on collision with "fear not." Staring at him, no hair, no eyebrows, no eyelashes. God made our faces so expressive and distinctive; What a divine designer, creating dimension, using color and tiny hairs. Did you know that the absence of eyebrows on familiar faces disrupts our ability to recognize them? Eyebrows convey our mood and set the tone for our faces. When those details are gone, life's expressions fade. I'm watching my son fade away, turning gray like the people in "the Nordstrom" waiting room. I want off this ride!

I share this level of detail because I want to be honest about what we face, not skimming over those verses on suffering that go down crooked in our throats. Christians don't like to share when they question God during times of great suffering, fearing there is an imaginary "mirror-mirror on the wall" revealing our true reflection to the world, exposing what we look like in the morning before our makeup and our morning cup of Joe. Questioning God has been going on since God made man. Now that is the ultimate irony! Job is arguably the most famous book on suffering ever written and contains some of the most vivid visions of God answering Job's questions.

> *Then the Lord spoke to Job out of the storm.*
> *He said: 'Who is this that obscures my plans*
> *with words without knowledge?*
> *Brace yourself like a man;*
> *I will question you,*
> *and you shall answer me.'*
> —Job 38:2-3

This passage makes my spine quiver. Can you hear the boom in God's voice? "I will question *you*, and you shall answer *Me*." Here's where I wish that classroom strategy applied—*keep your head down*. It doesn't.

My friend also said suffering isn't "glamorous or heroic." It's not. It's the ugly cry. It's the trembling fear, down on my knees begging for grace and mercy. I'm wondering if, in our efforts to hide or disguise our suffering behind false confidence, avoiding at all costs, someone seeing an authentic reflection of our fears; I wonder if we are missing something *big* here.

In 1 Peter 5, it states,

> *Be alert and of sober mind. Your enemy, the devil,*
> *prowls around like a roaring lion looking for someone to*
> *devour. Resist him, standing firm in the faith, because*
> *you know that the family of believers throughout the*
> *world is undergoing the same kind of suffering.*

> *And the God of all grace, who called you to his eternal*
> *glory in Christ, after you have suffered a little while,*
> *will himself restore you and make you strong, firm, and*
> *steadfast. To him be the power forever and ever. Amen.*
>
> — v. 8-9

Writing is my conversation with God, my search for truth and understanding. *God, I don't understand why this is happening. God, this hurts so bad. God, I am scared! Did I do something wrong? If I did, I take it all back!* He has been faithful to speak to me and guide me to some level of understanding and some answers to my questions. I think there are things we just aren't going to understand here on Earth, and in those times, I must accept that I'm not God. I don't know everything. I don't see the world from heaven's view. We claim that we wish we were God, so we could control the outcome and write our own story, ensuring a happy ending. I probably thought being God was a good idea before all this suffering. Now that I see it—no, thanks! He can be God. The phrase in the title from a Brandon Heath song, "Give Me Your Eyes." I used to sing it with him. Catchy tune. I realize the song is about seeing people the way God does. But now, *no way.* There is no way I could live even for a second seeing what God sees, the amount of suffering.

In 1 Peter, there are some directives given and some instructions. "Be alert and of sober mind," meaning *take this seriously.* His reference for what you are watching out for is the devil, and he likens him to a lion seeking to devour us. These words couldn't be much more precise; that lion wants to tear into your skin, eat your flesh, and consume you. Not much left to interpretation.

Resist him: How do you do that? I am finding that we should be talking a lot more about the verse "take every thought captive." A big part of resisting the devil is not letting him have control of your mind. It is a battle of words, often fought in silence and solitude, kept secret. Some fears plague us and wake us in the dark of night, and we rarely share them with others. It is a war, and the word "captive" is apropos.

Captive—a person, taken prisoner, or an animal that is confined.

That devil prowls around like a lion. He is conniving and cleverly camouflages himself from view. The battle is almost won if he captures your mind and fills it with lies. To resist him, we must fill our minds with biblical truth and make no room for his lies. Replace his words with the Truth of Jesus Christ. Resist! Take every thought the devil speaks captive. This is war!

I want to say I've read *The Art of War,* but I haven't. I've heard it is full of helpful military strategies I hope I never need. James Clear wrote a synopsis of the book, and that's as close to reading it as I will get. In his summary, a couple of statements stood out.

"All warfare is based on deception."

Isn't it interesting it doesn't mention a physical weapon? Deception is the weapon, and the devil is the master deceiver.

The instructions from Ephesians, chapter 6—

> *Put on the whole armor of God, that you may be able to stand against the wiles of the devil. For we do not wrestle against flesh and blood, but against principalities, against powers, against the rulers of the darkness of this age, against spiritual hosts of wickedness in the heavenly places.*
>
> — v. 11-12

The other point highlighted by James Clear is,

- "If you know the enemy and know yourself, you need not fear the result of a hundred battles. If you know yourself but not the enemy, for every victory gained, you will also suffer a defeat. If you know neither the enemy nor yourself, you will succumb in every battle."

The Art of War is not the inspired word of God, so with that in mind, I sift through the military strategy presented with caution. But change it to say,

- If you know the enemy and know your God—you need not fear the result of a hundred battles.

God makes it very clear the devil is our enemy and that he plans to devour us.

- *Knowing* God and the truth of His word is the *"How"* of trusting him and ultimately winning every battle.

Let this be a witness to who God is.

Whom Shall I Fear?

In *the course of a lifetime*, you could never track everything you teach your children, planned or unplanned. You hope they pick up your good attributes and habits and somehow miraculously don't copy the bad ones. Everything you put into them, you pray prepares them for life, a life where they seek Jesus, no matter what, and hope they don't sleep on your couch all through their twenties.

A friend posted about teaching his son to hit a baseball. My mind raced back to the hitting videos, the practices, the games, and the great memories filled with ballpark dirt. Followed by the question, "Did we teach them to seek Jesus as much as we taught them the fundamentals of baseball?"

> *"Did we teach them to seek Jesus as much as we taught them the fundamentals of baseball?"*

We came home from the hospital a week ago. Ryan had just endured five days of chemo, hooked up to an IV machine continuously pumping cocktails of medicine that keep nausea at bay, some to protect his organs, as chemo can't differentiate between cancer and the heart. The plan is to kill every new growing cell in his body, cancer. There are casualties along the way. Did you know that you lose all your hair because chemo kills every rapidly dividing cell in the body, including hair? I knew chemo made your hair fall out; I didn't know why. During this stay, we learned that Ryan would have 17 chemo-treatment weeks over about 40 weeks, delaying his return to the University of Kansas to a full year from now, *a crushing blow.*

That night, when we got home, behind closed doors, I heard Ryan listening to "Whom Shall I Fear?" by Chris Tomlin. The lyrics blasted loudly from his iPhone, and I dropped to my knees. The words overwhelmed me, and his choosing to listen to them humbled me. I never envisioned my child fighting cancer. I envisioned baseball. We made sure he knew how to hit and throw a baseball. That is all well and good, but I am so glad we made sure he knew *who* to believe in and *who* to seek fiercely. In this struggle, the suffering of life, his belief and faith in God are what will get him through. Thank you, God, for making yourself known to my son.

Arm Wrestling

I*'ve taken up arm wrestling inside my mind.* I don't recommend it. Arm wrestling is a battle of wills, a display of brute strength. Which arm will force the other one down, or which arm can outlast the other? Inside my mind, there is a constant argument. My vision is clear; nothing in life is the same. It's hard to argue against the obvious that surrounds me. In the quietness of my days and nights, doubts and questions about this plan shout out, taunting me. I can't say I'm bitter; Job says it best in chapter 23, verses 3 and 4, "If only I knew where to find Him; if only I could go to His dwelling! I would state my case before him and fill my mouth with arguments." Job sums it up perfectly!

There is no way Job knew how his words would ring true in my life thousands of years later. My version includes, respectfully, but with an overture of *"why"* mixed into the stating of my case. "Couldn't we have considered another path, another journey? Why this one? Why *my* son? And while I'm asking, why are you taking us here? When *will* this end? *How* will this end?"

On one side is fear, unanswered questions, wielding a sword of grief, loss, and suffering, laced with the oppressive length of this path and the weight of this journey. On the other side, there is Jesus. I'm unsure if anyone out there is envisioning this fight with the same visual clarity as I am. There is some serious bloodshed in this brawl. Or maybe you're responding with a resounding "Jesus! That's an easy choice; why would you even allow such a wrestling match to take place? *Are you still not getting the* 'Trusting the Lord with all your heart' lesson?" I can't help but hear the Church Lady on *Saturday Night Live* in my head, "Well isn't that *special*, you still don't trust Jesus."

For me, it's a fight to the finish. I can't run from it, escape, eat, shop, TV, or sleep myself out of this battle. A greater battle for my thoughts has never been waged. It is moment by moment, not day by day. At my weakest, I utter only the name *Jesus*, usually in the dark of night; sometimes, I have the strength to whisper, "I trust you, Jesus" over and over. There! That's my strategy. It's not elaborate, but when used—and *used* is the key—it does work. Notice the clarifying statement, *"when used."* It is a choice to use this strategy, or the fight is over in seconds, no contest.

Trust has been a repeat topic for me and may continue to be. I'm anticipating peace and joy to be equally challenging. The reality is there are struggles we can't distract ourselves from. We all do it. Take the easy way out. Eat a monster cookie; take your mind off it. A monster cookie may not do it for you. Whatever our vice is, our crutch, we put off facing our fears, numb the pain, and sometimes deny there is a problem at all. But then, sometimes, God puts us in such a storm where there is no escape.

> *Trust has been a repeat topic for me and may continue to be.*

"Then he got into the boat, and his disciples followed him. Suddenly a furious storm came up on the lake so that the waves swept over the boat. But Jesus was sleeping. The disciples went and woke him, saying, "Lord, save us! We're going to drown!"

He replied, "You of little faith, why are you so afraid?" Then he got up and rebuked the winds and the waves, and it was

completely calm. The men were amazed and asked, "What kind
of man is this? Even the winds and the waves obey him!"
— MATT 8:23-27

Envisioning this scene, I'm in good company. The disciples had Jesus
on the boat with them, and they still got scared; that makes me feel better.

For though we live in the world, we do not wage war as the
world does. The weapons we fight with are not the weapons
of the world. On the contrary, they have divine power to
demolish strongholds. We demolish arguments and every
pretension that sets itself up against the knowledge of God, and
we take captive every thought to make it obedient to Christ.
— 2 COR 10:3-5

The weapons we fight with are not the weapons of the world. Whisper
the name of Jesus. He is our only strategy.

"You don't really know Jesus is all you
need until Jesus is all you have."
— TIM KELLER

There Will Be Tears

"C*ount it all Joy."*

In case someone has similar questions about this joy we are to
be counting, there seems to be a lot of suffering these days—disease,
death, abuse, poverty, injustice, and Christians dying for their faith.
While it is hard to relate to fearing I will die *for* my faith, disease and
death are not far from me. Disease greets me each morning, and death

is proclaimed daily in our world so much that sometimes we barely acknowledge or notice it. Sorrow, I have felt such sadness at times, waves of it crashing over me with the consistent rhythm of the ocean and the power to drown. As Christians, how are we to suffer? What example are we to show the world? God's word is full of trials, and praises are sung amidst them. Joy.

> *Count it all joy, my brothers, when you*
> *meet trials of various kinds.*
> —Jas 1:2

I find myself critiquing my "joy" performance like an Olympic judge. As I Rolodex through my mind, one of my favorite images is that of Paul and Silas singing praises in prison, a dungeon; I have no concept of *how bad* it was, but they were *in chains*! In contrast, I see myself in the comfort of my own home, weeping under a blanket. What is wrong with me? Where is my joy?

There are times when I feel *His* overwhelming strength, I see *His* hand, I trust, I know Him never to leave me, and I thank Him for His provision, even the chance to hurt and grow closer to Him. And then a wave crashes against me, and the sea of sorrow swallows me up; once again, my body slips through my life preserver into the deep, where there is no peace and no joy, and I'm choking on panic.

These thoughts have played in my head off and on for almost a decade, but more recently, a crescendo. I am getting embarrassingly low scores from the judges who dwell in my mind. *"This is a day the Lord has made. I will rejoice and be glad in it."* Why can't you get this maneuver? This failure has driven me to the scriptures like a starving man to a buffet. Nothing can distract me from the table set before me, searching for a comfort to fill me so I can survive. And then, there it was! A food I have never seen on this buffet.

The Apostle Paul speaks,

When they arrived, he said to them, "You know how I lived the whole time I was with you from the first day I came into the province of Asia. I served the Lord with great humility and with tears, although I was severely tested by the plots of the Jews."
— ACTS 20:18-19

Tears? Paul *cried* when he was tested? How have I missed this dish? Then again, in verses 37 and 38, *"They all wept as they embraced him and kissed him."* Wept! Another miss! Where had this dish been hiding?

What grieved them most was his statement that they would never see his face again. Paul *cried*. I know God gave us tears. I do not believe God is some authoritarian ruler in heaven showing us no Grace, expecting a "chin up" attitude and a punch in the arm. We are saved by grace; *"His grace so no one can boast."* But at the same time, I felt this internal pressure to perform a perfect 10, to display joy, sing praises, and *praise You in the storm*—but the words ring in my head as a "Failure Anthem."

So, as I digest this newly discovered dish, I cautiously share it with you, as it is not meant to discourage anyone from pursuing joy or praising in the storm. But in case you, too, have been chewing the Beef Jerky of Joy, chewing, chewing, chewing, and swallowing hard—There *will be tears!*—and He catches them in a bottle and records them all.

Yes, Paul sang praises in prison, but he also cried. Let this be a witness to who God is and His GREAT LOVE for us.

You keep track of all my sorrows.
You have collected all my tears in your bottle.
You have recorded each one in your book.
My enemies will retreat when I call to you for help.

This I know: God is on my side!
I praise God for what he has promised;
yes, I praise the Lord for what he has promised.
I trust in God, so why should I be afraid?
What can mere mortals do to me?
I will fulfill my vows to you, O God,
and will offer a sacrifice of thanks for your help.
For you have rescued me from death;
you have kept my feet from slipping.
So now I can walk in your presence, O God,
in your life-giving light.
— Ps 56:8-13

Give Me a Story

"When one door of happiness closes, another opens;
but often we look so long at the closed door that we do
not see the one which has been opened for us."
— HELEN KELLER

For a couple of decades, I've carried around the desire to write a book about how *good* God is and how His plan is *always been better than mine.* It's been an ever-present item on my list of to-do's, a tugging on my soul. I would start, stop, save, and delete, and though I thought I knew my topic well enough to share it with others, nothing ever held it together. It was like trying to bake a lasagna without a pan. Up to now, I've shared more about Ryan's cancer battle and the wrestling matches I had with God, and I will get back to that story, but before I go on, it's essential to set the stage for our life before cancer. We didn't start Ryan's Race with fresh legs. Please indulge my "DeLorean" trip back in time to eight years earlier, in January 2008.

I asked God to give me a story so I could tell others how good He is; I just never imagined He would send me here to find out what that really meant. I didn't think He would send me here.

In 2001, the album *Almost There* by MercyMe hit the sound waves. "I Can Only Imagine" was the number-five song on the album. The song is the best-selling and most-played Christian single of all time. Bart Millard, the writer, wrote the song in ten minutes. In 2018, the movie *"I Can Only Imagine"* was released, grossing 86 million dollars. The story depicts the writer's life of suffering under the abusive hand of an alcoholic father. It's a heart-wrenching story that ends in reconciliation between Bart and his father. Before his father's death due to cancer, he ultimately sees Jesus. It's a story only God can write. I love the quote from the movie when Amy Grant hears Bart say that he wrote this song in ten minutes. "Bart, you didn't write that song in ten minutes. It took a lifetime." Some will be able to measure the weight of this truth when you read it, and some won't. Understanding it, really fathoming it, takes both time and suffering.

I asked God to give me a story so I could tell others how good He is; I just never imagined He would send me here to find out what that really meant.

But the number-two song on the same album changed my life. Man, it's a great song to sing in the car. The words are easy and sung in the perfect key to belt it from your soul. It's a simple message. Ready for it? "Here am I, send me." Yep, that's it. Lots of repeats. "Here am I, send me." That CD was one of my favorites because I had been proclaiming those exact words to God! "Here am I, send me!" I felt them to my core and meant them just as sincerely. When that song was released, Cooper was 2, Jackson was 4, and Ryan was 6. We were living *the life*! The baby bag was almost out the door. (I miss those babies.) What I would give to go back and snuggle them close and hear their baby cackles. I would know better now how to treasure those moments. You don't know how good it is until that good fades, and you realize those days aren't coming back. But life was good, *really good*, and I was ready for God to *send me!*

"*But I didn't think you'd send me here.*"

I share my story with the hope that what I learned through my suffering would shed light on your suffering and help you cling to God. I don't want one ounce of this pain wasted. God is the only one who makes beauty out of ashes.

The story of the song "I Can Only Imagine." It would be hard to think of a better example of a modern Christian story—*meaning not Job*—about a man sharing his suffering and sorrow, and God in His infinite mercy, His unmeasurable love enables *writing that beauty in ten minutes!* That kind of beauty comes only from ashes. That beauty dares us all to imagine *"What it will be like to walk by His side"*—that kind of beauty we can't imagine.

"Here am I, send me"—I meant those words, but I had no idea He would send me *here*. Some of you think I'm talking about Ryan and cancer, but I'm not. In 2008, Jesus delivered Caelen to our front door. What I haven't told you is how that all happened and how we knew it was Jesus.

Ever *Pleasant* Help

In *my office at home,* right next to the kitchen, so I can see them, are my favorite works of art. One created by Jackson (our middle son), stick figures of he and I holding hands under a rainbow, drawn back in the day when Jack was spelled with a backward "J" and looked like "Tack." On my desk are the 3 x 5 note cards that Ryan hid all over the house for me when he left for basic training two days after high-school graduation. They all say the same thing, scrawled in his hand, in a now-faded pencil, "I love you! Ryan." On another wall is a framed collage of seven coupons made of construction paper: "I will take care of Caelen today. Do anything you want." Cooper (our youngest son) made those for me not long after she arrived. Amazing how a child—whose age wasn't even in double digits yet—knew I was in desperate need of help, when many far older still had no idea at all. I never redeemed those coupons officially. I framed them instead, as they are one of the most-treasured gifts I've ever been given. The last piece of art, also by Cooper, in his best second-grade handwriting, *"God is our refuge and strength, an ever-present help in trouble."* Psalm 46:1 Except if you look closely, you will catch that, instead of "ever-present," it says, "ever-*pleasant* help in trouble." I can't help but chuckle at the irony of God being an *ever-pleasant* help in times of trouble, given no one ever describes trouble as pleasant.

A flat tire on the side of the road *isn't pleasant.* A dead battery in the winter snow *isn't pleasant.* An engine light popping up on the dashboard on a road trip isn't pleasant. Funny how all these examples that come to my mind are examples of unexpected inconveniences—and you have no control over them. Their frustration is compounded because they are stopping you or delaying you from heading down the road toward your destination. These unpleasant and unexpected inconveniences frustrate us and make us ask, "Why did this have to happen today?"

From *January 23rd*, "Streams in the Desert"

"God is . . . an ever-present help in trouble. Psalm 46:1 But He allows trouble to pursue us, as though He were indifferent to its overwhelming pressure, so we may be brought to the end of ourselves. Through the trial, we are led to discover the treasure of darkness and the immeasurable wealth of tribulation.

"We may be sure that He who allows the suffering is with us throughout it. It may be that we will only see Him once the ordeal is nearly passed, but we must dare to believe that He never leaves our trial. Our eyes are blinded, so we cannot see the One our soul loves. The darkness and our bandages blind us so that we cannot see the form of our High Priest. Yet He is there and is deeply touched. Let us not rely on our feelings but trust in His unswerving faithfulness. And though we cannot see Him, let us talk to Him. Although His presence is veiled, once we begin to speak to Jesus as if He were literally present, an answering voice comes to show us He is in the shadows, keeping watch over His own."

It was on *January 25th*, 2008 that Jesus delivered our surprise package wrapped in pink. Yes, this is a big rollback of the clock. We had no idea the length of time we'd spend in darkness.

As it said in my devotional, "Streams in the Desert," *my eyes were often blinded, and I couldn't see "the One my soul loved."* It was difficult to trust Him or see *any* faithfulness. The more time that passed where I could not see Him or hear His voice, the harder it was to believe *He* was anywhere close to me, in the shadows or out in the open. I couldn't help but question our decision, thinking surely God wouldn't *purposefully* give us an assignment this difficult.

One day, about four months in on this troubled journey, I was filling out paperwork for her new Social Security card. There were blanks for her previous names and mothers and fathers. I had to print two forms off the internet because there weren't enough blanks for all the names she had before she became *a Ramshaw*. At this point, we had so little information about her history. In my hand, I held a piece of paper we were given that stated her birth mom's name, height, weight, hair and eyes, and birth date. Being adopted myself, I knew the importance of every detail. At three days old, I got *my* new name. Caelen was now about to turn four and getting yet another name.

I couldn't help but question our decision, thinking surely God wouldn't purposefully *give us an assignment this difficult.*

As I stared at the paper, I couldn't make sense of her birth mom's birthday. I read it. Then I read it again. It wasn't computing. Her birth mom and I were born on the same day! How could I have missed this? Being adopted, the smallest of details like height and weight were giant clues to an unknown person that was once your connection to life. To know so little about *the one person* you might resemble, a detail, a clue, helping you to imagine an invisible face, is a very valuable piece of information. How could this detail have been overlooked by me, who knew its importance?

For some of you, who are trying to comprehend the significance, I will draw a picture. As I sat in my office, experiencing a *hmm*, what's the word I'm looking for? Let's try, "This isn't how I thought it would be, God!" or to quote "Streams" directly, "surely God wouldn't *purposefully* give us an assignment this difficult."

I was disillusioned by how this story was unfolding, one where all signs of God and His *ever-present help* had vanished, *this date, this revelation.* His announcement, "I am here. I have never left. Today, I am letting you in on a *little detail* that I think will show you I have always been here. I *knew* you would be alone, discouraged, and questioning my presence, thinking that maybe you misunderstood My plan for your life—*before* she was born, *before* her mother was born, *before* you were born."

I coordinated the details. They were there all along, but I kept them hidden until today, for *My* purpose. It is to remind you, just how *ever-present* I am. Yes, you and her birth mom are born on the *Same Day!* I am in the details of life. I weave Myself into all sorts of details throughout creation. Some are seen, and some go unnoticed or are yet to be discovered by the human mind. Some give me the credit for the creation, and some get confused and give the credit to the creation. Make no mistake, I knew when you were to be born, when her mom was to be born, and when she would be delivered to your door. "I am ever-present."

Our trial with Caelen compared to our trial with Ryan's cancer were night and day. God seemed distant with Caelen. I moved? He moved? I didn't see Him much at all after her dramatic arrival. All I saw was my failure and felt complete isolation. "He who allows the suffering is with us throughout it. It may be that we will only see Him once the ordeal is nearly passed, but we must dare to believe that He never leaves our trial."—"Streams in the Desert," April 14th

During Ryan's cancer, God was so close every moment, even if I hated the circumstances. He showed up in the details of life so often and so God-like, we just didn't walk very far before He was showing himself again and again and again. But no matter how often God shows up in the struggle with Ryan, I am overwhelmed by sadness. I feel like a Faith-Failure.

Fast forward to January 26, 2016, eight years almost to the day (we are about a month into treatment.) Ryan goes to the ER with a fever. We have been instructed that, with any temperature above 101, we go to the ER. We hoped that a few meds and some IV fluids would lower his temperature and send us home.

Unfortunately, it did not. For the next eight days, he'd be in the hospital, part of that time in the ICU, fighting pneumonia and acute respiratory disease. So sick he couldn't get out of bed or even lift his arms. I don't think we realized how close to the edge of death he might have been. They were some of the hardest days, in part because it was to be his week off for recovery between chemo treatments. It was an unexpected and unwelcome time of trouble. It was Jennifer's birthday that week, the first one to be celebrated as a couple, and he couldn't get out of bed, let alone go purchase a special birthday gift. It was a week of great suffering, high fevers, and a vision of just how serious this cancer battle could get.

So, if He is that *ever-present help*, why so much suffering? Couldn't it be easier?

"But He allows trouble to pursue us, as though He were indifferent to its overwhelming pressure, so we may be brought to the end of ourselves."

"Streams in the Desert," January 23

At the end of ourselves! Really, God?

And by faith, even Sarah, who was past childbearing age, was enabled to bear children because she considered Him faithful who had made the promise. And so, from this one man, and 'he as good as dead' came descendants as numerous as the stars in the sky and as countless as the sand on the seashore.
— HEB 11:11-12

"As good as dead" can't get much closer to the end of ourselves than that. From as good as dead, came descendants as numerous as the stars. God just keeps repeating His story to me. It's not about *you* and *your* strength. It's about *Me* and *Mine.*

"To give us the spiritual gift we desire, God may have to begin far back in our spirit, in regions unknown to us . . .

Long before we begin to be aware that He is answering our
request—has answered it—and is visiting His child."
— GEORGE MACDONALD,
"MAN'S DIFFICULTY CONCERNING PRAYER"

"We don't want our lives to change at all."

2007

Life was good, *really good*. As I type, I can't help but think about how my thoughts are not *Your* thoughts, and my ways are not *Your* ways. You can hear those words two ways, God is speaking them, or you are. The perspective, the vantage point from which you see life, dramatically changes if you speak the words from your point of view vs. how they are meant to be said, from God's perspective, His heavenly view.

"My thoughts are nothing like your thoughts," says the LORD.
"And My ways are far beyond anything you could imagine."
— Is 55:8

A few months before our front-door delivery, a test was given in our adult Sunday school class. It was a marriage test, in which the husband and wife answered questions separately and then compared answers. Richard and I were married only a short time before we realized that we answered most questions *differently*. "Tomayto, Tomahto." Sid, the Sloth in *Ice Age*, says it so well with his memorable lisp, *"You complete me."* God has a way of completing us with an attraction to someone who is often our exact opposite.

So, we took the test, and one of the questions was, "What would you like to change in your life in the next five years?" Richard and I both answered, "Absolutely Nothing." See? I told you—life was good. We even agreed we were living large. The boys were so fun, they were now 8, 10, and 12, and we were driving on cruise control. As I look back over my life, remembering the things I've said out loud to God, like, "Give me a story to write about how *good* you are," followed by "I don't want my life to change at all"—they rank right up there with the dumbest things I've ever said to God. I realize He knows my words before I utter them, but a tiny part of me thinks that I can sneak a thought past Him, if I don't say it out loud. I can't help but picture God telling His assistant, if He has one, "Put in my file on Cathy Ramshaw; she wants to write a story about my 'goodness,' and she doesn't want her life to change 'at all.'" God had to chuckle at that one.

"My ways are far beyond anything you can imagine." And the story God wrote for me has taken a lifetime.

"I can only imagine."
— BART MILLARD

God Can Spit You Out on Whatever Beach He Wants

A*dopted at three days old*, I had a different story than most babies. My parents didn't tell me about the day I was born; they told me how God put me in their family. It was mostly my dad telling me this, but in a nutshell, he would say, "Cathy, your mom couldn't take care of you the way she wanted to or how God would want her to, so she prayed to Him and asked Him to put you in a Christian family that could." He told me that from the beginning. I don't remember it any other way. It was so much my story that I knew nothing else about how my life began. I never questioned why I was with them and not with my "real mom."

I never felt *thrown away*.

I believed my mom did her best for me. My earliest prayers were for her. I prayed God would take care of my mom as He had taken care of me. I knew I was loved and cared for, and I wanted her to be okay. I didn't spend my childhood worrying about her, but I distinctly remember asking God to take care of her. That story has always been my truth about who God is and what He can do. God can spit you out on whatever beach He wants—just ask Jonah.

> *And the LORD commanded the fish, and*
> *it vomited Jonah onto dry land.*
> —JON 2:10

Can you imagine? What a ride that was!

When you're adopted, people often assume you're going to adopt. I never understood the application of "If this, then that" to adoption. Then when you have three boys, the other assumption is, "Don't you want a girl?" Growing up with three brothers, I was used to spontaneous wrestling matches that shook the house. I wasn't a pink-tutu kind of mom. So, no, I don't need a girl.

In the '90s and early 2000s, international adoptions became prevalent in the Christian community. We knew many families that had adopted children. Most were baby girls from China. "Don't you want one?" our friends would say. I didn't have that urge or feel an unmet need for pink in my life. I loved being a boy mom!

My dad said that before I entered the picture, he and my mom passed a department store window with a mannequin of a mom and her daughter wearing matching dresses. I don't know the whole conversation, but I do know "Let's get one" was said by my dad. God did the rest from there. If I had been a boy, I would have gone to another family. The concept that God can put you where you're "supposed to be" was a life truth for me.

Richard and I discussed and even pursued adopting domestically, but only for a short time. I couldn't help but feel like I was taking someone else's child, someone who was dreaming of pink and begging God for a baby. We were good. *We didn't want our life to change.* Once we made that decision, I recall a conversation in our

> *"God will have to drop a baby girl in my lap if we are supposed to adopt."*

backyard with some good friends about adoption. I remember where we were standing when I said, "God will have to drop a baby girl in my lap if we are supposed to adopt." I spoke those with the same conviction as I spoke, "God, give me a story so I can tell others how good you are," "Here am I, send me" and the infamous "We don't want our lives to change at all."

Dropping Her into Our Lap

So, on January 20, 2008, God started His plan for His airdrop.

A close friend who ran a local adoption agency was at our home for a Bible study. I call her the "baby pusher," and I mean that in a good way. Many babies need a home, and she was the right girl for the job. She was an excellent advocate for adoption. She burst into my living room, phone in one hand and Blackberry in another, her standard position. When she got off the phone, she said, "We have a family in crisis, and they want to disrupt."

"Disrupt?" I said. "What do you mean, 'disrupt'?"

She explained, "They want to give their adopted daughter back." In horror, I questioned,

"*You can give them back?* They could have given *me* back?" My imagination tried to picture what would cause a family to "disrupt." Under no circumstances could I imagine giving a child back.

The other day a friend who runs a ministry in Haiti for orphans posted on Facebook a request for prayers, as they had just suffered a

7.2 earthquake. I said a prayer. I will admit, it was not a passionate prayer. It sounded like I was *ordering fries with that*. I thought to myself, *Why wasn't I more thoughtful about this request?* The answer came back to me: "Because you can't imagine it. You can't see what the people see in Haiti." This is the best way to explain my perception of disruption. I couldn't imagine giving a child back, but I wasn't seeing what they were seeing. I didn't know what was happening in their life. I asked to see a picture of this little girl. Truthfully, I was half expecting a horn to be protruding from her forehead. Instead, a little 3-year-old strawberry blonde with a big smile was sitting on a bike. For the rest of the night, this *disrupting* story bothered me. I could not understand or shake the vision from my head.

My prayer for this little girl was simple: "God, you can spit her out exactly where You want. I don't have to solve this for you. You are God. You love her more than I do. She is Your child, and You will put her where she belongs." And for the record, I 100% believed that.

Your Hands Made Us All

W*e are still back in 2008*—just don't want you to get lost in the belly of this whale.

The next day, January 21st, my devotion was based on the verse, *"We are like clay, and you are the potter; Your hands made us all."* (Isaiah 64:8) I was reading Max Lucado's "Grace for the Moment" devotional. He is a good thinker and paints a picture your eyes can see. As I read through the short lesson, I thought of the little strawberry blonde. I felt comfort knowing God doesn't leave you broken. Whatever was going on, God could fix it. He's the potter; I believed He wouldn't leave her broken.

The day passed, and another came, and the little girl was still heavy on my mind. I kept telling myself, "God doesn't need you to fix this. He has a plan for her, and He can ensure she goes to the right home." We do all sorts of things to help others. We can make a meal for a family who has lost a loved one or offer to help someone move, relatively easy acts of service that have a definite end in sight. I had no moral pull telling me this was my problem to solve.

Another day passed. In addition to "Grace for the Moment," I was reading "My Utmost for His Highest."

January 23rd's devotion read:

> "The greatest characteristic a Christian can exhibit is this completely unveiled openness before God, which allows that person's life to become a mirror for others. When the Spirit fills us, we are transformed, and by beholding God, we become mirrors. You can always tell when someone has been beholding the glory of the Lord, because your inner spirit senses that he mirrors the Lord's own character. Beware of anything that would spot or tarnish that mirror in you. It is almost always something good that will stain it—something good, but not what is best.
>
> The most important rule for us is to concentrate on keeping our lives open to God. Let everything else, including work, clothes, and food be set aside. The busyness of things obscures our concentration on God. We must maintain a position of beholding Him, keeping our lives completely spiritual through and through. Let other things come and go as they will; let other people criticize us as they will; but never allow anything to obscure the life that "is hidden with Christ in God" Colossians 3:3. Never let a hurried lifestyle disturb the relationship of abiding in Him. This is an easy thing to allow, but we must guard against it. The most difficult lesson of the Christian life is learning how to continue "beholding as in a mirror the glory of the Lord. . . ."

Why wasn't I forgetting this little girl and moving on? With caution, Richard and I took a secret trip to see her with our own eyes. But as we proceeded, I repeated the phrase, "God, you are going to have to Billboard this for me." I didn't want to take someone else's child. God had a plan, and He didn't need my help getting her to the beach *He* wanted. With "Billboard this for me" firmly in mind, we journeyed down an unfamiliar road, "keeping our lives open."

We pulled into the drive, and, staring back at us from the front door was the little strawberry-blonde we had seen in the picture. Inside hanging on the wall were three headshots of each child, and smiling back at me was a face that looked so much like Ryan I couldn't believe it. I elbowed Richard and whispered with my teeth clenched to keep my lips still, "She looks just like Ryan." Within minutes, I was being escorted by her hand to her room, just the two of us. Proudly showing me her room, she tapped my thigh, pulling me to the floor. She demonstrated that I was to be on my knees. "Pray for my parents." This scene was not how my mind had written our first encounter. But with her persistence, we prayed for her parents. No, I don't remember the prayer. I'm sure I did most of the praying. I couldn't help but feel like God was writing something. While we had girl time, Richard spoke with the dad and gained some understanding of this need to disrupt. I won't share the personal reasons; let's say they were looking at an earthquake around them, and they couldn't manage.

We asked a few questions about the birth mom. Me being adopted, what little information you can glean about what your mom looks like is always high on the list of questions. I remember when I first learned that my mom had brown hair and blue eyes and was 4'11" tall. That little bit of information was all I knew about her, but I could picture someone short, with dark hair and blue eyes. So, of course, I asked, "What do you know about the mom?" "Not much, but she is 4'11"." Was God writing a billboard? There aren't many full-grown women coming in at the under-5-foot mark.

We took this happy and very active three-year-old to Dairy Queen. The girl liked her some catsup! Ice cream was a hit as well. Both of us were at peace as we sat in the booth and watched her eat. I still couldn't get over how much she looked like Ryan. My boys don't match, a redhead, a brunette, and a blonde. She looked more like Ryan than Jackson and Cooper did.

We drove home, and I repeated over and over to Richard, "I need God to *Billboard* this for me." We decided that the next step to take was to tell the boys about what we had done that day to see how they reacted. We explained that our family was complete, that we didn't need to add anyone, and that no decisions would be made anytime soon. Our boys lit up with excitement telling us how they could rearrange their rooms and where she could sleep. Inadvertently the boys informed us that Ryan had expected to graduate to his own room in the basement as part of his Christmas gift last year. I guess we missed that billboard. They spent the entire evening in our bed, discussing what it would be like to have a sister. At one point, Jackson asked, "Could we get a boy instead?"

We planned to have her come on Friday after school for a couple of hours to meet them. We wanted to take our time with this. We planned to bake some cookies and play some games. I suggested we get a couple of small gifts for her and asked for ideas. Cooper enthusiastically proclaimed, "A kitchen. A play kitchen!" I asked for something smaller, and his next big idea was a "Dora the Explorer Tent"! I offered up, maybe a pair of play sunglasses. I don't know what I expected, but I didn't expect this level of enthusiasm. Billboard this for me, God. I *gotta* know this is You, not my emotions.

January 24/My Utmost for His Highest

"*The vision Paul had on the road to Damascus was not a passing emotional experience, but a vision that had very clear and emphatic directions for him. And Paul stated, "I was not disobedient to the heavenly vision" Acts 26:19 Our Lord said to Paul, in effect, "Your whole life is to be overpowered or subdued*

by Me; you are to have no end, no aim, and no purpose but
Mine." And the Lord also says to us, "You did not choose Me,
but I chose you and appointed you that you should go . . ."
—JN 15:16

Scripture is God-breathed, and it is a living word. It's so powerful and amazing how a verse you've read many times before can jump off the page at you. Not always, but sometimes it feels like God is speaking directly to you.

"Your whole life is to be overpowered or subdued by Me;
you are to have no end, no aim, and no purpose but Mine."
And the Lord also says to us, *"You did not choose Me, but*
I chose you and appointed you that you should go . . ."
—JN 15:16

I couldn't help but ask, "Are You choosing *us?*"

"Are You giving us specific directions? Are You saying our life should change and be overpowered by You and Your will? Only *Your* purpose? Are You asking us to go? Is the reason I can't stop thinking about this child because *You're choosing to spit her out on our beach?"*

Pure Grace

Remember the *"Baby Pusher"?* She called me on January 24th. "Do you know what her first name means?"

"No."

She informs me, "Wearisome." Her middle name is Grace. "Wearisome Grace." Well, it certainly fits her life. After being bumped from mom to mom, she had to be weary.

One of my best friends growing up and into adulthood had the last name "Kaelin." No one called her by her first name. No one called me by my first name, either. I was Troutt. She was Kaelin. She definitely had the cooler name of the two. All us girls, the Cathys, the Staceys, the Julies, and the Jennys, said that if we ever had a girl, we would name her Kaelin. This was long before the *Brittney* and *Taylor* trends hit.

I didn't want to take her name from her, but if I changed the last letter in her name to an N, she became Caelen, and the meaning changed from "Wearisome Grace" to "Pure Grace." Was it a coincidence that her name was so close to Kaelin? Was it a coincidence that Catherine also means "pure"? Are you changing "Wearisome Grace" into "Pure Grace"? Is this Your billboard? I *gotta* know it's you. I won't do it unless I know it's you, God. I don't want to do this on my own emotion. Write it in the sky for me in larger-than-life, bold font!

Surprise!

J*anuary 25th*: My Utmost for His Highest

"As servants of God, we must learn to make room for Him—to give God "elbow room." We plan and figure and predict that this or that will happen, but we forget to make room for God to come in as He chooses. Would we be surprised if God came into our meeting or into our preaching in a way we had never expected Him to come? Do not look for God to come in a particular way, but do look for Him. The way to make room for Him is to expect Him to come, but not in a certain way. No matter how well we may know God, the great lesson to learn is that He may break in at any minute. We tend to overlook this element of surprise, yet God never works in any other way. Suddenly—God meets our life ". . . when it pleased God. . . ."

"Keep your life so constantly in touch with God that His surprising power can break through at any point. Live in a constant state of expectancy and leave room for God to come in as He decides."

So, it's January 25th, and she's coming after school to bake cookies. I'm at Walmart getting sunglasses and cookie ingredients, and my phone is beeping like crazy. I'm on the phone with my brother; it's his birthday. I see Richard call. Then the Baby Pusher. Then Richard. I, of course, said nothing to my brother because I didn't want to make this decision with any other outside influence but God. Only God's Billboard! As the beeps continue, I think, *they've changed their minds.* I call Richard back, and this is when God walks in and says, "Surprise!"

Take Care of Her

Richard *said they called.* They are on their way here. They have packed her bags and said their goodbyes, and they are not taking her home. I'm not sure what my first thought was, but I distinctly remember my blood changing from regular blood to jet fuel. "What? 'They aren't taking her home'? How does that work? Who is supposed to keep her?"

The next couple of hours were a bit of a blur, and I'm not going to share the details of that January afternoon because it doesn't add to the story. I *can* share that, in a few hours, my house was deep cleaned, as stress often fuels a cleaning rampage in me. That combined with jet fuel in my veins, I was a machine! And as I explained, I couldn't see their earthquake; this didn't make sense, *yet.*

That afternoon, the parents signed away their rights at our kitchen table. She was officially in our custody, so we could make medical decisions and act in case of choking on a grape. Don't ask me why choking on a grape was my big worry!

The mom gave me a funeral hug, one of those long ones, when it's hard to let go, because you're saying goodbye, forever. She pulled back, and we held forearms. Tears in her eyes, "Take care of her," she said. I responded, "No, God will take care of her. If you plan to count on just me, you won't be able to live with yourself. You must know God will take care of her, not me. She is His child."

And they left.

I Love *CHOCOLATE!*

M*y first official act of mothering* this pink child was going potty. What was it I said last summer? *"God will have to drop a baby girl in my lap if He wants us to have one."* Now, do you see the importance of sharing that statement? So again, my first official girl-mom job was taking her to the bathroom. As we all know, little girls and boys operate entirely different in more ways than one. As she sat face forward on the toilet, I bent down to her eye level and said we would have some pizza for dinner and make some cookies. She replied with, *"I LOOOVVVVE CHOCOLATE"!*

She said *love* and *chocolate* like she was tasting it right then, each syllable drawn out for emphasis. I replied with an equally emphatic, *"I LOOOVVVE CHOCOLATE, TOO!"*

And so, it began.

Bedtime Story

R*eading a Bible story to the boys* was a nightly bedtime activity. When they were little, the story of David and Goliath was their most requested story. They loved it when Richard bellowed the words in a deep voice, "You come against me with sword and spear, but I come against you in the name of the Lord!" That was a very exciting part of the Bible for young warriors like themselves.

As we gathered her up with her pink polka-dot suitcase, we unzipped the bag to discover pink zip-up footy pajamas. I was sure this was the most pink we'd ever had in our house. We put a blow-up mattress on the floor of Cooper's room. It had been quite a day, and I thought it was starting to wind down when Cooper said, "Where's the Baby-Bible? We *have* to read her a story."

Truth? I thought to myself, *Can't we skip this?* But eight-year-old Cooper was emphatic. Luckily, I knew where it was, and Cooper excitedly snatched it from my hands. "I know *exactly* what story to read!" There he sat, the Bible in his lap, frantically flipping through the pages, all of us gathered in his room. Enough time went by that I said, "Cooper, *any* story will do. Really, just pick one."

"No, I've got the story!" He finally finds the story he wants, and the boys each took turns reading a page of the story of Joseph, not David and Goliath. It's the Baby-Bible, so the story was simple and short. Joseph was thrown away by his brothers, abandoned, left in a pit for dead, but God had a different plan. God had big plans for Joseph, He would use Joseph to save His people from starvation. The story concludes with the line from Genesis 50:20, *"What man meant for evil, God meant for good."*

As the Bible was closed, she exclaimed, "That's my story," in a sweet three-year-old voice. We would soon discover she had a limited vocabulary. The family before us had done lots of work to get her to where she was, but she was still significantly delayed. They are a good family. They tried. I don't want you to think poorly of them. I keep thinking of that earthquake; if you can't see it, it's hard to imagine how hard life is for those trying to survive. So often, when we can't understand the hurt and the struggle, we fail to show understanding or compassion as we should.

"That's my story!" I know that, in her mind, the boys had just read her a bedtime story. That's the only thing it could be. But I believe that God was speaking to me as I heard Him say, "Cathy, this has happened for centuries, people thrown away and left for dead in a pit, sometimes by their own family. You are just getting a front-row seat. Despite man's wrong choices, I can still use broken, imperfect people to save." It was beginning to feel like he was "choosing" us to do that.

"Cathy, this has happened for centuries, people thrown away and left for dead in a pit, sometimes by their own family. You are just getting a front-row seat. Despite man's wrong choices, I can still use broken, imperfect people to save."

And the Lord also says to us, "You did not choose Me, but
I chose you and appointed you that you should go . . .
—JN 15:16

Our Beach

God *often must spell things out for me*, and I repeatedly said, "Billboard this for me, God. I *gotta* know this is You."

I didn't sleep much that night. I still had jet fuel running through my veins. Not able to sleep or even relax, I got up at about 4:00 a.m. In all the chaos from the day, I still needed to read Max Lucado's entry for that day.

True confessions: I read "My Utmost for His Highest" for January 25th, on the 24th, looking for a billboard message. Would God be bold and tell us one way or another what to do? God was talking to me, to us, with more clarity than usual. When Richard and I recall this week, we speak of God's presence in our home being like nothing we had ever experienced before. We both cling to that, and when earthquakes come, and they come often with her, we remind each other of how clear and overpowering God was that week.

"As servants of God, we must learn to make room for Him—to give God 'elbow room.' We plan and figure and predict that this or that will happen, but we forget to make room for God to come in as He chooses. Would we be surprised if God came into our meeting or into our preaching in a way we had never expected Him to come? Do not look for God to come in a particular way, but do look for Him. The way to make room for Him is to expect Him to come, but not in a certain way. No matter how well we may know God, the great lesson to learn is that He may break in at any minute. We tend to overlook this element of surprise, yet God never works in any other way. Suddenly—God meets our life '. . . when it pleased God.'"

Keep your life so constantly in touch with God that His surprising power can break through at any point. Live in a constant state of expectancy and leave room for God to come in as He decides."
My Utmost for His Highest—January 25th

When I read those words on the 24th, I had no idea God would break into our lives with this surprise. He stepped right into our family in a way we never expected. When people ask how this all happened, I always say the short story, "Jesus walked right up to our front porch carrying her in His arms and said, "This one is yours." When God does that, I don't know about you, but I don't have the nerve to argue or question if He has the correct address. If anybody but Jesus had asked us to do this, we would have quit long ago. When I get to heaven, I'd like to have coffee with Noah and ask him how often he wanted to quit building the ark and how he kept going.

I'm not 100% sure about this assumption, but I will say what I think you are thinking right now. Many of you might read that statement, "If anybody but Jesus had asked me to do this, I would have quit long ago." and question if we heard God's call correctly, given how difficult this journey would be, and if He did give her to you. why aren't you more joyful about the assignment? No commandment states, "Thou shalt smile while being stoned" or "Thou shalt not ask for this cup to pass." The Bible does go into detail about suffering and sacrifice. There was a lot of it! It would be a lie if I told you that Richard and I haven't wanted to quit. God gives us hard things. Sometimes He sends us to a place we didn't even know existed and never imagined He would send us there.

> *"If anybody but Jesus had asked me to do this, I would have quit long ago."*

I was notorious for making *"My plan."* But this week was different. God walked into our home in a way we never expected. God met our life when it pleased Him and how it pleased Him. We had asked Him to be clear—"billboard style": write it in the sky, and His power broke through. He chose us. He chose to spit her out on our beach.

Adopted by God

In his faithfulness to me, He put an extra thick coat of chocolate frosting on the cake. When I opened Max Lucado's devotional, sitting alone in the dark of my living room, I read the January 25th entry title, "Adopted by God," I honestly thought, *Okay, okay—I got it. This is the Billboard I asked for.*

The devotional reads,

> *"The Spirit himself testifies with our spirit that we are God's children."*
> — Rom 8:16

"When we come to Christ, God not only forgives us, He also adopts us. Through a dramatic series of events, we go from condemned orphan with no hope to adopted children with no fear. Here is how it happens. You come before the judgment seat of God full of rebellion and mistakes. Because of His justice, He cannot dismiss your sin, but because of His love, He cannot dismiss you. So, in an act which stunned the heavens, He punished Himself on the cross for your sins. God's justice and love are equally honored. And you, God's creation, are forgiven. But the story doesn't end with God's forgiveness.

It would be enough if God just cleansed your name, but He does more. He gives you His name."

He does all of this out of His *"Pure Grace."* God's Billboard, written in the sky for us all.

And They All Lived Happily Ever After

The *perspective you bring to a situation* and your experiences affect your expectations. My expectation was, "We would all live happily ever after." My life up to that point resembled a fairytale. But that's not what happened, not even close. People tell me to write a book about Caelen. I have always responded with a firm "No" because the story isn't pretty. I'm not pretty in the story. It didn't turn out at all as I had expected. Not that I had much time to ponder an expectation, but what happened was nothing I could have even imagined. After her surprise delivery, it is hard to see God in the story at all. I never thought He would send me here.

We spent the first year scratching our heads at what we were seeing. I didn't just scratch my head; I was pulling my hair out. We didn't recognize the behaviors we saw. Caelen did not feel pain. A goose egg on the forehead due to a miscalculation of the corner of the kitchen bar produced no tears; instead, she laughed. She never fell asleep in the warm sunshine of a car ride. She was instead rocking constantly front to back, never still. *Never.* Every time she saw a policeman, she said these words. "Police are bad. They chase you. They put you in jail. They take the baby." And if she saw a man with long hair in public, she would say, "Don't leave me here!" This is the only time she would ever seek our comfort or protection. She didn't want to be touched or held. If you insisted on holding her hand to cross the street, she would pinch your pinky between two fingers, nothing more. It was as if our hands were diseased and feared. She had two emotions—anger and hyper-happy. The hyper-happy (manic) never ran out of steam until it turned into a rage I didn't recognize and a three-year-old shouldn't know how to feel.

We'd talk to friends and family and say, "Something's not right." People always responded with, "She's fine." "She'll be fine by kindergarten." My personal favorite was, "You're just used to good boys." What we saw was not a gender difference. It's so interesting how people question what they can't see. Richard used to stand in a grocery store, and when he saw a screaming child misbehave over the denied candy purchase, he would inevitably say, "Give me that kid for a week, and he won't act like that." He doesn't say that anymore.

We had her for a year, and we were exhausted. Our "good life" had disappeared. Some friends invited us, just Richard and me, for a week's vacation. My parents kept her that week. I will never forget my mother's reaction to me when I returned. She grabbed both of my arms, up by the shoulders, as a football coach does to a player before he sends him out on the field to battle (something she has never done before or again since) and looked straight at me and said, "Why didn't you tell me?"

"I'm pretty sure we did."

This is why I don't want to tell you this story. That phrase "You have to see it to believe it" applies here in a way I don't think can be fathomed. Sometimes the more you describe it, the crazier you sound. No matter how well it is described, until you see it play out repeatedly, you honestly can't believe it. Onlookers are quick to judge a situation they cannot understand. The only people who understand are the other parents trying to "fix" their child, who has endured severe trauma resulting in RAD. This underground community of parents, living through the identical earthquake are the only people safe to share your story with.

Cleveland Clinic describes RAD as follows:

"Reactive attachment disorder (RAD) is a condition where a child doesn't form healthy emotional bonds with their caretakers (parental figures), often because of emotional neglect or abuse at an early age. Children with RAD have trouble managing their emotions. They struggle to form meaningful connections with other people. Children with RAD rarely seek or show signs of comfort and may seem fearful of or anxious around their caretakers, even in situations where their caretakers are quite loving and caring."

From the outsider's point of view, a child with RAD appears to be friendly, seeking to connect. As hard as this is to fathom, even after reading multiple books on attachment and trauma and attending parenting conferences, the following statement has helped me to understand Reactive Attachment Disorder a little better. *During the first three years of life abuse and neglect caused by the mother causes the child to fear the mother, (main caretaker), the source of their pain. A stranger never left them alone to cry, suffer, or be hungry. In their mind, a stranger is safe; the mother is the enemy who traumatized them. When this happens in the pre-verbal stages of life the brain's "software" programs the mother figure as the abuser. The mother is the source of fear even when the new mother is loving and caring.* When you think about it, and I do a lot, this is one of the sickest things you can do to a child.

*"The parent-child connection is the most powerful
mental-health intervention known to mankind."*
—Dr. Bessel van der Kolk
(Psychiatrist specializing in child trauma,
author of *The Body Keeps Score*.)

Read it. Your perspective on life and others will change.

Recipe

When *Ryan was diagnosed with Ewing's Sarcoma*, the doctor explained that there was a specific chemo recipe to follow to kill the tumor, and if the doctor from our hometown followed it, we could go home. There are a lot of contrasting elements between cancer and trauma. One of the most significant and difficult is that there is no recipe to follow for trauma. When people suggest I write a book to help other parents struggling with a child affected by abuse and neglect, I have a massive wall built up against that idea. The foundation of that wall rests on the fact that I don't have the answers. I can't fix this. There are many things to try: behavior modification, medications, and a great variety of books already written on the subject. However, I have found that very rarely can you use the same recipe. Each child is different. Each day is different. The triggers, the hormones, the moods, and the events of the day can change everything. While we have learned some beneficial methods for keeping ourselves calm and Caelen regulated, there is no set recipe to follow. There are no breaks from the mental illness/brain trauma, which is an integral part of her daily functioning. It is ever-present. In medical terminology, NED stands for No Evidence of Disease. NED is a finish line in cancer. Unlike NED, there is no finish line with RAD. There is always evidence of the disease.

The chemo-concoction given to Ryan used to kill the tumor; sometimes, it kills things it's not supposed to, but it's not like there is a choice. It is either the chemo-concoction or death. The goal is killing the tumor while you hope and pray that the treatment doesn't kill the patient. The chemo given to a child for Ewing's Sarcoma is so potent that an adult can't survive it. A child replicates cells so quickly that they can recover from treatment. It's hard, but their bodies can do it. Because the adult can't recover as quickly or, sometimes, at all, chemo is given at a lesser and slower rate of frequency. Subsequently, the adult's ability to beat cancer diminishes, and the chance of survival is much lower. (Ewing's Sarcoma is a pediatric cancer, but in even more rare cases, an adult can get the cancer.)

Contrast this scenario with abuse and neglect. For a child who endures abuse and neglect during the first three years, especially the first year, the damages are more severe and long-lasting. An adult, teenager, or even a child in grade school experiencing abuse and neglect can survive better than a baby or toddler, because they have developed coping and reasoning skills that the baby's brain has not. The baby's brain is pre-verbal. They can't tell someone what hurts. Think about it, how does a baby communicate pain? Crying. The brain is a conditioned organ that stores experiences. If the baby learns that, *When I cry, I am hurt more by my caretaker*, the brain learns that crying makes it worse. So, during the most vulnerable time in life, those first three years, the abused and neglected baby brain is learning how to survive—not connect, trust, and regulate. The brain experiencing trauma is rewired to do something it's supposed to do only while under attack. It is rewiring to survive in its abusive environment. The bond that is supposed to develop between the mother and child is not happening. Either way, there is no recipe for the rewiring of the brain later. There is no tumor to kill. The behaviors the child displays are exactly what their brain learned to do to survive. How do you cure that?

Certain functions, like trust, attachment, language, empathy, eye contact, emotional responses to pain, pleasure, soothing, and even the ability to play—all of that is developing in those first years. When those are not taught or experienced as the child is developing but is instead learning to survive, teaching those skills later is a constant battle. You can teach a child a skill, like throwing a ball, how to hold it, and what leg to step with, and the child learns the motion, creating muscle memory, like riding a bike. Trying to teach a child to feel something that was supposed to have been taught over thousands of healthy interactions, repetition over the years, in the very first stage of life, becomes an entirely different interaction between mother and child at this later stage of development.

A child being cared for and loved learns something as innate as feeling sad during a separation from its mother or even satisfaction after a meal; they learn awareness of themselves and others.

A child being cared for and loved learns something as innate as feeling sad during a separation from its mother or even satisfaction after a meal; they learn awareness of themselves and others. During those interactions, they are taught healthy emotions. They are learning responses to love and touch and comfort. Pick up a baby kitten that has been loved and cared for since birth, and they purr. Try to touch a feral barn kitten that has never been touched and count the scratches on your arms.

"Trauma compromises our ability to engage with others by replacing patterns of connection with patterns of protection."—Stephen Porges, known for developing the "Polyvagal Theory"—explaining what happens in the body and nervous system when there is a perceived threat or danger, what it does to our sense of safety, and the impact on our behavior.

"I do it!"

"I *do it!*" a phrase proclaimed from her 3-year-old mouth; a war cry fueled by her truth that no one was coming to help. "I do it!" Painfully, it is not like your typical defiant toddler demanding independence. I wish it were. Healthy independence is practiced by a three-year-old, while it can try our patience as we wait for them to complete the task or become exasperated enough to ask for help, declaring independence is a necessary rite of passage as the child learns to do things independently. It is supposed to happen.

One of the many tragic consequences of Caelen's first three years was that her brain learned she could not trust her mama(s) or fathers; they were not coming to her rescue. Her mamas are the source of her pain, neglect, and abandonment. When she said, "I do it," it was a volcanic eruption from her core, a shield she wielded, protecting her from harm. "I do it because I do not trust you!" "I do it because no one comes when I cry for help!"

> *"Some of My children find Me more readily during dark times,*
> *when difficulties force them to depend on Me. Others feel*
> *closer to Me when their lives are filled with good things."*
> — FROM "JESUS CALLING"

The words "I do it" roared inside my head as I read this devotion. I recalled how much I despised her "declaration of independence." *Despised* is a strong word, but yes, *despised* is accurate. Her distrust of me was unwarranted. I had done nothing to deserve this, and it hurt me; frustrated me. I was *not* those mamas! Why can't she see that? All I was trying to do was love, protect, and provide for her. Her distrust wasn't fair. Unable to penetrate her belief that I was to be feared, that I couldn't be trusted, her life experience had rewritten the software of her brain to say, 'Mamas hurt you. You can't trust them.' Men were worse. They evoked a fear in her eyes that a child shouldn't know. A fear, seen in the eyes of the hunted encountering their predator, fear for their life.

On what should have been an uneventful bike ride one Saturday morning, eight months after her front-porch delivery, there was an accident, a compound fracture of the forearm, and a cast for six weeks.

(She didn't cry.) Devastation for Mama #5, as swimming was the only activity this new addition enjoyed. I must repeat this for dramatic effect. Swimming was the *only* activity she enjoyed. She did not watch Veggie Tales—or *any* tale, for that matter. If she was given a book, she became a paper shredder. The child did not sit for any activity. Jumping off the diving board and swimming to the ladder was what she did. This injury sent me into desperation, crying, *What will I do now?* The role of the "untrusted mama" was destroying me!

And then, something unexpected happened.

"I do it!" by necessity became "Help" almost instantly. I didn't see that one coming.

On my desk at home sits a black-and-white picture of a little girl holding up a boulder. She leans into the mountain of rock, arms outstretched above her, giving the appearance that she is holding the boulder in place. Ridiculous, yet it was a picture I identified with, as I thought of myself as that little girl. Not that I could ever hold up a boulder, but I was determined and independent. "I've got this one, God. Don't worry about this boulder rolling down the hill. You go take care of the world's troubles. I got this. I do it." I had planned to frame it as a reminder of myself holding up the rock, refusing to leave my post as Mama #5, persevering, enduring. "I do it!"

In this journey as Mama #5, I have done too much on my own strength. Although I haven't found it yet, there must be a Bible verse supporting the belief that God wouldn't give me something I couldn't do on my own. Aren't there bumper stickers that say, "God never gives you more than you can handle?" As my arms remained in place, dutifully supporting the boulder, exhausted from the weight, but refusing to let go, I held my position, attempting to love, comfort, and help her, but she wouldn't let me do it. Her entire being pulsated with "I do it!" She wanted no help, no comfort, no nothing; until that fateful bike crash that would literally break her "I do it" in half, just like her arm. And that's what happened. Our daughter couldn't button her pants. She had to let me do it.

For those of you who haven't connected the dots yet, yes, I am just like her, and maybe you are, too. How often have I treated God like he is the untrusted Father, questioning His love, provision, and protection? I show him unwarranted distrust all the time as I worry and fret, spinning my yarn of life, planning out my days, because somewhere in my mind, I still believe, "I do it." How is that for honesty? We have this vision for what life should be, and we, I, hang onto that image with a vise grip; as I tell myself I know best, I tell God, "I do it."

God does value perseverance;

> *"Let perseverance finish its work so that you may be*
> *mature and complete, not lacking anything."*
> —JAS 1:4

God *does* want us to patiently endure.

> *"For what credit is there if, when you sin and are harshly treated,*
> *you endure it with patience? But if, when you do what is right and*
> *suffer for it, you patiently endure it, this finds favor with God.*
> — 1 PET 2:20

But there is also this . . .

> *Then Jesus said, "Come to me, all of you who are weary*
> *and carry heavy burdens, and I will give you rest. Take my*
> *yoke upon you. Let me teach you because I am humble and*
> *gentle at heart, and you will find rest for your souls. For My*
> *yoke is easy to bear, and the burden I give you is light."*
> — MATT 11:28-30

If we were sitting in a coffee shop and I was telling you this story, you could hear my frustration that, no matter how often I pick her up from school, she's worried I won't. I could give you a list as long as my arm of examples of her not trusting me, but the examples don't matter because her reasoning always concludes with "I can't trust you, you hurt me, you're the mom, my enemy." When I step back and contemplate this lack of trust, I can understand that her brain doesn't just see me. Her brain remembers all the other moms and what they did. She does not recall a specific abuse she received from each mom. She doesn't tell me stories about why she can't trust them or what they did to her. The memories happened pre-verbal; she has no words for them, but the memories are there.

Picture her brain as a tightly woven ball of yarn, layer upon layer, round, and round the yarn builds and builds, weaving her thoughts together, her memories of neglect and abuse. Those yarns of abuse and neglect are woven into her like the veins that carry her blood. They are part of her. If you struggle to believe this is possible, ask yourself how your child learned to trust you—it's the same process, a different color of yarn.

God is teaching me some profound, painful lessons through suffering. Remember the words from the devotional, *"Some of My children find Me more readily during dark times when difficulties force them to depend on Me."* I'm that child learning in the dark. People don't typically share the lessons they learn in the dark. They keep them to themselves out of pride mostly. Let's face it: The lessons you learn in the darkness of suffering aren't like chocolate cupcakes, scrumptious morsels you want to share with your neighbor. Usually, it's the realization of how sinful we are. Who wants to share that with their neighbor? I, like Caelen, want to control everything in my life. I, like Caelen, don't trust as I should. The longer I am Caelen's mom, the more I see that I am just like her. I wouldn't say I like admitting this. I'd rather keep that to myself in the dark.

Is God up in heaven talking to Jesus, saying, "Well, I guess we're going to have to break Cathy's arm so she can't button her pants on her own anymore?" Ryan's cancer rivals Caelen's broken arm—not that those two things are alike, but that, when Ryan got cancer, I stopped saying, "I do it," and cried for help. I didn't walk away from holding up that boulder after careful consideration and weighing my options. No, I collapsed right there under it. There was nothing I could do; just like Caelen could no longer button her pants, I could do nothing to heal Ryan. "I do it" instantly became "Help me!"

When the Lord broke my arm, so to speak, it rendered me helpless, and I put the picture in a drawer. I have no plans to frame it anymore. I don't want to be that girl, holding up the boulder, like that's my part of the deal with God. It's not. He doesn't intend for me to hold up anything. His burden is light. He *can* be trusted. There is no "I do it" Bible verse, and that saying, "God never gives you more than you can handle," is a lie.

Dear Lord, forgive me for exasperating you with my lack of trust. So many times, I have served You in my own strength. I am sorry. I have misunderstood Your calling on my life. Yes, I am to endure, and persevere, but not on my own. "I do it" is not Your plan. As I have executed my own plans, questioning the truth of Your "light burden," I am learning it is the burden I choose to carry alone that is heavy.

Yes, Lord, the pain and struggle of trying to love a child who sees love as a threat is exhausting. I pray you take away her hurt. I pray you heal the brokenness deep inside her mind. I pray she will trust You.

Yes, Lord, seeing Ryan's life change so dramatically, seemingly everything taken away, has made me understand that I no longer want to attempt even a moment without You. I cannot bear this burden alone.

I pray, Lord, that You heal and restore anything within Ryan's and Caelen's body that is against Your will. I pray that I can see Your provision and trust Your strength. I proclaim Your glory, Your grace. You are a good and loving God who can be trusted.

In Jesus's Name, Amen

"All our worry and fret is caused by calculating without God."
— OSWALD CHAMBERS

Who Is *That* in the Mirror?

Whileile the broken arm helped break her of her mantra "I do it," she still has an undercurrent of distrust that runs beneath the surface and suspicion that somewhere out there is a better family, a better deal. She can say she trusts us, but those words evaporate into nothing and survival dominates her being the moment she perceives any sign of deprivation. She struggles to believe that we can see how to fix it because of our ability to understand life from a more informed view. Does she think we wouldn't do everything we could to help? My frustration mounts with her as her distrust permeates every single encounter. And then I see a little girl telling God, "I do it," "I know better," "I have a plan," except that little girl is my reflection in the mirror.

> *If your child asks you for bread, would any of you give him*
> *a stone? Or if your child asks for a fish, would you give him*
> *a snake? Even though you're evil, you know how to give*
> *good gifts to your children. So how much more will your*
> *Father in heaven give good things to those who ask him?*
> — MATT 7:9

I Thought You Told Us
to Go Here

Ass years passed and we saw so little change in her, I no longer recognized myself in the mirror. I felt like a complete failure. How could God have given us this little girl we can't fix? Can't help! What we were living every day was not anything close to what our life had been. The boys retreated to the basement, escaping the earthquake. Every day, Caelen's trauma reared its ugly head. Not only was I struggling to deal with the shaking of our home's foundation, but I was also seeing less and less of the boys. I saw it as a trade that I had to make. My time with them was sacrificed to care for her and protect them from her turmoil. A laying down of the life I had known. It felt like I was trading my life with them for taking care of her. I had to protect them from the trauma of the earthquake as much as I could while trying to reach a child I couldn't understand.

I was seeking God, and it felt like he was doing nothing and saying even less. The week she arrived in 2008, when *"He met our life . . . when it pleased God."* Where was He? I thought you said, *"you wouldn't leave her broken."* This is about as broken as a person gets, and now, she has broken me.

In those years, I thought about Noah building the ark. He was 500 years old when God commissioned him to build the ark. What must Noah have thought when God gave him those instructions for the dimensions and told him about the animals, two by two? At some point, Noah had to think, *You know I'm 500 years old—right?*

It took Noah 100 years to build that ark, give or take *a decade or two.* I had been trying to be Caelen's mom, to love and care for her, for a couple of years, and I was *worn out.* I would think about Noah and how tired his body must've felt building that ark. How tired did he grow of swinging a hammer day after day? The morning would come, and I would stare at the wall of my bedroom, not lifting my head. I couldn't. I had to talk myself into starting the day. I would repeat the verse, *"Today is the day the Lord has made. I will rejoice and be glad in it."* (Ps. 118:24) Over and over for months, years. I chewed that verse like a hard piece of bubblegum that had lost its flavor long ago, and my jaws ached. I was not rejoicing. I was not glad to be in this.

I knew what chaos waited outside my bedroom door. It was the same chaos I saw the day before and the days before that. All I could think was *Noah didn't want to get up, either.* His body *had* to ache. There had to be days when he was lying in bed, questioning *why God chose him.*

That was my question. Why did you choose me? One of the worst things to say to someone suffering or struggling is "God picked you because he knew you could handle it." *Ya know what? That's not true.* Not one piece of that is true! God knew exactly how hard this would be and how long this journey would last. It would last my lifetime. I was crumbling beneath the weight. He did not choose me because He knew I could handle it!

The song "Oceans, Where My Feet May Fail," sung by Hillsong, paints a vivid scene of Christ calling us out on the water. It is such a calming melody, and the words are a love song, except when the ocean waves rise and you can't feel His embrace—what then? When life is hard, and all you can think is, "I thought You told us to go here!" "We are sinking, God!" "Why would You tell us to go here?" "You knew! *You knew!*" "I can't fix her!" "I can't help her!" "This isn't how it was supposed to be. *Why did you send me here?*"

No *Hope*

For a time, I quit reading Bible verses with the word "hope" in them. Yep, I'd skip right over them. I wasn't interested in hearing about His hope anymore. There is no hope of this getting better, so it's just best we don't talk about it. I didn't keep this a secret. Richard knew; my close friends knew. I wasn't hiding it. I couldn't hide it. It was just a fact. I had no hope, and I couldn't see any reason to believe hope would show up anytime soon. I hoped that she would get better, fixed, and that life of being the boys' mother, their happy, functioning mother that I once was, would return. But that wasn't going to happen.

We couldn't go anywhere as a family unless there was a daycare or some activity for her. Sitting in church? Not happening! Vacation? You can't put her in a car seat for hours; she won't stop rocking back and forth, and while you think that is no big deal, after 8 hours of driving and her rocking non-stop, you're a crazy person. "Just go to sleep. Go to sleep!"

Within months of her arrival, we knew regular vacations were out of the question. When we had our conversation with the boys about the possibility of adding a little girl to our family, the one where Jackson asked if we could get a boy instead, the next night Jackson asked if adding her would affect our vacations. Richard confidently said no, adopting her would not affect our vacations. We had no idea how much our lives would change. If we did go on vacation, we had to have something she could do. Kanukuk is a Christian camp, and each summer they provided "Family Camp." The kids had access to all the fun activities in the morning, while the parents participated in a study of some sort, kind of an extended church service meets Sunday school, and then the afternoon was family fun time. Caelen was young enough that she could attend their daycare. Sounded like a good plan for the entire family.

On our first morning there, the pastor they had flown in for this week of camp introduced himself. He started by telling us about what to expect this week. "This week, I am going to preach on only *one word.*"

Real Funny, God!

I*'m giving you only* one guess *at what that word was.* I slumped in the pew like a teenager told to stay home on Friday night. I couldn't believe this entire week would be on *Hope*. "Hilarious, God!" Hopefully, you can see the humor in this.

Personally, I think it's just another indisputable reason to say there is a God, and He seemed to think He could convince me *not to lose hope.*

> *Therefore, with minds that are alert and fully*
> *sober, set your hope on the grace to be brought to you*
> *when Jesus Christ is revealed at his coming.*
> — 1 PET 1:1

Wait a minute, *Set your hope on the grace. . . . at his coming!* Where is the verse that says to set your hope on the grace of Jesus Christ because He is the potter and isn't going to leave her broken? I need some serious help down here. I want the verse that says that hope is coming long before Christ's return! I want the verse that says *put your hope in Him* because He is going to fix this!

See, I told you, this reflection of mine in the mirror ain't so pretty. Why would I share this story?

> *We remember before our God and Father your work*
> *produced by faith, your labor prompted by love, and your*
> *endurance inspired by hope in our Lord Jesus Christ.*
> — 1 THES 1:3

Endurance inspired by hope in our Lord Jesus Christ. I was only two years into this journey, and I was out of endurance. I spoke with the "family camp" pastor one night, sitting at a picnic table outside the mess hall. I told him about the little joke God had played on me. I told him about our life. I wasn't proud of my life or my thoughts, but a starving man is going to ask for food, even if he is ashamed of the clothes he's wearing. I don't remember the entire conversation, but I remember this.

I wasn't proud of my life or my thoughts, but a starving man is going to ask for food, even if he is ashamed of the clothes he's wearing.

"Is your hope in yourself, or is your hope in Jesus Christ?"

Good question. But I had been crying to God for help, and there had been no answer. No help! My hope question had *one* answer I wanted from God, "I will fix her." "I won't leave her broken." "I'm giving you your life back." Okay, I know that's *three* answers.

I was willing to put my hope in Christ—

As long as, He followed *my plan* and *met my expectations.*

As long as, He gave me the answer I wanted.

As long as, He solved the problem on my timeline.

As long as, He gave me *"Happily Ever After."*

Life Is Good?

H*ow can I tell this story* of how Jesus made a "Special Delivery" to our front door, and now it looks like our "good life" will never return? It's so difficult; I'd thrown my "Life Is Good" shirt away long before Ryan's cancer, because wearing it made me feel like a liar.

What good can come from my sharing our difficulties? I ask myself these questions all the time. In the following pages, I share how it was only when God took me through the *valley* of the shadow of death that I learned to declare His glory *during* my *deepest pain.* Once again, I hear,

> *"Some of My children find Me more readily during dark times when difficulties force them to depend on Me."*
> –JESUS CALLING

Let's climb into the DeLorean for a trip forward to January 2016, *exactly* eight years after Caelen was delivered to our front door, back to Ryan in the ICU. Caelen is still in treatment out of state. Jackson and Cooper are holding their own and swimming on the High School swim team. . . . and I can't believe God has sent us here. What did I do to deserve this?

Really Ugly Wrapping Paper
January 26, 2016

It *was an off-week, no chemo,* and supposed to be a "good week." Ryan had made plans, the first in weeks, a KU basketball game, the anticipation of normal, no chemo, no hospital, and Jennifer's birthday. Instead, we are admitted overnight due to a low-grade fever, a precaution. As the night wore on, his fever spiked to 103.3; our precautionary overnight stay turned into days of high fever, draining him of his breath, so weak the monitors no longer detected it. With masks, gowns, gloves, breathing machines, isolation, and ICU, we reached a new level of disbelief and fear.

Joy! Lord, how? Joy, in all of this? Life drains from his body; his eyes grow dull. Count it all, Joy? Why does God call us to rejoice in times of trial? And what does that look like? And *how?*

We serve a God who sent His only son to die for us. Christ has felt every sadness we have ever felt; it's too hard for my small mind to comprehend. In the garden before his crucifixion, He sweats drops of blood, asking the Father,

> *If you are willing, remove this cup from me;*
> *yet not my will but yours be done.*
> — Lk 22:42

> *Christ, being found in human form, he humbled himself by*
> *becoming obedient to the point of death, even death on a cross.*
> — Phil 2:8

Fixing our eyes on Jesus, the pioneer, and perfecter of
faith. For the joy set before him, he endured the cross.
— HEB 12:2

Joy. The word is stalking me! I'm *choking* on Joy. I can't pretend to understand or fathom all Christ endured to fulfill God's plan—His obedience to death. Christ alone in the garden, His disciples just feet away, *asleep,* Him *crying out* to the Father. My grief, alone in a dark hospital room, watching my child, sick, suffering as he slept. Standing at the end of his bed, my hands touch his feet, begging God not to make him suffer this pain.

Standing at the end of his bed, my hands touch his feet, begging God not to make him suffer this pain.

There amid my desperation, I beg for our circumstances to change. *Why Lord?* And *Joy?* It doesn't make sense, a paradox of epic proportion, and I am failing *again!* It felt like a never-ending conversation that I was having with God. My dismay, with His call to Joy, a secret argument, battling inside me, trying to convince Him why this is an *unrealistic expectation.*

Until the transfer to the ICU, the journey from one end of the hospital to the other. Alone again, gathering Ryan's belongings from his room as hospital staff wheeled his bed out the door to take him to the ICU. I was approaching the long hallway joining the two towers of the hospital, a passageway to a new level of unknown. Almost like a friend standing next to me, just as I passed through the threshold, I heard, *"I'm not asking you to be happy about this."* No, it wasn't audible, just clear, no explanation, no elaboration, but those words, "I'm not asking you to be happy about this," percolated in my mind on a low boil for days.

Why does God call us to have joy and rejoice amidst our trials, hurts, and pain? After days of sorrow, I'm getting closer to an answer. I think the joy in our sorrow is a gift that comes wrapped in some *really ugly wrapping paper*—horrible, painful circumstances. When He calls us to joy right in the middle of our tears, we must seek Him, only Him, for that joy.

- You can't fabricate joy when you are watching your child suffer.
- You can't fill yourself with joy on your own strength.

God isn't calling us into some fake exterior, a painted-on smile with a parade wave to the crowd. What is appealing about a God like *that?* What is *loving* about a God like that?

In the garden, the Father doesn't remove the cup, but He does provide the *strength* for Christ to fulfill His purpose. In these last two months of a hard trial I never envisioned, I must keep my eyes on Christ, or the doubts and fears *destroy* me, *debilitate* me, and leave me with no hope. I have no chance of survival without Him, not for one day.

My *hope* is in Him, as this is *not* all there is. There is *hope and life beyond this world*. My *strength* is in Him, as it is *only when I am entirely focused on Him and not on my circumstances* that I can stand.

My *joy* is in Him, as I know that He is the only thing holding me up through this journey. No, I am not happy about this, but He isn't calling me to happiness. It is me who has confused happiness with joy—He is calling me to Him.

No matter the circumstances, I can have joy because my hope is in Him, not me. When focused on Him because of who He is and all He has done, even "immersed in tears," I can have joy.

"immersed in tears, yet always filled with deep joy." —Paul
— 2 Cor 6:10

Is Everything Going to Be Okay?

I*t's 2:00 a.m., and I've been reading* about cancer for hours. Statistics. Survival rates. Treatments, standard and experimental. We've been at this for more than two months, and I am still searching for the answer. My eyes are bleary from reading; what was I looking for? I was searching for that one article that would tell me, "Everything is going to be okay."

In the "Commonly Asked Questions" section of every article or book, the question that everyone wants the answer to is *never* there, "Is everything going to be okay?" It should be at the top of this list. Just tell me it's going to be okay!

Distraught from my reading material and needing to take my thoughts captive, I replaced my search, taking my mind back to a song I would listen to over and over in those first few weeks after the diagnosis. Back when I couldn't breathe, and, if I shut my eyes, my imagination took me to the worst-case scenario and a pain I could not bear. The only escape from those thoughts is to replace them with something else. "Just Be Held" by Casting Crowns. I played that song, forcing the fear from my mind.

The song answers the question *Where is God?*

"I'm on the throne." In the early days the title of the song, "Just Be Held" were the words that brought me comfort. I was in a state of helplessness. *Be held* was the extent of my ability. Down the road a ways, I replace my fear, reminding myself of where He sits. I'm on *the throne.*

Translation. . . . "Everything is going to be okay."

As a believer in the death and resurrection of Jesus Christ, the fact that He is on the throne is my answer. Yes, everything is going to be okay. Now, I will not lie here in my bed when I should be asleep and tell you this doesn't hurt, that it's easy, or that this revelation has magically transformed my situation. I'd like for everything to be okay *tomorrow.* Back to normal. I'm sick of "new normal." I didn't know how good I had it. I want my "old normal" back, please. No, the reminder that He is on the throne doesn't make this hurt less, but it reminds me of how this all ultimately ends and that it will be okay *because* He is on the throne.

Everybody's "It" is different, like snowflakes—no two are exactly the same. You have hurts and worries, too, and you desperately want someone to tell you everything is going to be okay. We all want that magic pill. Swallow, and it's all better. He knows we'd like it to be that easy. I can't imagine what supernatural control it takes for Him *not* to just fix it. As a mom, I want to *"fix it"* for my kids, especially when they are hurting or struggling. If I was God, I'm not sure I could *keep* from making every day perfect for my children. Think about how great it is to see our children happy and successful, and how *hard* it is when they aren't. That leads me to believe that there is a *hidden value, a treasure* more significant than the ease of life, to be discovered in this struggle, to *believe* He is on the throne, *no matter* my circumstances; a treasure *so valuable* He *allows* us to suffer, even when He can fix *anything.*

Be still and know that I am God. Say it again! *Be still and know that I am God.* Those words put me in *my place* and Him in His. They give much-needed perspective and the reminder that *He is God,* and I am not.

Psalm 46:10 starts with *"Be still and know that I am God,"* but the verse doesn't end there. It continues, and most of us forget there is more to it. I mean, none of the decorative pillows say more than the first part of the verse. *"Be Still and Know that I am God."* Here it is in its entirety.

> *Be still and know that I am God; I will be exalted*
> *among the nations; I will be exalted in the earth.*
> — Ps 46:10

What does it mean to be exalted, and *why* is it added here?

—**Exalt:** To elevate by praise, to glorify.

We are acknowledging God's power to save. Does that mean tomorrow I will wake up, and all will be well and good, and we can forget about all these cancer treatments? We both know the answer is *No*. But when it comes to those commonly asked questions of life, "Is it *going to be okay?*" reminding ourselves of who God is, all He has done, and where He sits helps us answer that question, no matter *how* our life looks that day.

> *Then I heard every creature in Heaven and on earth and under the earth and on the sea, and all that is in them, saying: To Him who sits on the throne and to the Lamb be praise and honor and glory and power, forever and ever!*
> — REV 5:13

Thank you, Jesus. Everything is going to be okay.

Unsatisfactory in Rejoicing

So, *I have this tea towel* that was a gift that says, "Rejoice Always." I never really liked it because it reminds me I *don't*. If "Rejoicing" was on my grade-school report card, I would receive a "U" for "Unsatisfactory." A verse I do like. . . .

> *Do not be anxious for anything, but in everything, by prayer and petition, with thanksgiving, let your requests be made known unto*

God, and the peace of God which transcends all understanding,
will guard your hearts and minds in Christ Jesus.
— PHIL 4:6-7

Remember, it's the verse I memorized while exercising with Cindy Crawford back in the 90s. I had to work to remember the *"with thanksgiving"* part. It's an awkward placement, almost an afterthought, but then *not*. Truth, I think I liked that verse so much because it feels comforting; if you ask God for stuff the right way, *"with thanksgiving,"* He's going to make it all work out—so stop worrying. He gives you peace as a bonus. *What's not to like?*

Imagine my surprise to see just two verses above my
favorite verses, those two words, *"Rejoice Always."* How
have I missed their proximity to each other all these years?
Is there a connection? It actually says, *"Paul's exhortation,"*
Rejoice in the Lord always: and again, I say rejoice!
— PHIL 4:4

—**Exhortation:** to emphatically urge someone to do something.

Back to drying my dishes with *that* tea towel that makes me feel like a failure. It had been a hard couple of days. Lots of tears. Lots. Earlier that day, I wrote a prayer listing how God satisfies us, a combat mission for my sadness—listing the things that truly satisfied my soul, His gifts. The *magnitude* of His glory and *goodness* was bold in my mind.

Now later, standing at my kitchen sink, sorrow fueling my anxious soul, tears rolling down my face, I slowly put my mind on my list of soul satisfactions. And then, right in the middle of my sorrow, my anxiousness, I could "rejoice." My mind saw *His goodness*, and peace came, not an "*Awww* angels singing in a bright light" kind of peace. I think the word "transcend" sounds like Angels *should* appear—or at least *a bright light*. But a sense of peace came as I thought of His provision on Earth and the Heaven to come!

I was rejoicing. No dancing. No tambourines. Just my mind seeing His *goodness,* rescuing me from despair. Despair is a terrible place to live. A peace that came when it didn't really make sense and certainly wasn't expected. A peace that *transcends understanding;* I couldn't have said it better myself.

> *Finally, brothers and sisters, whatever is true, whatever*
> *is noble, whatever is right, whatever is pure, whatever*
> *is lovely, whatever is admirable—if anything is excellent*
> *or praiseworthy—think about such things.*
> — PHIL 4:8

—There's a list that satisfies.

> *Whatever you have learned or received or heard from me or seen in*
> *me—put it into practice. And the God of peace will be with you.*
> — PHIL 4:9

Rejoice Always! I will see those two words as an exhortation to receive one of God's great gifts: *Peace.*

I Could Have Had a V-8!

God *has a funny way of talking to us;* a verse will keep showing up, someone says something, or a phrase in a song stands out. It's a repeated message or sometimes just a word. During Ryan's multiple hospital stays, "Humble"/"humility" popped up everywhere.

Watching TV used to be an entirely different experience than it is today with our streaming options. You had little control over what commercials you had to sit through. There were no remotes and getting up off the couch to switch channels wasn't happening, no "skip Ad" options were available, and so you were at the mercy of the advertisers. One of the catchier commercials I remember was for V-8 Vegetable Juice, a time before anyone even considered drinking kale in liquid form disguised with apple juice. The commercial was everywhere, and it played all the time. A simple message, "I could have had a V-8!" combined with a smack to the forehead.

It was successful in the '80s and resurrected in the 2000s, but, instead of hitting yourself, the scene plays with a Mommy eating a French fry. Her baby responds with a smack to her mother's forehead, "You could've had a V8!" Again V-8 sales soared.

God just kept conking me on the head with *humble, humility.* I interpreted the Word to mean "submissive," "quiet," a behind-the-scenes kind of guy. Bearing my soul, I don't think I gave the *word* humble much value, despite really liking the verse, Micah 6:8.

> *And what does the Lord require of you? Act justly,*
> *love mercy, and walk humbly with your God.*
> — MIC 6:8 PARTIAL

Amid numerous hospitalizations, circumstances so far outside of my control, imagine my surprise that God kept conking me on the head with *humble.* Really, Lord? *Humble?*

—*humilitas*, the Latin word for "humble," is defined as "low, small, slight, and flattened in appearance" vs. *today's definition* of humility, as feelings of insignificance, inferiority, and subservience. Neither is appealing by today's standards. Just sayin'.

There aren't a lot of bestsellers out there called *Ten Steps to Being Flattened and Subservient*, but amid circumstances so far outside my control, I could not be more "*humilitas*," flattened. I could do nothing to change my station in life.

I ran into a young man that I knew as a young boy. I used to be his Sunday school teacher. He was married and had four kids. His baby girl was born with a severe heart condition, and they have gone through a year of hard, gut-wrenching times. There we were, just the two of us, a God appointment, talking about how arduous this journey is, watching your child fight for life and suffer, and, out of his mouth, he said it. "It's humbling." I punched him in the arm like Elaine punches Jerry on Seinfeld and said "YES! That's it!" He went on to say, "You are thrown into a situation you have no control over, living out of a backpack, held up in a hospital where time stands still, and you can do absolutely nothing to make it better." Adding, "You and I are workers. Get-it-done kind of people." Let me qualify that this young man is one of the hardest-working guys I know, coming from two of the hardest-working parents I know, so I'm not sure I meet that standard, but I'm glad he thinks I do. He went on to say, "We aren't the ones who ask for help. We're more the self-sufficient type. We just get to work."

There it was, further confirmation God *was*, in fact, conking me on the head with *humility*.

Back to Micah 6:8 *"And what does the Lord require of you? To act justly, love mercy, and walk humbly with your God."* I like this verse because when life gets confusing, it asks and answers the bottom-line question, "What does God want?" And the answer in my mind looks like a walk on the beach, and I mean that literally. He wants to walk beside us through life. *Well,* not so fast. If you look closer at what "humbly" means, it changes the journey *a lot.*

Matthew Henry's commentary states this; "humbly conform ourselves to the will of God" and "every thought within us must be brought down, brought into obedience to God. This is what God requires and without which the costliest services are vain offerings."

"Humbly with your God." I think I pictured it more like God and me walking through life, acknowledging, He *is* God after all, the creator of all, my salvation, my strong tower, the list is endless. But "conform ourselves to the will of God, every thought?" Didn't God want to know *my thoughts? My plan?* Tell me I'm not the only one. So many times, I've been running down my road of life and looked back and said, "Come on, God. Catch up! I've got a plan! I will tell you about it on the way!"

So many times, I've been running down my road of life and looked back and said, "Come on, God. Catch up! I've got a plan! I will tell you about it on the way!

When tough times hit, you realize *you* have *no plan*. The verse *"Your ways are not my ways, Your thoughts are not my thoughts,"* well, that reality gets *real big, real fast,* and you realize you don't understand as much as you thought you did. Your plan, even if it is to save the world, end world hunger, or bring world peace, how did Matthew Henry say it?—*"Vain Offerings*—if your thoughts aren't brought into obedience to God and you aren't conforming your will into God's will."

Watching your child suffer [or fill in your own story of suffering], there is an endless supply of "sufferings" to choose from. You cry out to God and say, "I don't understand this plan! I'm afraid, but I will trust you. I'm *flattened,* Lord. I don't want to do this, but if I must, I am thankful You are walking with me, holding my hand. It's not the walk on the beach I planned, but it's what You ask of me, and I know Your plan is always better than mine.

Peace Out of a Drive-Through Window

"I*'ll take an extra-large order* of peace with that!" Sometimes just a thought, a vision captures me, takes me prisoner, like a net engulfs a butterfly—there is no chance for escape. It's an overwhelming memory, and it's what my eyes see right now before me. Fear whooshes in like waves crashing inside my head, and I want to scream! I collapse to the ground in the fetal position. So many tears! Where are they stored, Lord? You have storehouses of snow and hail; are my tears there, too? Reaching for You on the throne, stretching out my arms like a toddler begging to be lifted. Please! Please pick me up! Just pull me up there with you and whisper how You will make beauty from these ashes because I can't see it.

I like to tidy things up before opening the front door to guests. How about you? I don't want visitors seeing my mess, dirty dishes in the sink or laundry in a pile. But here, I feel God urging me to open my front door, giving you full access to the conversations I am having with Him. There isn't much I can control in my life these days, but I can open my front door and let you see the furniture of life turned upside down in utter disarray, nothing remains in its place. If God wants this shared, then I don't want to waste a single tear.

Before the mess a typical start to my day was prayers, listing out the Fruit of the Spirit like they were side orders on a menu. "I'll take fries with that—and don't forget that special sauce." Sometimes I placed my order so fast, it was as if I was at the drive-through window—no time to walk in and sit down.

"I would like an extra-large order of peace, please."

There! I've put in my order for peace. That should be good for the day. I will have peace.

Peace I LEAVE with you, My peace I give you.
—JN 14:27
Now may the Lord of peace himself give you peace at all times.
— 2 THES 3:16
May the God of hope fill you with all joy and peace.
— ROM 15:13
And the peace of God will . . . guard your hearts and minds
— PHIL 4:7

My mind hears the verses about peace, and I believe all of them to be true.

- Leaving peace.
- Giving peace.
- Filling me with peace.
- Guarding me with peace.

All of these are *giving* words. He is the giver, and I am the receiver. Ask, and you shall receive, right? Sometimes, God rains down peace on your soul; a gift from His grace—nothing you earned. But there is also a spiritual discipline to peace. There is more to peace than receiving it.

Seek peace and pursue it.
— Ps 34:14
You will keep him in perfect peace whose mind is stayed on You, because he trusts in You.
— Is 26:3
Through prayer and petition, the peace of God will guard your hearts and minds, in Christ Jesus.
— PHIL 4:7

- SEEK
- PURSUE
- STAYED
- PRAYER
- PETITION

All *action* words!

There have been fearful days when I have envisioned Jesus on the water in the middle of the storm, and I say out loud, "I trust you, Jesus.

I trust you, Jesus." When peace escapes you and fear tries to swallow you, get out the big guns, and say it out loud. *"I trust you, Jesus!" "I trust you, Jesus!"* Your brain will fight this. You will say it doesn't matter if I say it out loud or not. *It matters.* Say it.

There have been days when His living word keeps fear at bay, when my eyes are more like His, and I see Him clearly, when I am immersed in His word. *And songs.* He knew songs would calm our racing hearts and bring peace. He hides them inside us and brings them from the depth of our soul at just the right time. "Turn your eyes upon Jesus, look full in His wonderful face," a song first published in 1918 and included in hymnals for decades, for good reason.

Once again, the peace comes when I write. I begin full of fear, overflowing, like waves crashing over the side of a boat—sinking me. I'm overwhelmed by grief, sadness, and exhaustion. I pour out my tears, and sometimes there seems to be an endless supply, but when I truly seek Him, miraculously, I receive peace—a gift! He stamps our conversations on my heart with a branding iron, and I return to them, reminding myself *this is what you believe and know to be true.* It still hurts, but I am not hopeless. The ugly cry is over for now. The grief and fear will return, but so will the Peace, when I turn my eyes to Him.

"Turn your eyes upon Jesus,
Look full in His wonderful face.
And the things of earth will grow strangely dim,
In the light of His glory and grace."
— HELEN HOWARTH LEMMEL, 1918

Suffering Was the Plan

I*'m not particularly eager to suffer*, but who is? For those who don't know me well, I faint at the sight of blood—mine *or* yours. Don't describe your wound or injury; I don't want to hear it. And whatever you do, don't show it to me, and ask, "How bad is it?" I am not your gal.

Good Friday . . . Christ's Suffering. For being a Christian almost my entire life, I can't say I spent a lot of think-time on Christ's suffering. Until Mel Gibson's movie *The Passion of the Christ*, I didn't understand the extent of the crucifixion and the torture that went with it. And while we are being honest, I didn't put it together that the plan for the *crucifixion* was already in place long before Adam was naming the animals. I saw the events as an actual timeline. Christ came when He arrived in the manger, nine months after the angels appeared to Mary, explaining what was about to transpire. Seriously, Mary wins the award for the being the most surprised, *"I'm pregnant?"* And when did God come up with that idea? I wasn't sure. It never occurred to me that He, Christ, was always there, waiting in the wings, so to speak, God's failproof rescue. Somehow, I missed the references to Christ in the Old Testament in my Sunday School lessons. *Omnipresent* is difficult to communicate on a Sunday school felt board.

How to make sense of the Father's plan to sacrifice *His* Son, through suffering, for my sake, my sin? Since the beginning of time.

Yet the Eternal One planned to crush him all along.
— Is 53:10

Yet, it was the Lord's will to crush him with suffering.
— Is 53:10

Read any translation; it never softens. The suffering was planned and fully known from the beginning.

*Yet it was the Lord's will to crush him and cause him to
suffer, and though the Lord makes his life an offering for
sin, he will see his offspring and prolong his days, and the
will (good pleasure) of the Lord will prosper in his hand.*
— Is 53:10-11

One of my life's foundational truths. . . . "God's plan is always better than mine!" I base that on some obvious deductions made on my part about His role in the creation of everything and the fact that I couldn't get better than a "C" in college chemistry. It's a simple deduction that needs no explanation. I can't say that His plan always looks better than mine on the surface, and I do have some good ideas, but to argue that, somehow, I know better or more than Him is a ridiculous thought from every angle, so I choose not to argue the point. God is all-knowing, and He loves better than I do. Life is simpler when I don't argue with that truth.

Yet, it was the Lord's will . . . His plan to crush Him, His son, with . . . Suffering.

My recent experiences go beyond the expected "mother worries." Broken bones, not making the team, and watching your child drive a car without you—those are somewhat universal mother worries. But when someone hears that my child has cancer, many exclaim, "That is my worst nightmare." No one says it to your face, but you see it in their eyes or whispered behind your back. They are talking about your reality being *their worst nightmare,* almost always followed by "I don't think I could do it." Newsflash—you aren't given a choice to pick another card.

Within two days of the official "C" word becoming part of our life, I was at church in the administrative office, working on a Facebook Page for Ryan, where we could update people and list prayer requests. At the time, I had never really been a big Facebook user. I had an account, but I was far from proficient. Plus, my brain wasn't working well. A friend of a younger generation was helping me set up a prayer page for Ryan.

As we sat hidden in a cubicle working, our pastor and one of the other staff members entered the office. Both men were long-time friends of our family and had boys the same ages as ours. As they walked through the office, not knowing I was there, our family was the topic of conversation, both expressing that they wouldn't know what to do if their son had cancer. They volleyed their questions back and forth, just as I probably would have if it were them and not me, theirs and not mine. The moment struck me hard as I listened to them question what they would do if it were *their son* with cancer. What was *I* going to do?

While watching my son suffer in the dark of a hospital room, machines beeping, him sleeping, my silent tears cinch my throat muscles tight, binding my sobs from bursting forth in a loud wail. Crushed by a sorrow I never anticipated or envisioned. *How could I?* No mother imagines the depth of the darkness where I stood.

How could God's plan be to crush His son with suffering? I want to say I understand that level of sacrifice, especially this week as Good Friday approaches, but I can't comprehend it. Now that I am experiencing my own earthly version of watching my son suffer, that God's plan was in place *from the beginning,* the suffering is even more significant. *Why?* Because God *knew* it was coming the entire time!

Listen to Garth Brooks sing "The Dance." The entire song debates the question, 'Is knowing ahead of time, how it's all going to end *better* than not knowing?'—Because you can choose not to dance the dance of life, avoiding the pain of the loss. Or is *not knowing* better? So that you get to experience the dance of life, even if pain comes with it. The songwriter, Tony Arata, determines he is glad he didn't know what was to come, because if he had, he would have never danced the dance.

It was Brooks' second number-one hit, and he has been quoted to say, "'The Dance' will be the greatest success as a song we will ever do. I'll go to my grave with 'The Dance.' It will probably always be my favorite song."

My point in mentioning it is God *knew* how it all would go. He left *nothing* to chance. And He *still did it*, for you, for all of us.

So, we interrupt this broadcast with a word from our sponsor. Why in the world would I write this book? I still cry as I edit and re-edit the words, some written *seven years ago*. My vision is blurry from the tears, and my muscle memory kicks in as my throat cinches closed. There are days I don't want to sit here because the pain is still real. Just because it's in the past doesn't make it not hurt, which adds another element to God's great sacrifice. The crucifixion is in the past, but the pain of the memory is not gone. I would argue that the pain is more intense for God now, as He watches those He loves, the ones He made the sacrifice for, ignore, mock, and reject this sacrificial act of love. Want to really hurt me? Tell me what I've done for you doesn't mean anything to you. Now, imagine God sacrificing His Son, only to watch the world reject the greatest gift of love known to man.

So why write this? It's for those who question what they would do when a tragedy they never imagined interrupts their life. How do we face suffering, survive, and not lose faith in the God we trust when the plan doesn't make sense or feel loving? I will not state that there is a set formula for enduring suffering or that I did it perfectly if such a thing exists. Suffering is messy, full of snot and ugly cries. There is no perfection in suffering. But I have witnessed many who don't face the suffering and opt to ignore it, stuff it, eat it, shop it, and drug it. An endless number of books have been written about what to do after trying one or more of those as a solution or remedy to soothe the pain. If you manage to avoid one or more of those options, then the question is, how do you survive? Stress like this affects your mind and body, and there are long-term effects like PTSD, fear, anxiety, and the like. In the wake of those side effects, marriages fall apart, and relationships are strained or abandoned. For some, they pretend the stress of it doesn't exist, wearing a façade for as long as possible, but eventually, that fake outside wears out like an old coat. And then, saddest of all, people walk away from the Father, unable to reconcile their circumstances with a loving God or refuse Him outright, saying there is no God. After the painful sacrifice of His son, the turning away from His son in His greatest time of need, somehow, we can't see that He did all that so He would never have to turn away from *us*, in our greatest time of need. We turn from Him in dismay, anger, and unbelief, and question, *Was He ever good?*

So, first, the suffering was "Plan A" all along, and second, we wrongly assume that since this was always the plan, it didn't hurt God. Why would an all-powerful God make a plan that hurt Him? I never thought about how God felt watching His son suffer until I watched mine suffer so intensely. It's hard to envision Christ on the cross, the way it must have looked, with lots of blood, torn flesh, and the jagged ripping of His skin, His muscles exposed. Instead, we see, maybe, the shape of the cross, with no Jesus hanging on it. I'm not saying we do this on purpose, deleting Christ from the cross. It's painful, and our brains have a way of avoiding pain when they can. We don't see the suffering—kind of like we can't see an earthquake in Haiti. We try to comprehend it, but we don't see it and feel it like God does.

> *I never thought about how God felt watching His son suffer until I watched mine suffer so intensely.*

Today, in real time, I can't see past my son's pain. I would do anything to make it stop, and I can't help but wonder, *Couldn't God think of another plan?* As I sit here, up close, watching Ryan hurt, it makes me question, *Weren't there other options?* My thoughts aren't His thoughts—we've established that. I don't know how to make a brain work, a hummingbird fly, or a sunset appear and disappear effortlessly. My brain couldn't begin to conceive out of the darkness how to make light, but God could and *did*, and yet His plan was suffering and sacrificing His Son. That would not have been my Plan A.

Who makes a plan for suffering? The Father did. I don't pretend to fathom that. He is God. He could change the plan. Christ, He could have changed the plan. During the temptation in the garden, He could have said, "I'm out!" But he didn't. God, in Genesis, when He looked at the man and said, "It's not good for him to be alone. I will make him a helper," it sounds to me like He altered *the plan*. Think about how long the Father and the Son had to anticipate *the plan*. Forever! They always knew the plan.

Even Christ said, *"Abba, Father." he cried out, "everything is possible for You. Please take this cup of suffering from me. Yet I want Your will to be done, not mine."* (Mark 14:36) All this, as He sweats blood—that's a real thing, the sweating of blood.

Hematohidrosis; may occur in individuals suffering from extreme levels of stress. Around the sweat glands, there are multiple blood vessels in a net-like form, which constrict under the pressure of great stress.

I've been under more stress than I can manage lately; thankfully, there is a pill for those moments. Maybe we'd see more cases of hematohidrosis in our modern day if there weren't so many pills. There was no pill for Jesus.

+ I can't fathom the anticipation of the plan for Christ's suffering, as the Father or as the Son—either one, I can't.
+ Fathoming the depth of Christ's suffering. . . taking on everyone's sin. I *really* can't understand *that* one.
+ Fathoming the Father's love for me, that He would sacrifice His only son, willingly making *it* the plan. I would never make that the plan.

However, it was our sicknesses that He Himself bore.
And our pains that He carried; Yet we ourselves assumed
that He had been afflicted, struck down by God
and humiliated.
—Is 53:4

But He was wounded for our transgressions, He was bruised
four our iniquities; the chastisement (punishment) of our peace
was upon Him; and by His stripes we are healed. All we like

*sheep have gone astray; we have turned every one to his own
way; and the Lord hath laid on him the iniquity of us all.*
—Is 53:5-6

Using the word "our" softens the guilt, the responsibility of the sin.
It spreads it out. Let's face it; it is always easier to accept the unwanted
responsibility of doing something wrong if everyone around you did it,
too. Even a young child quickly shouts, "He did it, too!" So, let's call it
"mine," not "ours." He hung there for my sins.

Have peace; think of that. How often have I struggled for peace during this suffering, begged for it, and never even considered that Christ
was beaten, so that I could have it. And then say this line, slow. *"And by
His stripes (lashes) we are healed."*

*"As a result of the anguish of His soul, He will see it and be satisfied;
By His knowledge [of what He has accomplished] the Righteous One
(Christ), My Servant, will justify the many [Justify—making them—
and me—righteous, upright before God, in right-standing with Him],
For He will bear [the responsibility for] their (my) iniquities (sins)."*
—Is 53:11

So, let's recap—

+ The Plan. . . . Wounded . . . Suffering . . . His Son's Death.
+ The Lord. . . . Satisfied.
+ Christ's Soul for My Sin.
+ His Beating for My Peace.
+ His Stripes . . . *Lashing.* Ripping of skin and tearing of flesh for
  my healing.
+ His Accomplishment. I'm justified, upright before God.

And if all that wasn't enough, when suffering turns to the crushing
fear of this life's end, your own—or worse, your child's—it was His

Plan all along to crush His own Son, so that when death comes, and it comes to us all, we could have life eternal, our only hope and true peace.

What an amazing plan!

> *For God, so [greatly] loved and dearly prized the world, that He [even] gave His [One and] only begotten Son so that whoever believes and trusts in Him [as Savior] shall not perish but have eternal life. For God did not send the Son into the world to judge and condemn the world [that is, to initiate the final judgment of the world], but that the world might be saved through Him.*
>
> —JN 3:16-17

If you have never believed and trusted that Jesus could be your Savior, so that you can have the assurance of eternal life, *hope* and *peace*, it is my prayer that you might consider all He has done for you and accept His Plan; it's His Gift. His lashing for your healing. His suffering to save you. It was always His plan to save *you*.

Dear Father in Heaven, thank you for sending your Son to suffer on the cross for me. I ask you to forgive me of my sins and thank you for this gift of suffering and sacrifice so that I can have peace and the promised hope of heaven. In Jesus' Name. Amen

> *For (as a believer) you have been called for this purpose, since Christ suffered for you, leaving you an example, so that you may follow in His footsteps.*
>
> — 1 PET 2:21

Thou Shut the Door
Upon Thee

April 4, 2016

I *try to smile, push down the sadness* welling in my throat, as I shut the back door of the silver sedan. The Uber car pulls away; Richard, my sweetheart of 27 years, and Jennifer, Ryan's of 8 months, leave for the airport. Ryan and I will be living in Houston for the next couple of months so he can receive a unique cancer treatment called Proton Beam Therapy.

Uber! Defined as *better, larger* or *greater than.*

Nothing felt better as they drove away. Everything was larger and greater than anything I had ever had to navigate, and I felt small and less than as I stood on the sidewalk outside the far end of MD Anderson Cancer Hospital. You must see it to believe it. This 344-acre hospital is enveloped inside The Houston Medical Center's 1000 acres of hospitals, stretching tall into the Texas sky like a cowboy's ten-gallon hat. It is a world of its own, people rushing in and out each day, racing against the clock, fighting death, while the rest of the world lives. My brain could not absorb the "Uber-ness" that surrounded me.

Cars and shuttle buses, staff motioning vehicles in and out, whistles blowing like it's a popular New York hotel, complete with bellhops assisting their guests in and out, in time to make it to their Broadway show. Except no one is going to Broadway here. There are even valet services for anyone who wants to avoid navigating one of the many high-rise parking garages. Arrive at peak time in the morning, and you'll have time to drink your entire coffee on the slow tight twist to the top of the garage in search of an open spot. How could so many people be heading to the Cancer Show with these horrific reviews?

After the chemo treatment, Ryan and I exited the hospital later that night with a backpack full of saline attached to a portable pump and instructions for me to de-access the port in his chest approximately 22 hours later. We'd never done this before, he with a portable pump disguised as a backpack full of college books and me pretending to be a nurse, with instructions far outside my training as a mother that had included Band-Aids, Tylenol, or a kiss to make it all better.

The long gray hallways all look the same, leading us to the unfamiliar apartment #139. We entered and shut the door behind us. He's supposed to be in college, reading books, not toting saline. He'd left home already, we'd said our goodbyes, and I had accepted the new normal of mother of a young college student because it was where he was supposed to be. *This* is not where he is supposed to be. *I* am not who he is supposed to be with. He's supposed to be with his friends, finding his new role in life, not fighting for it.

Ryan, asleep in the one bedroom, I lay on the couch, four white walls 12 feet high, built around me like a prison, rushing traffic outside the sliding glass door, not the quiet of our country home. Heavy footsteps above, not my children, a stranger I will never meet. At all hours of the night, what sounds like an office chair rolls across the floor over and over. My son has cancer, and I know why I'm awake. I want to yell at the ceiling: *Why are you awake? Go to sleep!*

I live in a state of mind where I can't reconcile my surroundings with who I am and asked to do things I am not prepared to do, like de-access the port in my son's chest! I don't do needles! I faint at the sight of blood. Didn't anyone do their research before casting me in this role?

Even the refrigerator screams, "stranger!" A half-gallon of milk, coffee creamer, and two yogurts. I don't know who you are! My fridge hasn't been that lonely in a decade! My grocery cart used to be so full of milk that the check-out girl would ask if I ran a daycare. "Well, sort of. I have three teenage boys."

It is as if God picked us up and removed us from life, like that game you never win at the arcade. The one where the claw drops down to grab the stuffed toy that is just out of reach, except this time, the

God-sized-claw didn't miss. He grabbed us firmly and moved us out of our life. The claw got us!

I wake Ryan when it is time to de-access the port. In Ryan's chest, close to his heart, is the port that ushers in the poison, followed by saline fluid. Hours and hours of saline forcing the poison out, keeping it from killing his organs, we hope. It's called *chemo*, which, in my mind, was "medicine" before I knew about the cancer world. It's poison, not medicine, meant to kill cancer, but it kills many things. Cancer kills lots of things.

It is as if God picked us up and removed us from life, like that game you never win at the arcade.

I sat beside Ryan in one of the two unfamiliar kitchen chairs, uncomfortable and straight, not meant for long family conversations around the table. I miss our chairs, our home. The nurse had shown me what to do back at the hospital. She made it look so quick and easy. But Ryan was not her son, and she did not faint when she saw blood. I told myself I could do it, much like I would tell myself I could handle giving blood without fainting. It never worked. How embarrassing it was to say to the nurse, "You'll need to lay me down before you draw blood. I faint."

I touched his chest, where they had opened him up and inserted the port, back in December. I remember how quickly the procedure was scheduled the day after meeting Dr. T. The poison was rushed in the next day, with no time to wait. It had all moved so fast, with an undercurrent of urgency, like the men waving the cars in and out in front of MD Anderson. With large arm movements, motioning cars forward, the message is clear, "Move along. This is urgent"; no time to stop.

I sat next to Ryan, and my eyes blurred with tears. I couldn't see anything I was supposed to be doing. I took deep breaths. I told Ryan I was sorry and that I could do it. "Let me catch my breath." He calmly waited and then patiently showed me again what I was supposed to do. He never got mad or frustrated and patiently waited as I tried to calm myself, but as I type, recalling this moment so vividly, the same hot tears blur my vision, and I remember how my cheeks contorted my face, forcing my eyes shut and the tears out. I couldn't do it. I was so afraid I'd hurt him that I could hardly touch the port. I failed. I was so "less-than" what he needed. As Ryan always would, no hint of disappointment spoken in his calm voice, he quietly said, "I'll do it, Mom." He had every right to be frustrated with his less-than mother trying to be a nurse.

Five weeks before cancer, Caelen began a treatment program for RAD. I was failing at being her mother. With the words "mass on your spine," the door to Caelen slammed shut and was barricaded, my mind unable to manage both. The instructions to "go find our equilibrium" might as well have been "de-access his port in 22 hours." I am failing at both. She is now eleven, and when she became part of our family, God did not reveal all that had happened to her or what we were about to endure. All He said was, "This one is yours." At that time, the unspeakable neglect and abuse and the extent of the damage to her were hidden from us. "He covers our eyes until it is time to see." He's done that more than once in our life. I mention it again because it is a significant part of the story. We had no idea of the extent of her "trauma," a word we rarely used BC, *Before Caelen*; we had no comprehension of its power to take the life right out of a child and replace it with chaotic rage and constant hyper-vigilance. Had we known the long-term effects of her trauma on our family we would have told Jesus you have the wrong address and shut the door.

Who would shut the door on a little girl? The day when family number four didn't take her home, you'd think we would have seen red flags going up everywhere. Her family of 8 months, we couldn't imagine what could cause a seemingly high-functioning and loving family to walk out of her life.

About eight months into our Caelen journey, the fatigue and frustration mounted. There must be something about the eight-months marker. Our inability to understand what we were seeing or why we were failing to reach her consumed me. Her previous father's words were not so hard to understand now. They were exhausted and out of ideas. They didn't know what they had. We would have quit if the assignment hadn't come from Jesus. The day she arrived, her trauma, disguised by a pink and white polka-dotted suitcase, two pink outfits, and pink footy pajamas, she was a grenade camouflaged in pink, and we didn't know it. Two days after being abandoned at our home, she said, "My mom and dad are playing hide-n-seek." That was the only and last time she mentioned them. We had no idea what explosions were ahead. We did not understand the significance of a child never crying for her mother or father, never crying at all.

The lifelong side-effects of abuse and neglect, a poison that filled her body, killing her soul and no saline to flush it out, and the effects of her trauma, which we knew nothing about, took over our life the same way it took over her brain. We did all we could to help her heal from the abuse once we found out what it was; that took several years of digging. After eight years of trying every therapy from human to horse, we were not making enough progress. We felt we were running out of time to help her. She needed full-time professional evaluation and long-term help, and we needed a break.

October 18, 2015—God made His big move. What is God's big move? It's when your circumstances change so dramatically in an instant, a life situation that, until His big move, could not be budged. She was accepted into a treatment program that had been impossible before because we couldn't afford full-time treatment. God provided a place and financing for her treatment. We would not understand his timing until December 5th, 2015, why God had made such a dramatic change in our circumstances with Caelen.

Caelen living somewhere else was not a permanent situation. It was the best solution we could find to help our daughter heal. It was a difficult decision, and we were judged severely for it, but if your child has cancer, would you deny them treatment because it made you look bad in other people's eyes? Who leaves their child, right? Who gives their son poison? We took her to the best place for treatment. Our goal was to provide her with the best life she could live, and we needed the best help we could find.

Her brokenness, in some ways, is more complicated and difficult to understand than cancer and more challenging to heal. Chemo makes your hair fall out. Mentally ill children make you pull your hair out. There is no reason to sugar-coat it. Cancer treatment can get a patient to remission or NED, no evidence of disease. Therapy and medications for the severely mentally ill get them to what we hope is a higher level of function, an improved ability to cope and regulate, and a slim hope for healing. Abuse and neglect never go into remission, and there is always evidence of disease. There is no poison strong enough to kill the memory of it.

When we left her in the best place we could find and were told to go home and "find our equilibrium," I don't think it was the first time they'd given those instructions. *Lost equilibrium* must be a common symptom for parents of children with RAD (Reactive Attachment Disorder). *Equilibrium* isn't found in the hospital fighting cancer. How could God allow these circumstances? I had just left my daily grind of feeling utterly inadequate as Caelen's mother. Failing daily, it was hard to even look at myself in the mirror. Who are you? Why can't you love her more? Or, more accurately, *why can't you fix her?* Who authors a story like this?

Now, almost all of our life had been stripped away. We were living in a world surrounded by other cancer patients, fighting a war that leaves people with life-altering wounds, taking away your hair, dignity, health, and appetite for anything; ruthlessly, cancer takes away your plans, i.e., *your control.* You don't plan to attend the wedding you received the invitation to; you don't plan for the 4th of July, you don't plan to watch your kid run track or play baseball, you don't plan to go to the grocery store or even plan your next meal. It's not like the flu—expecting a recovery in a week or less, postponing that date night to the following weekend. Your entire life is placed on hold with no end date. The plan is to put every ounce of effort and attention into the task of fighting cancer; That's the plan. The only plan, and it sucks the life out of you.

God has been holding me in all this unpredicted, unexpected, isolated, aloneness, and incapability to plan anything. All of this is not unexpected by Him. Oh, and no, I can't answer that question of "Why?" Why is this the plan? Was it really God's plan? Is this the luck of the draw? You, the creator of my child, did you miss those malfunctioning cells that make Ewing's Sarcoma? Did you, the creator of every star in the sky, who hung the moon, overlook chromosomes 11 and 22, mismatching as you knit him together in the secret place of my womb? No, I can't ask those questions and expect an answer written in black and white. It's nowhere to be found between Genesis and Revelation. I've looked.

But I ask Him daily to speak to me, to show me His purpose for me during this time alone with Him, behind closed doors with Him. God has firmly shut the door to life and sat me down. He pulled me out of all I know, and I am looking straight at Him in a way I have never done before, with an intensity my other life would never allow or accommodate. Would I ever be brave enough to ask for this alone time with God? *No way.* I am not that brave. But it has made me question why I am so afraid. He is right here holding me. He shows up every single day, and so does my fear. How many times does He have to show me just how present He is before I trust Him?

Mark 9 accounts the following scene:

So, they brought him. When the spirit saw Jesus, it immediately threw the boy into a convulsion. He fell to the ground and rolled around, foaming at the mouth.

Jesus asked the boy's father, "How long has he been like this?"

"From childhood," he answered. "It has often thrown him into fire or water to kill him. But if you can do anything, take pity on us and help us."

"'If you can'?" said Jesus. "Everything is possible for one who believes."

Immediately the boy's father exclaimed, "I do believe; help me overcome my unbelief!"

When Jesus saw that a crowd was running to the scene, he rebuked the impure spirit. "You deaf and mute spirit," he said, "I command you, come out of him and never enter him again."

The spirit shrieked, convulsed him violently and came out. The boy looked so much like a corpse that many said, "He's dead." But Jesus took him by the hand and lifted him to his feet, and he stood up.

I believe. Forgive me of my unbelief.
— MARK 9:24

Does it get any more honest than that? I no more say I believe than I am asking for forgiveness for my unbelief. The irony of it all is I have also asked myself, "How many times do I have to show up for Caelen for her to believe I'm coming? Why won't she trust me?" See the irony? Caelen endured extreme abuse and neglect for so long that her brain told her to stop crying because it only made it worse. I wonder how long it took for Caelen to stop crying because no one was coming. When did *she* lose hope? Was it weeks? Or months? The brain is a magnificent wonder and built to help us survive in this lost and sinful world, but the injustice of it all is hard to comprehend. Even Caelen, in her simple mind, asks, "Why didn't God make you my first mom?" I don't know, Caelen. I don't know why.

I beg God to heal both of my children multiple times a day. I also beg Him to show me He is right here with me, and He does. All of these thoughts have been swirling in my head for weeks. God knew exactly where I would be sleeping on April 4, 2016. He knew how alone and isolated I would feel. He knew all my thoughts long before I could put them to paper. He knew how much I would need to hear from Him on April 5, 2016. He knows I am begging for miracles from Him; He is all I've got.

4-5-16 The next morning, "Streams in the Desert," exactly four months after my big plan to make a nice dinner on 12-5-15.

> *"Go inside and shut the door behind you and your sons"*
> — 2 KINGS 4:4

Come on, God! Seriously! Are you really listening that close? As I typed those words last night, were you thinking the entire time, "I will answer you in the morning?"

April 5th "Streams in the Desert":

"They had to be isolated from everyone, separated from human reasoning and removed from the natural tendencies to prejudge their circumstance. They were to be cast into the vast expanse of starry space, depending on God alone, in touch with the Source of miracles."

"This is an ingredient in God's plan of dealing with us. We are to enter a secret chamber of isolation in prayer and faith that is very fruitful. At certain times and places, God will build a mysterious wall around us. He will take away all the supports we customarily lean upon and will remove our ordinary ways of doing things. God will close us off to something divine, completely new and unexpected, and that cannot be understood by examining our previous circumstances. We will be in a place where we do not know what is happening, where God is cutting the cloth of our lives by a new pattern, and thus where He causes us to look to Him."

"Most Christians live a treadmill life—a life in which they can predict almost everything that will come their way. But the souls that God leads into unpredictable and special situations are isolated

by Him. All they know is that God is holding them and that He is dealing in their lives. Then their expectations come from Him alone."

Like this widow, whom I can't ever remember reading about before (it's short and worth the read, 2 Kings Chapter 4)—"We must be detached from the outward things and attached inwardly to the Lord alone to see His wonders." *Soul Food*

> *"God sometimes shuts the door and shuts us in,*
> *That He may speak, perchance through grief or pain,*
> *And softly, heart to heart, above the din,*
> *May tell some precious thought to us again."*
> — "Streams in the Desert"

This! This is my conversation with God, the Almighty. This is how clearly He responds. No, He has not told me He will heal Ryan. Yes, that is the question, the only question that plays in my head like a record stuck on a scratch. *Heal him fully,* I beg. No answer. But He does tell me, He's doing a work, a work He's done with His beloved since the creation. He is cutting the cloth of my life to a new pattern; The pain is so deep I must look only at Him, until He opens the door to life again.

Singing Back-Up

Sometimes *God disables our plan entirely* to get our undivided attention. Bending down out of heaven, He cups our ear like a mother cups her child's and whispers, "I love you." Except we don't know that's what's happening until we recognize it's His voice. "Oh, you're talking to me."

Tonight, walking on the treadmill in the apartment workout room, I had big plans. Everything I intended to do while walking, my planned multitasking, failed miserably. An unplanned conversation ensued between God and me. Truth, it was a lot of me talking to me. He was just a spectator to my conversation with myself. Do you ever notice that you tell yourself you are talking to God, a warped version of prayer, but it's just you talking to yourself while God eavesdrops?

Inside my head, a spinning conversation, talking about the suffering, how bad this hurts. Bewildered, I am sharing my woes with myself, in disbelief that this is His plan. He knew this would happen and didn't stop it. I interrupt myself: "He is still a good God," saying it in hopes that the words will help me believe it today.

In my ears, Spotify plays "Top Christian Tracks."

Immediately Francesca Battistelli begins to sing her hit "If We're Honest."

In just one song, the Lord of All was cupping my ear, whispering a response to my one-way conversation with myself. My face tightened to hold in the tears as God cupped my ear, telling me that the truth can be harder than a lie. Well, isn't that the truth? As I write, I'm not writing this to you. I'm writing it to me and letting you eavesdrop. I must be honest, because I can recognize my lies, so what's the point? Faking it is a waste of time and energy.

The book "On Writing Well" came as a Christmas gift from my husband. It has sat safely in my nightstand drawer since 2001. My dream to write a book had several false starts. But the story was always intended to be about God, how life with Him is far better. His plan is better than yours because He's way smarter and loves you more. You see, I knew this truth back in 2001, still no book materialized. Where were the words, the story? No grand revelation flowed onto paper faster than my fingers could write. As much as I knew God was good, I think He

> *As much as I knew God was good, I think He knew that secretly, I wasn't sure about the "all the time" part and didn't know how good He was.*

knew that secretly, I wasn't sure about the "all the time" part and didn't know *how* good He was.

True confessions: I used to belt out "Witness" by Nicole C Mullen while walking on my dirt road. There are a lot of "Yeah yeah yeah yeah yeah's." That was what I was best at. I didn't know all the verses, and there were parts where I am sure the words I sang were nowhere close to the actual lyrics. Besides fainting at the sight of blood, I am also known for not getting the lyrics right. My husband's all-time favorite was when he and I were on vacation with good friends in Mexico, and one song was played everywhere we went. One day I finally asked, "Why does the song say, 'Hangin' on the bathroom door?'" Some of you are laughing right now. Some of you are waiting for the punch line. It'll come.

Back to singing backup for Nicole—the song has soul! The printed words don't do it justice. All I can say was I was singing right along with her, telling God I was answering the call!

Back to the story. The other day I was listening to an online writing class. As the class ended, the instructor recommended one book, only one, prefacing that it was old, but still very good. Any guesses? "On Writing Well," of course. God likes to make sure you know He is listening when you're having that one-way conversation with yourself, when you invite God to listen in on *your plan*. He never forgets and must chuckle to Himself. How many times will I continue with my plan before I get it? There *is no* "My plan."

My prayer—okay, really my *lament*—shared with Richard back in 2001, "I don't have a story." Warning! Don't ever say those words out loud! God might just give you one. My excuse—more accurately, my foot-stomping reply to God when He gave me years of a story with Caelen was "No one would want to read this story!" There is no happy ending. I have no answers. I am a complete failure at being the mother of the child Jesus dropped on my front porch! I'm not writing about that! Not!

Then Ryan! Seriously, God? A storm of fear rages inside me, so massive and overpowering that it can't be contained. If I don't speak it out loud, it will destroy me. If I attempt to conceal the crashing waves that overtake me daily, I will drown!

I never planned this story, as *no one* would *ever* plan this story for themselves; an adopted daughter with severe emotional disturbances on one hand and the oldest fighting a rare cancer, 200 cases in the U.S. a year on the other. Don't forget that it is the middle son's Senior year. Within three weeks of graduation, he leaves for basic training in the Air Force, followed by tech school and will be gone for six months. My big overwhelming sadness should just be *that*—my son graduating and moving away. That's what all the other moms on Facebook are crying about. Their senior is leaving. I want to be part of that "Boo Hoo Club." Just that is enough! Truthfully, it feels like, for eight years, I have missed out on all the boys' lives, consumed by the war Caelen wages each and every day. This isn't the story I planned, and it's not one I want to write.

On my text first thing this morning, following my one-way treadmill conversation, a friend shared this devotion with me.

"O tested soul, perhaps the Lord is sending you through this trial to develop your gifts. You have some gifts that would never have been discovered if not for trials. Do you not know that your faith never appears as great in the warm summer weather as it does during a cold winter? Your love is all too often like a firefly, showing very little light except when surrounded by darkness. . . . . . ."

"Wasn't it just a short time ago that, on your knees, you prayed, 'Lord, I seem to have no Faith. Please show me that I do?' Wasn't your prayer, even though you may not have realized it at the time, actually asking for trials? For how can you know if you have faith until your faith is exercised. . . . God sends trials so our gifts may be discovered."

"God trains His soldiers not in tents of ease and luxury but by causing them to endure lengthy marches and difficult service. He makes

them wade across streams, swim through rivers, climb mountains, and walk many tiring miles with heavy backpacks."
— PARTIAL "STREAMS IN THE DESERT" APRIL 10TH.

- Moral of the story: Never say, "God, I don't have a story," unless you're prepared for Him to give you one.
- Second moral: If you say you want to write about faith in God, prepare for battle and buy a good helmet.

Why are you part of this story? What good is a story if you never share it? God has sat me down and cleared my calendar. When Ryan sleeps, I write. I cherish this time with God. Don't misunderstand; I would change it all in a heartbeat if I could. I don't want to write this story. Ryan's cancer started *in utero*. It lay dormant for 20 years. I don't want anyone to think God gave Ryan cancer so I could write a book. I don't know why Ryan has cancer, 1 of 200 cases in the U.S. a year. Really? At his age, the location of the tumor on the spine, localized, chances of getting it are 1/32,000,000.

What I know is that He is here with us, giving us the grace to make it through one day at a time. "Can I get a witness? Yeah! Yeah, yeah, yeah, yeah!"

God Showing Off

Rex Hudler, "Hud," *the color commentator* for the Kansas City Royals, and Ryan Ramshaw have much in common. Both talk more about baseball than anything else. Both have red hair. Both love the Royals. Rex has a colorful way of giving a play-by-play, and Ryan loves his sense of humor. God put these two together in a way we never imagined, with a blessing beyond anything we could have ever planned.

> *"Consider it pure joy, my brothers and sisters, whenever you face*
> *trials of many kinds, because you know that the testing of your*
> *faith produces perseverance (grit). Let perseverance finish*
> *its work so that you may be mature and complete,*
> *not lacking anything."*

(Both Ryan and Rex consider James 1:2-4 their favorite Bible verse.)

Facing trials of many kinds, you learn there will be days when joy is easier than others. Today was a joyful day! Joy was overflowing everywhere, in abundance! Rex learned of Ryan and his cancer not long after his diagnosis. His first contact with Ryan was a voicemail he left for Ryan on December 17, encouraging him "to be a light for others" "Isn't that what He wants from all of us?" he said.

> *Facing trials of many kinds,*
> *you learn there will be days*
> *when joy is easier than others.*

God has a funny way of showing off in ways only God can, and over the beginning course of Ryan's early treatment, Ryan and Rex connected through crazy "coincidences," one of which is this week. It was wonderful.

Here we are in Houston, Texas, and guess who is playing the Astros in their season opener—none other than the 2015 World Series Champions, the Kansas City Royals! Ryan texted Rex, telling him he was here getting treatment. I have to laugh because it was just this fall that Richard bought one of the only autographed copies of Rex's book *Splinters* online to give to Ryan as a Christmas gift. It was such a big deal. We had no idea what was coming in December. So, it's a bit surreal to think, here we are in Houston, and Ryan is texting Rex, like they are old friends.

"He said we should come to the game, and he'd leave us tickets at the will-call window," Ryan said with his sly, unassuming grin. We walked into the giant dome, and now Ryan was smiling from the top of his World Series cap to the bottom of his toes. He points to the ticket, Row 2. "Do you think that really means the second row?" We kept right on walking until we found our seats right behind the Royals' dugout!!! Awestruck! Giddy! Of course, texting our family and friends. "You will not believe this!" We couldn't believe it, and we were there!

About halfway through the game, Ryan, my rule follower, gently nudged me with his elbow so as not to call attention, and whispered, as if he shouldn't be telling me this, but "Rex is texting me."

"Now?" I asked. "While he's working?" See, Ryan comes by his rule-following honestly. "Where is he?" Ryan subtly motioned with his head, "Up there." I, of course, turned to look up. "Where?" Ryan explained *where the broadcasters sit*—like I should have known this. The game is the season opener and is being nationally televised. Of course, this would not have occurred to me. Rex sends another text. Giggling his Ryan-giggle, "He wants us to wave." We had no idea that we were now on national TV and that Rex had been sharing Ryan's story on national television. God made sure everyone could see. We looked up to see Rex waving to us, and we waved back. It was God showing off, big time.

Next, my phone lit up with texts, saying we were on TV . . . then again . . . Rex mentioned us by name . . . Grandpa Ray was having dinner at the "4 Corners" café when he looked up at the TV screen at just the right time and shouted, "Hey, that's my grandson!" as he pointed to the old TV hanging on the wall. . . . Friends were screaming at their TVs. . . . even if they were alone . . . The guy beside us elbowed Ryan and said, "Hey, my friends sent me this. We're on TV." He couldn't believe it. We were famous! "Wait! We're famous because of *you*. They are talking about *you*!" We recounted the story of Rex and Ryan . . . You can't make this up.

Rex is known for his "Hudisms." He says and does a lot of funny things; that's what Ryan loves about him, his stories, the "Rally Bug," "Pure Protein," and Ryan giggles, and there is joy. Lots of Joy! But a Hudism you might not know is, "People will know you are a Christian by the way you love other people" (*Splinters*, page 170, Rex Hudler's memoir). Tonight we felt such love, not just because of the incredible experience but also because of all the messages. Your joy for us! Celebrating with us! Now that is some Amazing Love.

Waiting for a shuttle bus, we just sat reveling in the night. Ryan nudged me again. "Rex just texted me. He wants us to come to 'the yard' to meet 'the guys.'" The story just gets better and better. Next week he starts his 31-day radiation treatment and will spend the first five days in the hospital getting chemo as well. These memories will be our manna for the journey ahead, helping us persevere.

> *"Consider it pure joy, my brothers and sisters, whenever you face trials of many kinds, because you know that the testing of your faith produces perseverance. Let perseverance finish its work so that you may be mature and complete, not lacking anything."*
> —Jas 1:2-4

Red Sea

God *has been writing stories* since the beginning of time—stories that direct us to look up, see Him, get to know Him better, and trust Him more. Some scenes are more dramatic than others, life reaching a crescendo that takes your breath away.

Sometimes it's a great battle, and He, God the Almighty, makes the rescue, swoops in, provides, fights, and saves as only *He* can. When I reach Heaven, I envision sitting in God's big cinema in the sky to watch His greatest stories. We will all have front-row seats because He is God, and we are in Heaven, and He can do anything. "Now Showing! *The Parting of the Red Sea.* . . . "Critics give it five stars. Moses is played by Moses, not Charlton Heston."

The Israelites have escaped captivity; chased by the Egyptian army and entrapped by the Red Sea, they have nowhere to go. They cannot imagine a way to escape. And then God speaks! Can you hear the boom in his voice?

> *"Do not be afraid. Stand firm, and you will see*
> *the deliverance the Lord will bring you today. The*
> *Lord will fight for you; you need only be still."*
> — Ex 14:13-14

"*Stretch out your hand,*" He commands. Moses braces himself, the wind whipping his face, the sea spraying high above his head. In Heaven, we will not need 3D glasses or "smell-a-vision" as real seawater wafts above, and we're eating the best popcorn you have ever tasted.

The surging waters rushing back, the roaring winds drying the land, the Israelites marching in faith into the seabed to safety. Amazement in their eyes. The sheer awe of it all, as the Almighty holds back the sea. A thriller even when we know how it ends. Proclaiming in song, we hear in chorus, with the orchestra behind,

"I will sing unto the Lord, for he hath triumphed gloriously;
the horse and rider hath He thrown into the sea."
— Ex 15:1

God writes a page-turner of a story, inserting miracles as He pleases. He could have saved the Israelites any way he wanted. He could have

> *God writes a page-turner of a story, inserting miracles as He pleases.*

just zapped the breath from Pharaoh's lungs and put Moses in charge. But who retells *that* version of the story? Would we still be talking about it if it went, "Then Pharaoh died of a heart attack"? *Ho-hum.* God didn't have to add the car-chase scene to *The Parting of the Red Sea.* But imagine, as young and old witnessed this take-your-breath-away miracle, just when they thought there was no escape and death was inevitable. What must it have been like for them to keep reliving and retelling the story almost in disbelief?

The credits roll by: *Director and Producer—God, in His Sky-High Theatre.* He will replay all the miracles we missed in our lives, *in slo-mo, so we see it—really see it.* How many gasps of "I never knew He saved me that day!" are whispered as we munch our buttered popcorn? "Now I see why I missed that turn. That delay saved my life." The unforeseen will be clear. It all makes sense from Heaven's view. The purpose of it all is revealed, and the development of the characters is seen from God's eyes, the struggle, the suffering, the waiting for just the perfect time—*God's* timing. He changes us through experiences, making us more like him, revealing the ripple effect from there.

Last week, I heard Him say over and over, "I just parted the Red Sea. Did you see it?" He repeated himself to me several times. Just as God sent the plagues to manipulate and control Pharaoh,

> *I will harden the hearts of the Egyptians, and I will*
> *gain glory through the Pharaoh and all his army.*
> — Ex 14:17 NIV

I will gain glory because no one can take credit for the parting of the Red Sea but God. No Ho-Hum about it! God still set the scene for us in 2016. Chariots aren't chasing us, He isn't using the demise of a Pharaoh to display His glory, but He sets the stage for the big miracle, confuses the enemy, saves, provides, and sustains; for His glory, a story He wants us to remember, to retell, to build our faith, as the wilderness lies ahead, and *He* will provide the "Manna."

Later during that game, Salvador Perez, the Royal's beloved catcher, tossed a ball to our new friend Marv, the unsuspecting Royals fan sitting next to Ryan, who didn't know God was adding him to the cast of a miraculous story. He offered it to Ryan. Ryan said, "You keep it." Before we left, Marv asked Ryan to autograph his baseball. Humble Ryan said, "I don't know what to say." My reply, "That's easy, 'Royals vs. Astros. April 11, 2016, Ryan Ramshaw. The day we were famous.'"

So why do I tell you all this? To proclaim His glory for the things He has done. The telling of a story that makes you look up and see Him and remember the waters He has parted for you, reminding you He still saves us. He does it all the time. Sometimes, we may have left the theater for more popcorn, and we miss it, but He still parts the waters, and it is magnificent when we see it!

Eight Words

Be still and know that I am God.
— Ps 46:10

These *eight words carried me through* our suffering these past months. Over and over, in moments when breathing seemed more than I could manage, I clung to those eight words of truth. God tends to have to repeat himself with me. Throughout His word, He says *"Be still and know that I am God."* I'm glad I'm not the only one who needs to be told more than once. It's a message repeated for the masses, not just me.

"The Lord will fight for you, you need only be still."
— Ex 14:14

Some days, it is harder to do *that* than others. To believe *that*, to do the "Be Still." There are times when you can't help but be just like the Israelites. "Was it because there were no graves in Egypt that you brought us to the desert to die?" Translation . . . "Really, God? *This* is your best plan?" We critique the Israelites' attitude as if we are any different.

It is still so hard to

"Be still . . . remember 'I am God.'"
— Ps 46:10

Remember it . . . proclaim it . . . sing it!

Because the wilderness is coming, and there will be hard days when you don't want to go on; it will be the memory of God's Glory displayed in your mind that will get you through. Sustenance.

I will sing unto the Lord, for he hath triumphed gloriously;
the horse and rider hath He thrown into the sea.
— Ex 15:1

When you're in the hospital getting chemo, and you're tired and sick of the fight, and Rex texts, "Hos asked how you were doing this week." (That would be first baseman and Golden Glove Award Winner Eric Hosmer.) Well, that's what we call "Manna"—an unexpected, gracious gift from Heaven.

"Be still and know that I am God."

+ Remember it.
+ Proclaim it.
+ Sing it.

The "D" Word . . .

I*'ve skipped over them all my life.* Let's not go there. We can talk about this another day. You know the verses that talk about God's—*shhh!*—Discipline. I don't like to think that God would discipline me. It causes too much internal conflict. Let's blame it on the devil, the other "D" word.

If I'm good, I can avoid discipline, right? That's been my theory for a long time. As a kid, I saw no reason to break the rules. What could be worth the discipline that follows? I went home sick from the second grade because I told Mrs. Delaney a lie. No, I don't remember the lie, but I do remember walking out of the school next to my mother, wondering if I should confess that I was not sick or keep up the lie. See, there's always that—once you start down that road of dishonesty, it's hard to find a spot to turn around. Yes, my theory had held water for a very long time. If I am good, I can avoid discipline. If I am good, I can avoid bad things happening. They are the same, right?

And then there are verses that I don't skip.

> *Trust in the Lord with all your heart and lean*
> *not on your own understanding; in all your ways*
> *acknowledge Him, and He shall direct your paths.*
> — PRV 3:5-6

These verses, this is the flavor I favor.

This is where I dwell, because well . . . I like them.

Verses that warrant skipping, I do not deny their presence. They are there, but *going there* means I have to resolve this internal conflict, a crucial conversation with the Father.

> *My son, do not despise the Lord's discipline, and do*
> *not resent His rebuke, because the Lord disciplines*
> *those He loves, as a father the son he delights in.*
> — PRV 3:11-12

Guess where that one sits in relationship to the one I like, back in Proverbs Three? Only five verses down! Funny, I never knew they were neighbors. I must've skipped that block.

A biblical scholar, I am not. I don't speak Hebrew or Greek, and I have no doctorate in Theology, but I learned the other day that the Hebrew word for "discipline" in this proverb does not mean punishment.

Not punishment? Per Tim Keller, who is a biblical scholar, able to read both Hebrew and Greek, discipline does not mean punishment. I really do all I can to avoid punishment. Did I mention I rarely misbehaved as a kid because I hated getting in trouble? A stern "Catherine" spoken by my father when I was teetering on the edge of disobedience, and a snap of the fingers sent shivers down my spine.

If I'm honest, my definition tells me *discipline* means *punishment*, no matter what Tim Keller says. Who wants to talk about getting spanked last night by your parents? *Not me.* Let's do all we can to avoid that!

Are you still with me in this text, or are you skipping it? The "D" word? Discipline is *mucar* in Hebrew. It conveys the notion of *chastening*, meaning "instruction." About to skip to the next chapter? Stay with me. There is a purpose to this. The purpose of *mucar* is to make us more like Him. To teach us in wisdom and knowledge. God teaches us in our trials, our pain, our suffering, the stuff He can't teach when we're on "Easy Street."

> *Discipline is* mucar *in Hebrew. It conveys the notion of* chastening, *meaning "instruction."*

We don't like to speak about the fact that God allows pain, because that's hard to reconcile in our mind, it conflicts with our vision of a loving father. Our avoidance keeps us from preparing to expect it. *Okay, I'll just say it:* "I would do anything to avoid a spanking! Can't I just be good enough to avoid the 'D' word?"

God does not work that way, dang it! (I probably shouldn't say that.) *"because the Lord disciplines those He loves."* "Shoot! What's a good little girl like me to do? This discipline—*okay, okay, Tim Keller*—"not punishment" seems unavoidable because He loves me, us.

Why do I care? Because when the God we call good "All the time," can you hear it echo across the congregation? "He is good!" Followed by, "All the time." It's a regular rah-rah cheer in the middle of church. But when He allows cancer or neglect so severe it causes brain damage, into your children's lives, this mom asks, "Why are you disciplining me?" Followed by, "Please, Lord! If it is something I've done wrong, I'm so sorry. I won't ever do it again. Please don't let my children hurt. Don't let Ryan hurt to teach *me* a lesson. I will do anything for You to make it stop!"

When something amazing, absolutely miraculous happens—something that only God could orchestrate—it's easy to say, "God is good," when you are walking on Easy Street. I've shared only a sliver of the miracles God has performed on our journey with Ryan, and God *is good.* But there's that crucial conversation that goes unspoken for fear of the answer. Will the answer cause great conflict because it brings into question His being good *all the time?* Isn't there a qualifier in there somewhere?

I love the verse, *"God knit you together in your mother's womb."* What a display of God's sovereignty. Rejoice in the protection of His hand. Before we breathe a single breath, *He* knows us. *Miraculous.* There aren't many more picturesque verses in the Bible than God knitting you together.

Ryan's cancer originated when chromosomes 11 and 22 mistakenly connected, in my womb. *God knew.*

When life is traveling along, well, not Easy Street, but in a gear where you can use the cruise control and enjoy the scenery, there is no conflict *then.* His goodness isn't brought into question when life is good. When you experience the stop-you-in-your-tracks pain, a detour of epic proportion, those "D" verses cause a conflict.

> *"My son,*
> *Do not despise the Lord's discipline.*
> *Do not resent his rebuke.*
> *Because the Lord disciplines those He loves,*
> *As a father, the son he delights in."*
> — PRV 3:11

I foundationally despise and avoid discipline because it's painful and feels like punishment, not instruction. It seems reasonable to me that, if you try to follow the rules and do what is right, you should be able to avoid the D-word and please God.

But that is when my mind sees only *this* world. When I set my mind on eternity, and that discipline's purpose is to make me like Him, not forgetting that Christ suffered and the Father suffered for me, the conflict eases a bit. I'm not saying it goes away. Remember, lies make my stomach hurt.

Romans 8:18: *"I consider that our present sufferings are not worthy of comparing with the glory that will be revealed in us."*

Truthfully, not my favorite verse. Not a verse I skip, just one that I preferred remained at a distance. I keep walking closer and closer to it, seeing it more clearly with each step, trying to embrace it.

If you're brave enough to look up verses on discipline, right next to the D word, it's almost always followed by "those He loves." He "instructs" those He loves.

> *"My son, do not make light of the Lord's discipline,*
> *and do not lose heart when He rebukes you, because*
> *the Lord disciplines the one He loves, and He*
> *chastens everyone He accepts as His son."*
> — Heb 12:6

Whisper the Name of Jesus. . . .

W*e've been dropped off in a war zone.* We walk among the wounded, the enemy showing no mercy. Babies, toddlers . . . no one is spared. Violin players to soccer players or any member of the family tree are eligible for combat. Those whose life had just begun or those approaching the end, squeezing out the last drop of life's juice, questioning whether the fight is worth it. Some have been told that the fight is over even before it begins.

Muslim, Christian, Buddhist, some counting on positive vibes, and good thoughts. What was it I heard today? "Positive energy." Venezuela to Russia, South China to South Texas. Rich and poor, even a Sheik just next door. The sickest of the sick, trekking across continents to fight death, grasping for life. No lullabies played over the intercom announcing new life. Only those sung quietly in the dark by the tear-filled mother as she comforts her precious baby and begs for life.

Wounds worn on the outside, the pain of loss, not just hair; arms, legs, eyes, the complete function of their once-healthy body, lost. Scars worn like headbands across the bare skull. Throats and mouths struck null and void, silenced. All made by the same God, sharing together an eventual cry for help, fueled by life-shattering fear that this battle might not be won. The steady beat of the blinking cursor on my screen, usually unnoticed, seems as big as a yellow caution light in a deserted intersection in the middle of nowhere, a warning. I question myself about taking you into our war, what it looks like here. Should I include you in the journey of where we are going next?

I was staring up from my foam hospital couch. The morning arrived too soon, and, without conscious thought, my arms raised, emotion overflowing, crying "Jesus." A long, wearing, and painful day ahead for him that will end with me whispering *Jesus* over my son. Jesus, resting on him. Jesus, Jesus, Jesus. There are no other words to say. Good vibes are useless. No amount of positive attitude could penetrate this suffering; only Jesus can.

Why is it that calling on the name of the Lord is the last thing we do? A last-minute revelation, like, "Well, I guess maybe *God* might have an idea on how to fix this." I hope you hear that last statement with all the sarcasm of Jim Gaffigan performing live. He delivers sarcasm on a silver platter. Can you hear his inflection? *"Well, I guess maybe **God** might have an idea on how to fix this problem."*

How is it I am too busy to include Him in the details of my day? Instead, I opt for a made-by-me plan, requesting He might agree, bless it, and make it smooth and easy, just like I see it.

Everyone who calls on the name of the Lord will be saved.
—JOEL 2:32

Jesus. Jesus. Jesus.
"There's Just Something About That Name"
— BILL AND GLORIA GAITHER

The Big Cs . . .

If *we all could wear T-shirts* explaining who we are, how our day has been, our year, our life, would we treat each other differently? The T-shirts could say, *My Dog Just Died, My Husband Wants a Divorce, I Just Lost My Job.*

Would compassion flow more generously, as it does from our Lord, if we knew the details of the suffering of those crossing our path? Do we withhold compassion from some because of a fault we see in them? Translation: *Didn't you bring this upon yourself?* The proverbial "You made your bed—now lie in it."

Do we comfort each other, helping one another patiently, and endure suffering together, or do we wish it away, frustrated by the personal inconvenience caused by sharing the load?

Would we be more likely to share our suffering if there were no fear of being judged worthy of compassion?

Praise be to the God and Father of our Lord Jesus Christ,
the Father of Compassion
and the God of all Comfort,
who comforts us in all our troubles,
so that . . .
we can Comfort those in
any trouble
with the Comfort we ourselves receive from God.
For just as we share abundantly in the sufferings of Christ
so also our Comfort abounds through Christ.

If we are distressed, it is for your Comfort
and salvation;
if we are Comforted, it is for your Comfort,
which produces in you
patient endurance
of the same sufferings we suffer.
And our hope for you is firm, because we know
that, just as you share in our sufferings,
so also you share in our Comfort.
— 2 COR 1:3-5

MD Anderson is a small city within Houston, a cancer convention 365 days a year. No membership or T-shirt is required. The "Big C" joins us together. The other big "C" that is a byproduct of cancer is Compassion.

There is an invisible sign you wear here. It says, "I have cancer, too." Or maybe it says, "My child has cancer," or "My husband." The list of possibilities is long but requires no explanation. You don't have to speak the same language, look alike, eat the same food, live on the same side of the world, or believe in the same God. It's all unspoken and yet wholly understood: Compassion flows.

> *There is an invisible sign you wear here. It says, "I have cancer, too." Or maybe it says, "My child has cancer," or "My husband." The list of possibilities is long but requires no explanation.*

As I pulled up to a stop sign just outside "The Cancer City," my eyes meet the eyes of a woman walking beside my car. We could pretend we don't see each other, but we don't. I smile through the glass. She smiles the same one back. Without saying a word, it is known; she is breathing in fresh air for the first time in hours, maybe days, since seeing the sky. A deliberate deep inhale of the outside air, an attempt to record how good it feels inside your lungs, sunshine on your face. The experience is silently shared between strangers. Compassion flows.

I came home for just a few days. "Home Sweet Home." The words have a different meaning now.

A Graduation . . . A Celebration . . . An Exhalation . . . Life outside "The Cancer City."

"I just want to give you a big hug" is repeated again and again. We are showered in love: Comfort overflows. Cancer is a politically correct disease. It's public. It's obvious. It's accepted. No shirt required. I've often thought about how much harder it is to suffer from a pain not so obvious—not a loss of hair but a loss of soul.

There are all kinds of invisible wounds—"Hidden Hurts," I've coined them. The details go undiscussed. Let's face it. There are things we don't talk about. For eight years, as Momma #5, raising a child full of "Hidden Hurts," enveloped by them, consumed with no cure in sight, I cannot help but compare and contrast the differences I see. The effects of abuse and neglect have overtaken her nervous system, bowels, and brain. Multiple medications are used to help her function. Yet you would never know it just by looking at her. She looks just fine. She needs a T-shirt. She requires an explanation. What would the T-shirt say?

"I was left in my car seat for most of my first year of life." I can see that one on the discount rack in every color. I don't care if it is Hot Pink and comes with ribbon—no one is buying it.

Or how about. . . .

"Mom #1,
Gave me to Mom #2,
Because the dad of Baby #6,
Doesn't want Baby #5,
So how about you keep her?"
I don't see that selling like the shirts that say, "Cancer Sucks."

It was no fault of her own. Completely undeservedly, the first three years of her life sucked. I don't care if you put a rainbow or a unicorn on it, "Five mommies in three and a half years" isn't selling. The children's book *Are You My Mother?* loses its innocent humor when it is no longer fiction.

Eight years, trying to heal an invisible wound, a sore that has festered and grown since her birth. When did she stop crying? How long did it take? Days? Weeks? How many tears does a baby cry before its brain says, *Stop; no one is coming.* I can see why we don't talk about this. I'm uncomfortable as I search for words that accurately describe a day in a child's life that goes unseen, uncared for, and unloved.

We want to believe love heals all wounds. We want to kiss it and tell ourselves it's all better when it's not. It's hard to understand a hurt we can't physically see, like a father scanning his screaming child for a skinned knee. He picks him up, dusting him off. "You're not hurt. I see nothing. You're going to be just fine!" That! We want that! We *want to believe* that the absence of physical scars means she can't remember or feel the pain and will be just fine.

She remembers.

Her experiences made her who she is today, the same as your experiences made you; unfortunately, different ingredients were used. When you cried, your mom came, and your brain remembers that. Thousands and thousands of times, your mom came and spoke sweet words of comfort to you, assuring you that you are loved. Mommy is here. When she cried, her mom didn't come. Her brain remembers. When your mom said you were the most beautiful baby in the whole wide world, your brain remembers the love in your mom's eyes. When she heard nothing and saw no eyes lovingly looking back at her, her brain remembers. Is there any truth in "It's a good thing she was too young to remember"? No, that's a lie.

I love a good chocolate cake. I use chocolate cake a lot in my writing. It must be a good cake to receive Honorable Mention, one with homemade chocolate buttercream frosting piled high. But, if you leave out the eggs and the baking soda, the cake doesn't taste the same, no matter how much frosting you use. A baker would never consider cutting open that baked cake, pouring in those forgotten eggs, and closing it back up, thinking no one will notice. Then sprinkle baking soda on top like powdered sugar and expect rave reviews. The outside might look the same, but it will never taste the same.

That's the thing about "Hidden Hurts"; they are just that, hidden. Her outside doesn't match her inside. Her behaviors, the symptoms of those "Hidden Hurts," are not "sugar and spice and all things nice." They are anger, fear, anxiety, and a long list of unacceptable T-shirt terms. It's incredible how much easier it is to show compassion to someone who has lost their hair than to someone who has lost their soul.

I am overwhelmed by my own hidden hurt, the failure to heal her. The inability to show her compassion day after day, admitting I am not sure I have any comfort left to share. It's hard to fathom a little girl so typical on the outside yet so broken on the inside.

I am taking a risk here by saying something that will be hard to swallow. You won't like how it tastes. When your child has cancer, people come running with casseroles. Strangers buy you dessert at a restaurant. Your child's bald head is all the explanation needed. Cancer plays out on FaceBook. Cheers of encouragement are daily. Compassion flows.

Here, I say we have seen the body of Christ, and even strangers swoop into action, loving our family through this cancer journey. We have been showered in compassion and generosity with things we would have never requested. We are grateful. It has helped us endure.

I'm in the "Cancer City" parking garage, sitting in my car, dictating thoughts before I lose my nerve to speak them to paper. Tears pour out. Unaware, I look up through the blur, and there is a Texas-sized truck, the only kind they drive here, struggling to back out of the compact car spot. Really? What made you think that would work? A stranger jumps out of his car helping Mr. 10-Gallon-Hat wiggle from his sliver of a spot. You see it every day here in "Cancer City": immediate compassion, no questions asked, no judgment.

In "Cancer City," no T-shirts are required; everyone knows the battle being fought. And everyone knows it warrants compassion with a capital "C." It flows into action, changing how we respond to each other at a stop sign, a parking garage, or a hospital cafeteria. The suffering changes you, and compassion is shared freely, with no payback expected. It is how God intends for us to help each other endure.

After years with our daughter, my nerves are raw and exposed, and I have an exhaustion that cannot be healed with any amount of sleep. My reflection, I no longer recognize or like. How could I be so empty, so lacking in compassion? Is it something that eventually runs dry? I thought there was to be an endless supply.

The expectation, whether spoken or unspoken, is, "Isn't she fixed yet?" or "She looks normal to me!" One of the more popular: "God will heal her. Just keep loving her." To which I respond, "Would you say that to the mother of a child in a wheelchair or a child with Down Syndrome?"

I cannot heal her Hidden Hurts. I wish they made T-shirts for that.

Thank you, our Father of Compassion, for comforting us in all our troubles. Help us to show compassion and offer comfort to those in trouble. Help us share the hope found only in Christ.

Praise be to the God and Father of our Lord Jesus Christ,
the Father of Compassion and the God of all Comfort,
who Comforts us in All our troubles. So That . . .
We can Comfort those in
Any trouble
with the Comfort We ourselves Receive from God.
For just as we share abundantly in the sufferings of Christ
so also our Comfort abounds through Christ.
If we are distressed, it is for your Comfort
and salvation;

if we are Comforted, it is for your Comfort,
which produces in you
Patient Endurance of the same sufferings we suffer.
And our hope for you is firm, because we know
that, just as you share in our sufferings,
so also you Share in our Comfort.
— 2 COR 1:3-7

What Do You See?

What *do you see?* The mind sees what it is focused on, not what is in front of it. Several months ago, I would have told you we were barely holding on. Our situation with Caelen had reached a level of crisis we never imagined and had no solution for. We knew she needed more help than we could provide. She wasn't getting better, even though we were working harder. After eight years, God provided a place that could give her the help she needed. God's timing and provision, like giant puzzle pieces in the sky, moved about effortlessly by Him. She had consumed my every thought, my days focusing on her, facilitating every facet of her life. My nights were spent wrestling with whether my days had accomplished anything at all. The child who had become the oversize centerpiece of our lives, unable to see around her, was about to disappear from my sight. She had no Facebook page. She wasn't on anyone's prayer list for healing. Sometimes, I think people forgot that she was part of our family.

We had reached a checkpoint of sorts, a place to catch our breath, recover a bit before we started again. We had no idea of the race ahead, but God did. This was one of God's first miracles where He boldly shouted at me, "Look over here! I'm over here! Look at Me!" Our family entered Ryan's Race in an exhausted state. We did not have fresh legs for this marathon. I've quit asking God, "Why?" and I've landed on "What?"

What do you want me to do with this? There must be more purpose other than just surviving this journey. The life of caring for Caelen full-time had swallowed me whole. When we left her in treatment, it was like I was a snake shedding its skin, crawling out of the shell that covered me, a weighted blanket spread over my entire world, swallowing my days, only to be followed by cancer.

The To-Do's once so important evaporated, because nothing else matters when you hear, "The MRI showed a mass on your spine. We don't know what it is, but you are going to be very sick for a very long time" You never look back; whatever was at the top of your list for Monday is gone. You walk out of your old life and into an existence that doesn't look like life at all. Nothing is the same. It was like my brain had been erased; even the child who had consumed my every thought was gone.

Eight years, absorbed by one child, how to help her, how to survive her, and now my brain couldn't even see her; all I saw was Ryan and cancer. There was no space for anything else. The terms used for her mental illness, the names of her medications, and even the names of her doctors were no longer in my mental Rolodex. They had all been replaced, all new terms, new medications, new doctors. What was God doing?

The mind sees what it is focused on.

A study was done using two videos. One video showed two teams of students passing a basketball back and forth, and another video showed the same students passing the ball but added a girl with an umbrella walking right through the center of the screen superimposed on top. When the doctor asked the subjects in his study to count the number of times the ball was passed, an astonishing 79% failed to notice the girl with the umbrella. In the years since, hundreds of studies have backed up the idea that when our attention is occupied with one thing, people often fail to notice other things right before their eyes.—"Your Hidden Censor: What Your Mind Will Not Let You See" by Keith Payne)

My go-to distractions I had used to survive her were now useless. TV was one of my faves, followed by TV, or maybe a good show on TV.

Just get my mind on someone else, their life, their design or paint colors, their struggle, not mine. Zone out with someone else's thoughts. And with Caelen, *it worked*. Well, it never cured anything, her, or me; it just took my rattled brain to a place of distraction where I could no longer see her, where I stopped trying to figure her out, understand her, or fix her.

People can spend an entire lifetime thinking a distraction is their cure, but the reality is it usually makes you fat. That is, if you eat your stress. It makes you broke . . . if you shop your stress. It ruins your relationships . . . if you blame your stress. It makes you incredibly unproductive and even unemployed if you sleep away your stress. It isolates you from others if you do nothing but talk about your stress. Food, shopping, sleeping, blaming others, and non-stop talk about your stress are not cures for it.

Distraction does not change you or the storm you're in.

No distraction was big enough to take my eyes off Ryan's cancer. The storm raging inside my head was all I could see. A solid wave of fear followed by a tsunami of sadness could overcome me in an instant. Thoughts race; an ocean of tears are the waves inside my head that sometimes escape to my eyes, and other times they just crash back and forth, engulfing my every thought. What do you pray, and what do you do when fear rises with the crashing power of ocean waves?

> *No distraction was big enough to take my eyes off Ryan's cancer. The storm raging inside my head was all I could see.*

Some storms require you to stay and ride them out.

Prior to Paul being shipwrecked as a prisoner, while in route to Rome to face trial, a Northeaster arose (A very big storm!). . . . Paul speaks, "But now I urge you to keep up your courage, because not one of you will be lost; only the ship will be destroyed. Last night an angel of the God to whom I belong and whom I serve stood beside me and said, *'Do not be afraid, Paul.'*" (Acts 27:22-26 [partial])

There was a book written a few years back called, *Eat This, Not That.* It was brilliant because it tells you what to do, followed by what *not* to do. You can't just stop eating forever. You can't stop going out to a restaurant with friends. So, this book told you what was better to eat and what to avoid eating. Brilliant! So many times, we approach life with a hard "No." A firm, "Stop that!" When in reality, that is a terrible plan. Life rarely affords you the all-or-nothing approach with any amount of success. Failure is almost always guaranteed when I say, "That's it—no more chocolate!" Yeah, we know *that's* not happening. You can't just stop doing something. You have to replace it with something else first. You can't stare at a piece of chocolate cake and tell yourself, "Do not be hungry" . . any more than you can stare at the storm and tell yourself, "Do not be afraid."

*"[an] angel of the God to whom I belong . . . stood
beside me and said, 'Do not be afraid.'"*

I usually focus on the part of *"Do not be afraid,"* which causes me to see the very storm I'm afraid of when I should focus on the part that says,

"[an] angel of the God to whom I belong . . . stood beside me"

I'd like to see an angel! I think I could focus on *that.* But how do you do that when the storm surrounds you, a raging, life-threatening storm, with no break in the clouds and no angel, just His words, *"Be still and know that I am God."* Most of the time, I saw only "Be still." Being still is hard, especially in a storm, because our nature is to *do* something. Don't just sit there—we're sinking! But the verse doesn't stop with "be still"; it then says, "Know that I am God."

What do you know about God? Who is He? He's my savior, provider, redeemer, and protector. He is all-powerful, all-knowing; the list is endless because he is the Alpha and Omega. It all starts and ends with knowing Him.

What does He promise? He will never leave me or forsake me. I cannot be snatched from His hand. Nothing can separate me from the love of God.

Why do I trust Him?

As Abraham hiked the mountain to sacrifice Isaac, God provided. Joseph was sold into slavery by his family; God took what was evil and made it good by providing food for thousands during a famine. When Shadrach, Meshach, and Abednego were thrown into the fiery furnace, God let not one hair be singed.

> *For God so loved the world He sent his only begotten Son that*
> *whosoever believes in him should not perish but have eternal life.*
> —Jn 3:16

I believe you love me.

God sacrificed His son *for me*. Is He leaving me now? That is not the God I know, and it goes against what I believe is true. God loves me. He loves my family more than I do, more than I can even imagine loving them. That's a hard one to fathom. God loves my son Ryan more than I can imagine. I'm not anywhere close in comparison. On a truth like that, I think it's a "Zip it. Lock it. Put it in your pocket" truth. Meaning you can't reason through this because our human brains can never fathom the amount of love God and Jesus have for us. Simply put it in your pocket as truth.

The other truth that can be more of a tug of war is that Ryan belongs to You, not me, God. All my kids belong to God. When I feel particularly confident in my parenting, and all is going smoothly, and I'm even giving myself a little parenting pat on the back, it can be hard to remind myself that they belong to Him. I am merely a steward of their life.

The facts: Jesus, You died on the cross for me. You could have made another choice, but instead, You experienced all the evil forces of this universe and went to hell to save me, and the Father left You so that I would never have to experience what I deserved. You aren't leaving me now.

You may not answer the way I want or when I want, but I still trust you.

Shadrach, Meshach, and Abednego replied,

If we are thrown into the flaming furnace, our God is able
to deliver us; and He will deliver us out of your hand . . .
But even if He doesn't, we will never serve your gods . . .
— DAN 3:16-17 PARTIAL

The "Be still" part threw me off because it was my focus. Being still is possible only if you remember the second part.

"And Know that I am God."

To *know* something . . . you must *think* something. Remember the study, "When your attention is occupied with one thing, people often fail to notice other things right before their eyes." Fear, a big, scary, life-threatening fear, might be standing right before you, baring its teeth, but you don't have to focus on it. Choose to focus on Him.

> *Fear, a big, scary, life-threatening fear, might be standing right before you, baring its teeth, but you don't have to focus on it. Choose to focus on Him.*

I can see Him, or I can see my fear, but not both.

Sadly, I have to make this choice over and over because the fear comes back, waves its arm, and screams, "Look at me! Look at me! I'm over here!" Sometimes those are real fears I must face, and sometimes it's just worry.

Can any of you add a single hour to your life by worrying?
— MATT 6:27

The remedy is the same: focus on Him.

Dear Lord,

I lift up my eyes to the hills—where does my help come from?
My help comes from the Lord, the Maker of heaven and earth.
— Ps 121:1-2

Help me to see You, not my fear, not the storm. When I go through deep waters, You are with me. I believe I belong to You. You promise to never leave me. Forgive me when my eyes dart away to fear and the circumstances surrounding me.

- You call me out upon the water, just like Peter, and You tell me to focus on You.
- You do this out of love, not some cruel head game testing my concentration.
- You want me to focus on You because that is Your gift.
- When I see you, there is peace in the storm.
- When I see you, there is joy in the storm.
- Help me to focus on you.

In Jesus's Name, Amen.

Therefore, since we are surrounded by such a great cloud
of witnesses, let us throw off everything that hinders
and the sin that so easily entangles. And let us run with
perseverance the race marked out for us . . . fixing our eyes
on Jesus . . . the pioneer and perfecter of faith. For the joy
set before Him, he endured the cross, scorning its shame,
and sat down at the right hand of the throne of God.
— Heb 12:1-2

Messy, Hard-to-Understand
Hidden Hurts

Most times, *when I sit to write,* God has been nudging me for days or weeks. He stirs my mind with thoughts that repeat. Sometimes I push back, "Are you sure?" He then continues, "Yes, I'm sure," but never those exact words. He doesn't call an audible. I wish He did, or maybe send a text message.

"Yes, this is what I'm teaching you."

"Yes, I'm sure."

"Trust me."

"Yes, this is God"

He continues to stir in me through His Word, repeating thoughts orchestrating me to hear them somewhere outside my brain, a confirmation of our private conversation, until I sit down and wrestle it out.

Our family has been blessed to receive so many prayers, encouragement, and love as Ryan's Race Against Cancer plays out in our community and on social media. My older brother's house burned down a few years ago—his historic 1910 house that he had been restoring himself from the ground up. The community rallied around this man, whom they had watched spend 25 years living on a prominent corner, slowly and meticulously restoring an old house to its original glory. Then, one night, it was all gone. I heard him say, "Everyone should have their house burn down, just to see how many people care and want to help."

When your child gets cancer, no matter how amazing the love and care shown by others, you would never say everyone should have their child get cancer to see how many people care and want to help. Never.

But it is incredible to see the love. Usually, people say, "feel" the love. I *see* the love.

I go to the grocery store, and a parent of one of Ryan's high-school peers stops me and asks how Ryan is and how I'm doing. Next, he says, "I am praying every day." And I believe him; so many are begging our God for a miracle healing. We go to the Farmer's Market, and anyone who knows us stops to say, "We are praying," or yells across the lot, "Ryan is on our prayer list." On Facebook, people I haven't seen in 30 years are praying, strangers, acquaintances, praying. Please stick with me. There is a point to all of this, outside of me telling you how blessed we are.

I must mention the fact that we are prayed for by so many and loved. Yes, it helps us continue to fight, get up, and not feel alone or desperate. Uggh! Here is where I say, "God, are you sure?" "Are you sure you're sure?" You see, cancer is a disease without judgment, blame, or shame. Cancer is treated with punishing drugs that almost kill a person, but people understand it because they see how it ravages the body. But not every battle reveals the scars. This is where my heart starts to race, because I don't want anyone to think we aren't grateful for this outpouring of love. It has helped us carry this heavy load.

Buuuut—I can't believe there is a "but" on this—but there is . . . a big "but."

But my heart hurts for all those out there fighting things alone. Isolated. Not because they aren't loved, don't have friends, or we don't care, but because *what* they are fighting makes us uncomfortable, or we can't see the scars, so we doubt the hurt exists. Many hidden hurts are exactly that, not seen by the human eye. Or worse, some hurts come with a judgment on the person or parent.

- A kid fighting drug abuse . . . shame felt by the parents.
- Divorce, separation, infidelity; the shredding of two lives once woven together. I can't help but think it is worse than death, but we treat it like an expected high school breakup. Commonplace, "They're getting a divorce." Two souls, once joined, now torn apart.

- A rebellious child . . . the judgment of your parenting skills.
- Mental illness . . . depression . . . anxiety . . . learning disabilities—no visible scars.
- Miscarriage . . . too private to share, plus no one knew about the baby, yet.
- Financial trouble . . . what foolish choices did you make?
- Criminal record . . . Shame, judgment, a long list of never being wholly allowed back into the societal fold.

The list above, those are messy, and I know they are not all cruel diseases. Before I lose anyone, I know jail time is not a disease. I am not suggesting that everything is a disorder. The list is longer than I have made it, so forgive me if I've left something obvious off. Some may silently argue, "People must take responsibility for their actions." Yes, yes, yes. I'm not writing a get-out-of-jail-free pass or a "You're-excused-from-trying pass."

But messy, hard-to-understand, and sometimes completely-hidden-from-sight hurts are hard for us and sometimes come with a judgment. We go down a different grocery aisle when we see *that* person. We quit calling that friend because it's too hard, we don't know what to say, or we are tired of hearing them repeat themselves. How do I know these things? How else? I've done it, too.

> *But messy, hard-to-understand, and sometimes completely hidden from sight, hurts are hard for us and sometimes come with a judgment.*

We were in a coffee shop a couple of months ago in Texas. Ryan wasn't even with us. His bald head provokes all sorts of conversation and kind gestures from strangers. Sometimes, it's "that table over there bought your dessert." People want to help in any way that they can.

Anyway, we were lookin' like "furriners" to this Texan when he moseyed toward us. "What brings you folks to these parts?" *OK, not those* exact *words, but close.* "Our son is fighting cancer and getting treatment at MD Anderson." Stopped in his tracks, this college kid said, "Can I pray for you?" He put his arms on our shoulders and prayed a beautiful, thoughtful prayer. It makes me cry thinking about it.

A stranger. What a gift of love! What an example of Christ!

Messy, hard-to-understand hidden hurts are sometimes thought of as hurts that:

+ "If you would only work harder to fix it, you wouldn't hurt so bad." Eww!
+ A judgment on a parent—"The apple doesn't fall far from the tree." Eww!
+ Or a lack of understanding—"But I don't struggle with that. Why do you?" Eww!

Call them what you want, but they aren't easy, and they seem to be hurts that never truly go away. And let's face it: our society has a shorter attention span than a goldfish. I read that! I could question the source, but I see the proof of it all around me, including inside my own head. We lose interest in long-term struggles that don't get fixed and justify not getting involved because it's too messy, we think we can't make a difference, or it takes too much time.

The other day we were sitting at the dinner table, and I looked around at my three boys and thought, *God, I want Ryan to be healthy. I want him to have his hair and his eyelashes again. I want him to look like Ryan. I'm so tired.* And then I slapped myself. "How must Ryan feel?" He is the one physically going through this, and I'm complaining that it hurts to watch. But it does. It *hurts* to watch, and I want it to stop! But I would never leave him because it causes me too much pain. You would have to drag me away, by my hair, to get me to leave his side.

There are "things" in this world that can't be fixed, understood, or aren't fair. As I look around the dinner table, asking God to please restore

Ryan, there is a spot that has been empty since October. Caelen's life is a long list of "not-fairs."

When things aren't fixed, we tend to believe someone is doing something wrong. There must be a way to fix this. God would never give us a journey that doesn't get better. When you do what God says, there's a "Happily Ever After" clause written in. Unless you're doing something wrong . . . Right? Where is that verse that tells us if we are good, believing Christians practicing love as Christ, God will fix it all? Anyone? Anyone? Nevertheless, somewhere, we think this is one of God's promises.

It is hard not to ask, *Why?* Why won't God just fix this? What could it hurt if God just did a colossal miracle *right now?*

> *Where is that verse that tells us if we are good, believing Christians practicing love as Christ, God will fix it all?*

Ryan's Ewing's sarcoma started before he was born. Chromosomes 11 and 22 mistakenly combined, and those cells lay dormant until a growth spurt caused them to grow. *Voilà* . . . 20 years later, a cancerous tumor. Caelen is Hypomanic Bipolar, amongst a long list of alphabet-soup diagnoses at the end. I've never said that quite so publicly because I don't want to argue with someone questioning the diagnosis or question my motivation for sharing something so personal about my daughter. I know it's not the same as saying "Your son has a tumor," but *why* isn't it?

Ewing's sarcoma, although not hereditary, is genetic, and hypomanic bipolar is hereditary and genetic; neither Ryan nor Caelen asked for or could have avoided these unfair diseases.

We have lived with and probably always will live with a "messy, hard-to-understand, full-of hidden hurts" child, who will need a lot of help managing life and probably won't have a lot of people rushing to her side to help because she is hard and demanding. She can wear you out. We have also experienced a very public cancer battle and will also live with the ramifications of that disease and the damage caused by its treatment. What is the difference between the two?

Not all problems have a Facebook page. Some obvious hurts, covered in scars, are not as hard to endure as the hidden ones. It's hard to imagine that there are harder things than fighting cancer. I don't like to rate people's pain. Ratings tend to make us not share our hurts. Pain felt in complete isolation is harder than enduring poisonous chemicals surrounded by those who love you. For some, getting up tomorrow will be something they question they can do and will question it the rest of their tomorrows. For some, when they venture out to the grocery store or the Farmers Market, people might be tempted to pretend they don't see them, not because they don't care, but because theirs is messy, unexplained, hard, unsolvable, and we-don't-know-what-to-say-or-do kind of hurt.

So, we can't fix Caelen. No one knows how hard we've tried or how hard this is to accept more than us. Yes, she is coming back home. No, life will not be easy. Not everything is fixed here on Earth. We will get tired of trying to help her. Hard and messy things we can't fix drive us to God, drive us to trust Him when we are in despair and to not rely on our own strength—or, at least, that's what we're *supposed* to do. Sometimes it drives us to a deep depression, changing who we are, and destroying everything we enjoy in life and all we believe in. We choose to believe that this is all His fault, so why would I ever turn to Him?

Caelen is not the "Happily Ever After" we envisioned, but her presence in our family has made us better people. Not perfect people, but people who understand not all hurts show scars. Our compassion for others has grown over the years, as our understanding of these hidden hurts deepens.

I have had to learn that my hope is not hinged on fixing her, one of the hardest lessons of my life. It took *years*. Lots of wrestling with God, and for a time, Hope was banished. I mistook hope in myself for hope in Jesus. My hope is in the Lord, and this lesson provides something of far greater value than "Happily Ever After" ever will.

Heaven is our promise of salvation, where there is no more "messy-I-don't-understand-why-this-happened-hurt." One day, there will be ultimate healing. The kind of healing that will allow us to see the Caelen God always intended her to be and be the people God always intended us to be.

Until then . . . pray! Pray like crazy for each other, no matter how messy, hard to understand, or tempting it is to judge or avoid. *Pray!* Pray for each other.

> *We do not want you to be uninformed, brothers and sisters, about the troubles we experienced in the province of Asia. We were under great pressure, far beyond our ability to endure, so that we despaired of life itself. Indeed, we felt we had received the sentence of death. But this happened that we might not rely on ourselves but on God, who raises the dead. He has delivered us from such a deadly peril, and He will deliver us again. On Him we have set our hope that he will continue to deliver us, as you help us by your prayers.*
> — 2 COR 1:8-10

> *"God comforts us not to make us comfortable but to make us comforters."*
> —JOHN HENRY JOWET

Say Goodbye

In *September 2016, ten months after his diagnosis,* Ryan completed his chemo and was declared NED—no evidence of disease. The tumor remained in his body, but it was dead. Every 90 days, we would travel back to Houston for an MRI to confirm nothing had changed. Jackson, who was supposed to leave earlier in the summer for basic training and tech school, had been delayed until mid-September. I thank God for orchestrating that change. Nothing felt safe or secure during Ryan's treatment. Everything felt like it could slip from my hands at any moment and be gone forever. The thought of saying goodbye to Jackson in the middle of all this terrified me. What if it was the last goodbye?

We had a "Say Goodbye to Cancer" and "Say Goodbye to Jackson" party in the backyard, not a party theme I ever envisioned. We couldn't wait to say goodbye to the life of cancer. Saying goodbye to Jackson would be sad, but not forever. Jackson has given me some of the best hugs right when I needed them. I will never forget; it was Ryan's last round of chemo in Houston. Richard and the boys were on their way to Houston. Ryan was struggling with anxiety. Those extended stays in the hospital just got harder and harder. There were times I thought he'd jump out the hospital window if he could. There was nothing I could do, and I felt so helpless, and the frustration of not being able to relieve my son's pain was more than I could take.

I called Richard, as I knew they were close. He answered, "We're in the parking garage." I said, "Run!" "Run!" I couldn't bear one more minute of being unable to help him. It was killing me. Jackson was the first one through the door. If I haven't said it before, Jackson is a man of few words. The school might burn down, and he wouldn't consider it worth mentioning. Jackson is also physically strong. Through the hospital room door, he burst. He walked straight to me and hugged me tight. No words, no questions, just a big tight hug. Just what I needed. I will miss him! I have missed him and Cooper.

Jackson left for basic a few days after the party. Ryan put on his Air National Guard uniform the day after his final chemo at home and started working in the base finance office. It was too late to start college this semester, so he was off to work, even though he couldn't have felt good. I'm not sure he could even remember what it was like to feel good anymore. But it felt good to be an airman again, not a cancer patient. I remember taking his picture the morning he left for work. Moms take many pictures of their child's first days, but this first day was like none other. For the first time since December 5, I said goodbye to Ryan as he walked out the door for his first day back at life.

Our Ebenezer Stone

December 25, 2016

"Thus far the Lord has helped us."
— 1 SAMUEL 7:12

EBENEZER—The stone of help.

Each Christmas, Richard makes us all a Christmas gift, and this year he gave us all a rock, not a piece of coal in our stocking, a stone, an Ebenezer

Stone, a reminder of how God saved us. One side of the limestone had been cut smooth, and these words were placed there:

Thus far, the Lord has helped us.
— 1 SAM 7:12

Ryan had successfully completed his Ewing's treatment, and Caelen was back home; miraculously God had provided a place for her during his treatment. We were all still in one piece.

To God be the Glory.

Even if . . .

W*e made it to 2017!* We are so thankful we are all together! God provided our every need and more, but even if He hadn't, we would still serve Him.

If we are thrown into the blazing furnace, the God we
serve is able to deliver us from it, and he will deliver us
from Your Majesty's hand. But even if he does not, we
want you to know, Your Majesty, that we will not serve
your gods or worship the image of gold you have set up.
— DAN 3:17-18

2017

A Rock in My Pocket

During Ryan's first week in the hospital in December of 2015, "God-appointments" were scheduled every day as if there were some giant day-planner in the sky. You know what I mean: an appointment so unexpected and so perfectly timed, only God could do it. That week, an old friend came to the hospital to see me. She was a friend I had helped through some hard times of her own, off and on through life, someone I had shared my faith with, but I wasn't sure she could hear it then. I would never have expected her to visit, but then again, it is hard to predict who shows up in a crisis. There she was in the hospital waiting room. She brought me a rock that said, *"Be still and know that I am God."* I carried that rock in my pocket for a year or more, rubbing it and repeating its message. It wasn't a lucky rabbit's foot. It was my physical reminder to hold onto that truth.

Those words, *"Be still and know that I am God,"* were a simple phrase with so much power and meaning. Without God, there was no way I could survive.

A year later, with a memory, I can be transported back, collapsed in the hospital hallway. My head hurts, clinching back tears even now. Scenes from our journey fly by in my mind, like the pictures on my iPhone, as I scroll through them. In a flick of a finger against the screen, Blur. Blur. Blur. I propel them forward or backward in time. A photo catches my eye, a memory, and with a jolt, time slams to a stop. I am there, in that memory, feeling the pain of the moment just as I did when

I first experienced it. I am beginning to understand how Caelen is triggered by her memories—those memories we like to think she was too young to remember.

I am overwhelmed by the enormity of all that has been orchestrated, planned, and known by Him, since the beginning of time. Struggling to breathe, overcome with emotion, I know I am nothing without Him. I cannot stand. Thoughts, songs, and Bible verses hit me, and I double over at the waist. "Get Up! Get Up! It's over." "Snap out of it!" I hear Cher's voice from the movie "Moonstruck" as she slaps her co-star Nicolas Cage across the face. Why can't I snap out of this? This breaking down, collapsing into a puddle.

A photo catches my eye, a memory, and with a jolt, time slams to a stop. I am there, in that memory, feeling the pain of the moment just as I did when I first experienced it.

Fainting at the sight of blood is my signature move and has been since I passed out in the frozen blood bank on my third-grade field trip to the local hospital. The bus driver caught me on my way down. I have many memories of me passing out cold at the most inopportune times. I see myself lying across the threshold of the women's bathroom at the Denver Zoo. It's 2002, and five-year-old Jackson is going through a stage of constant contact with his 7-year-old brother Ryan. He can't keep his hands off him. Three-year-old Cooper is oblivious, probably making friends with a stranger. At just the right moment, a vertical wrestling match erupts as we order our lunch at the zoo cafeteria, which smells like the elephants are doing dishes in the back. Jackson steps backward in his Spiderman tennis shoes, stripping my toenail from my big toe until it, too, is vertical. This exchange of force against my toe ended with me passed-out, lying across the women's bathroom doorway. I had attempted to make it to my destination on my own. Mistake! Richard and three boys followed in tow. Standing above me, yelling, I could faintly hear them commanding me, "Get up! Get up!" as they motioned with their arms in unison.

We had once been a family of three healthy, happy boys, trying to navigate family vacations and hot weather, and a mom whose blood pressure plummets at the sight of blood. "The good ol' days," where recovering from a toe injury was our biggest challenge.

The "Be still" in "Be still and know that I am God" verse, Psalm 46:10, is translated as,

+ collapse
+ fall limp
+ become helpless
+ cease
+ and leave it in God's hands

For a year, I clung to this verse, and not until last night did I look up the meaning of "Be still" in this passage. I never imagined it meant "collapse, fall limp, helpless." Never in my life had I been "so still" as this past year—helpless, that is.

In contrast, when God parts the Red Sea for the Israelites, he says,

> *Do not be afraid. Stand still, and you will see*
> *the salvation the Lord brings you today.*
> — Ex 14:13

At the edge of the Red Sea, "Still" doesn't mean "collapse." It means exactly what it says, "Stand still":

+ firm
+ have a presence
+ you are part of this
+ be ready to go
+ no time for collapsing now

There were days when God parted the Red Sea for us—miracles explained only as an act of God. On those days, I could stand firm, watch in awe as the waters parted, and prepare to walk toward whatever was next.

God's instructions to *be still*, to know Him, and who He is, are not the same in every verse. They are the same words with different meanings used throughout the Bible.

> *Be still and know that I am God, and I will be exalted*
> *among the nations, I will be exalted among the earth.*
> — Ps 46:10

"Be still . . . *still* = collapse, fall limp, cease, leave it in God's hands.

and know . . . know = know me intimately, understand me, perceive me.

That I am God" . . God = *I am the same yesterday, today and forever, cannot be improved, the absolute standard of truth, goodness, and beauty.*

Contrast this with Exodus 14:13-14, *Do not be afraid. Stand firm and you will see the deliverance the Lord will bring you today. The Egyptians you see today, you will never see again. The Lord will fight for you; you need only to be still.*

Translated:

Stand firm . . . = Set yourself (No collapsing here; no fainting, please.)

The Lord . . . Lord = the God of Israel, far less personal.

Be still . . . still = be silent, struck dumb. I'm going out on a limb here, but if you're a lifelong imprisoned Israelite, recently escaped and running from the Pharaoh's army, and God parts the Red Sea for you. . . *you would be struck dumb, too.* I would have surely fainted!

I am a doer. I like to be involved. I like my plans, and I make lots of them. My previous experience with *Be still and know I am God* . . . was translated in "My Dictionary" as God saying, "Remember—I'm God, and I've got this." And me responding, "You are God; you've got this, but what do you need *me* to do, and have you considered this . . . as a possible solution or plan? I was thinking that blank might be a good option, just in case you are out of ideas." Collapse, fall limp, become helpless, cease, give it all to God . . . that was not my translation for *be still.* Not at all. God uses unexpected circumstances and undeserving people to declare His glory, to be exalted. He writes a great story! He even uses us as we lie collapsed, limp, and helpless. He uses all kinds of things that don't make sense.

> *And she gave birth to her firstborn son; and she*
> *wrapped him in cloths and laid him in a manger*
> *because there was no room for them in the inn.*
> — Luke 2:7

A baby, lying in a manger, was God's "Plan A" for saving the world. There is nothing more helplessly still than a newborn baby. Think of that for a moment—the savior of the world entered as baby, not a warrior, unable to do anything for himself or even utter a word.

> *For unto us a child is born, unto us a son is given:*
> *and the government shall be upon his shoulder: and his*
> *name shall be called Wonderful, Counsellor, The mighty*
> *God, The everlasting Father, The Prince of Peace.*
> — Is 9:6

Shekinah Glory

Father, you dwell in places that we don't expect, scary experiences like cancer that can destroy us. For David, it was a giant named Goliath. *"You come to me with a sword and a spear, but I come in the name of the Lord Almighty."* (1 Sam 17:45) There you are, dwelling with David, giving him the courage to fight and him giving You the glory of the victory.

You dwell in the loss of what we think is our life, losing our health and our peace in a home where we once found rest. You allow great loss and sorrow today, just as Mary and Martha felt with the death of Lazarus. You allowed Lazarus to lie dead for four days before raising him. You even cried for him. Your humanity felt sorrow, as death was not the plan. And then, for God's Glory, You raised him.

> *Did I not tell you that if you believed,*
> *you would see the glory of God?*
> *—Jn 11:40*

Seeing the glory of God—I'm not sure at what age or what point in my life I realized that seeing the glory of God is part of every single story in the Bible. When Moses asked to see God's glory, He hid him in the cleft of the rock so that when God passed by, he was sheltered from seeing Him, *"You cannot see My face; for no man shall see Me, and live"* Exodus 33:20. That's hard to imagine, a glory so great man cannot look upon it and live. Isn't the glory of God a good thing? How is it that it causes death? He is so good, His glory so divine, the contrast of our sin, filthy-as-rags humanity, compared to His holiness; we cannot look upon Him and live. The Holy of Holies collides with our sin, and we lose without Jesus.

> *In the year that King Uzziah died, I saw the Lord, high*
> *and exalted, seated on a throne; and the train of His*
> *robe filled the temple. Above Him were seraphim, each*
> *with six wings: With two wings they covered their faces,*
> *with two they covered their feet, and with two they*
> *were flying. And they were calling to one another:*

"Holy, holy, holy is the Lord Almighty;
the whole earth is full of His glory."
— Is 6:1-3

Moses had a tent that he placed outside of where the Israelites camped, and he called it the "Tent of Meeting." The Lord would show up in a pillar of cloud, again because no one can see His glory and live. Outside the tent entrance, God would talk with Moses. We all have an Earthly vision of the story of the Israelites escaping Egypt, thanks to Charlton Heston and the annual playing of the timeless *Ten Commandments* movie. This story still captivates us thousands of years later. Do you think Charlton Heston is mistaken for Moses in heaven? Does he reply, "No, I just played him on TV"? I digress, but after receiving the Commandments from God, Moses is described in Exodus 34:35, *"they saw that his face was radiant."* He radiated from God's glory.

You dwell in the fear and fatigue, as You were with Elijah. 1 Kings 19: *"I've had enough! Just let me die!"* As he slept, You sent an angel to bake bread for him, You gave him food and rest, and there You were, with him in his fear and fatigue, just as You are in mine, providing all I need, sustaining me.

You dwell each day in the hard things of life that take us to our knees, fill our hearts with sorrow and our eyes with tears, making us question the purpose of it all. The enemy hunts us down, seeking to destroy us, our peace, our hope, our faith, and our love for You. He heaves fireballs of fear, loss, worry, fatigue, and hunger, with the ultimate goal of total destruction, but there You are, dwelling with us through it all.

You are right here with us, in the middle of the pain and struggle, all of this an opportunity to experience and see the Glory of the Lord shine.

We don't have to go the Tabernacle to see the Shekinah Glory, to see where You dwell. You dwell with us; You hide us in the cleft of the rock. You cover us, shielding us with Your hand. You are here. You are right here with us, in the middle of the pain and struggle, all of this an opportunity to experience and see the Glory of the Lord shine.

"When clothed in His brightness
Transported I rise
To meet Him in Clouds of the sky
His perfect salvation, His wonderful love
I'll shout with the millions on high
He hideth my soul in the cleft of the rock
That shadows a dry, thirsty land
He hideth my life in the depths of his love
And covers me there with his hand
And covers me there with his hand"
— Lyrics from "He Hideth My Soul"

To God be the Glory.

You Don't Wear Mascara to a War Zone

March 2017

Silent conversations in my mind, a one-person ping-pong game, again. Didn't I already have this conversation? Hasn't this all been settled?

I will never leave you or forsake you.
— Heb 13:5 partial

*Peace I leave with you; my peace I give you. I do
not give to you as the world gives. Do not let your
hearts be troubled, and do not be afraid.*
—Jn 14:27

Isn't this what I believe? I've walked "the valley of the shadow of death," where I am to fear no evil. He is there. Remarkably, unexplainably, He is there in the valley, and yet I feel my legs under me; a cartoon mule, I sit firmly with my front legs planted before me, knees locked in place. Being pushed and pulled, I fight. I dig in with all my might as my eyes peer over the edge again into that shadowed valley. Please, not again. Please don't take us down there again. I *know* You are there, but You are here, too. Can't we stay up here?

We walk through the war zone today, hidden inside MD Anderson, Ryan's every 90-day check-up. It's been six months since the treatment was completed. Memories erupt before me like fireworks exploding against the dark sky. Emotion overwhelms me with a sorrow and fatigue I had never known. I'm transported back in time; there, in the waiting rooms, the hospital hallways, with the other mothers who can't believe their child has been invited to this cancer party. Disbelief in their eyes, mixed with a resolve to fight.

On the hospital shuttle, a son, wearing his university ball cap and t-shirt: *he's not supposed to be here.* This beautiful spring day, he is to be walking the sidewalks of a college campus. He hands his crutch to his mother as he struggles to make his brain work his leg. He pulls himself up the stairs of the shuttle bus. Mom follows behind, carrying the party favor. They sit right in front of us; his head falls to her shoulder, as it would have when he was a little boy. His bald head, not a newborn, not right, burns on his neck, explaining the slurred speech to his mom, the labored gait, and the crutch.

She calls home to update. "We counted. Almost done with 28 days of proton-beam radiation"—the same treatment Ryan had started almost exactly a year ago. "Stop crying. Turn it off!" I silently tell myself with the conviction of a mother yelling at her teenager to turn down the music! *What is wrong with you? You wore mascara today? Brilliant! What were you thinking? You're in a war zone. How could you be so stupid to believe you would escape this day without tears? No one wears mascara to a war zone!*

"Proton Beam" the driver announces. Mom and son slowly rise, each movement a struggle, a fight to make his body do what it used to do with ease. She holds him to steady him as he struggles down three steps. Steps he could have leaped from the top before entering the war.

I hasten through my thoughts, faith, and beliefs as I type. In a few hours, we will wait anxiously for the white coats to enter the exam room with the results of the scans, and you see, it doesn't count to say it then. You have to say it now, before, before someone else, who you can't depend on, tells you everything is okay. Your hope can't be in them or the scan results. It has to be in *Him*. You have to say it now. You must declare what you believe with all your might.

You will never leave me or forsake me! You are on the throne!

This is how I know it's going to be okay!

It's incredible how quickly I shift my hope to my plan, the things I can control and see. I start imagining what I will do if this or that happens. I've had to learn and relearn and remind myself over and over again that there is no hope in *my plan*. My hope is in the Lord.

Let us hold unswervingly to the hope we profess,
for He who promised is faithful.
— HEB 10:23

When this journey has been hard, "the ugly-cry-awful" kind of hard, it has felt like God goes an extra step to help me, remind me, touch my shoulder, and say, "Yes, it is me who is talking." I don't miss much about the profound suffering, really nothing, but I do miss those evident touches, God reaching down out of heaven to lovingly whisper, "I am here. I am right here."

Blocking out this war-zone waiting room with too many memories that I can't bear to relive, I hear precious Pandora play instrumental hymns, and He touches my shoulder once again.

When this journey has been hard, "the ugly-cry-awful" kind of hard, it has felt like God goes an extra step to help me, remind me, touch my shoulder, and say, "Yes, it is me who is talking."

'Tis so sweet to trust in Jesus,
Just to take Him at His Word;
Just to rest upon His promise,
Just to know, "Thus saith the Lord!"
Jesus, Jesus, how I trust Him!
How I've proved Him o'er and o'er;
Jesus, Jesus, precious Jesus!
Oh, for grace to trust Him more!
I'm so glad I learned to trust Him,
Precious Jesus, Savior, Friend;
And I know that He is with me,
Will be with me to the end.
— LOUISA M.R. STEAD 1882

I have told you these things, so that in me you may
have peace. In this world, you will have trouble.
But take heart! I have overcome the world.
—JN 16:33

—The white coats enter and declare "No Evidence of Disease."

Weddings

W*e all sat encased in white silk, lace, and toile.* Jennifer had found her dress! It was September 2017, and "The Wedding" was to be in June the following year. Ryan had finally popped the question. He waited almost a full year after his last treatment. It was a fairytale proposal made for a princess. Besides being a gift from God I had prayed for since Ryan's birth, she makes no bones about being *a princess.* I like her better for it. We had made it! We were amongst the living again! *There was going to be a Wedding!*

As we all sat in the glow of "Saying Yes to the Dress" the excitement and relief were proclaimed: "I'm so glad we have the dress." Men think women don't like to hunt. We do; we just don't use guns or wear "camo," and our trophies are much prettier.

The words, "I'm so glad we have the dress," pricked my heart as I thought, "I'm so glad we have Ryan." Attending weddings since Ryan's diagnosis was painful. We had attended only a few. In one, Ryan was a groomsman, and I bawled as I watched him on stage. He was *alive;* a groomsman at a wedding! All those days wondering what the future would look like, and there he was, so handsome, his tanned face, and hair, smiling, walking upright, no brace, no wheelchair, like nothing had ever happened. All the conversations with the white coats explaining all that could be lost were now in the past, and there he was, my beautiful son. The emotion overtook me. I had not brought enough Kleenex for the celebration. All my life, I had taken *so much for granted.*

You would never sign up for your child to battle cancer. But unexpected gifts came with the war—perspective and appreciation for the celebrations in life. I no longer assumed I would see Ryan get married. I begged God to see Ryan and Jennifer get married.

Scanxiety

It *was time for another one* of Ryan's 90-day MD Anderson checkups. It had been a year since Ryan had finished chemo. Driving the twelve hours every three months for his scans had become routine. It was September, and Ryan was attending college again. The four of us, Ryan, Jennifer, Richard, and me, were road-tripping, wishing it were for a different reason, but we tried to make the best of it.

Scan-xiety is a term used by cancer patients. The days before the scans cause anxiety you've managed to avoid until it is time to go back to the cancer world. You can be living life and not thinking about cancer every minute of the day, and then it is time for scans, and something clicks in your brain, and the fear you'd been holding at bay comes rushing back as if it had never left.

During this visit, the doctor said that the scans were clear. *Exhale.* But he qualified that good news with, "We see something in his blood. His counts are low. It could be he had a cold, and he is still fighting it. We'd like you to stay through the weekend."

No Words

The *weekend was torture.* As much as I wanted to put my mind on something else, the elephant on my chest wouldn't allow it. The days let me prepare. I didn't want to. I tried to tell myself this was nothing. I didn't want to prepare for cancer again. Something in my bones was allowing the disease to seep in. I could feel it.

When you practically live in a hospital, you learn about things like laundromats on the pediatric floor and the location of the kitchen where the parents could store their food. You are standing in your kitchen away from home, preparing your food beside strangers fighting the same battle as you. They don't look like you. They may not even speak the same language, but you all know what the other is thinking.

I can't help but recall one of my encounters with another mom. She wasn't from the United States. I wonder if I asked where she was from or if I would remember, but I have never forgotten her words, "We've been here a year." Those words were a punch to the stomach, freezing me in place. I don't know if it is shock, heartbreak, or fear that it could be you, but all physical movement stops, and your brain searches for a way to cope with what you just heard. It's as if someone declares "Freeze!" like it's a game of tag. No response is sufficient for that frozen moment in time. For all the words in the English language, synonyms and antonyms, adjectives and adverbs, there is no version of "I'm sorry" or punctuation that will suffice.

Some parents I met would share that this is their child's second or third cancer battle. I would listen to their story, and, as I walked back to Ryan's room, beg God, "Please don't make us do this again! Please, God—not ever again."

Human Cocoon

I*t was a Tuesday, and I turned 50 that day.* We anxiously waited for our doctor; we loved him, and I think he loved us, too. How could you not love Ryan and Jennifer? What a love story! They had fought cancer together, came out on the other side, and now there would be a wedding! He walked in, and the only word I heard was "Cancer."

Ryan sat on a chair, and Jennifer stood behind him, draped over his shoulders, their heads down like they were forming a human cocoon. I was on the run. The hospital hallways are almost always full of patients and wheelchairs and slow-moving bodies that appear to be dying. I made my way back to the secret passageways where the doctors traveled. It was rare to see anyone there, as close to home on a dirt road as I could find. I paced up and down the hallway, crying, desperate, remembering all the times I had begged God not to make us do this again. Telling him, I don't think I can do it again. Please, God. And now the moment was here. We were doing it again. All the begging and pleading had not stopped the cancer. We were going into battle again.

The hospital hallways are almost always full of patients and wheelchairs and slow-moving bodies that appear to be dying.

September 26, 2017

God will be with us through a new race. Ryan has Myelodysplastic Syndrome. We will get treatment here at MDA from a Leukemia and Lymphoma Specialist.

Next week more info would be available from the cytogenetic testing. The kind of MDS will determine treatment. (Cytogenetic testing is the review of a patient's DNA.)

Ryan's bone marrow is not working; they must fix it for him to survive. We will know what caused it next week. Probably the heavy doses of chemo he received for Ewing's sarcoma treatment.

Questions without answers swirl in my mind. I'm heartsick but not destroyed, as our joy does not hinge on this world. God has shown us He is faithful.

This was the predominant message of the day:

> *May the God of hope fill you with all joy and peace*
> *as you trust in him, so that you may overflow*
> *with hope by the power of the Holy Spirit.*
> — ROM 15:13

We drive 12 hours home, watching *Father of the Bride*. We still have a wedding to plan!

Turbo

After our two-day trip to Houston turned into ten days, we were back home for the weekend. As soon as appointments were scheduled, Ryan and I would return to meet with a new set of doctors. Remember the woman who called me and said, "I think God wants me to have you stay in our house"? After our thirty-day apartment stay in 2016, she texted. "Why aren't you staying with us?" *A complete stranger* all but told me to come to live in her house. I couldn't get my head around it. I guess if God sets this up, it will work out. So, we moved in.

Bethany and Mike welcomed us like family, and we felt it when we entered their home. They were a blended family with five children, all the same ages as our boys. It is a "belated" place to tell you more about them because we are now well into 2017 and started staying with them in May 2016. We never stayed in another hotel or apartment again. I mention this because when your entire life is torn from your grasp and the only thing you recognize from your old life is your car, staying in a hotel only makes you feel more alone and displaced. When we were in their house, we were home. We had a quiet place to rest between treatments, a beautiful kitchen with a refrigerator that looked like ours from home, full of good food. Bethany was an excellent cook and decorated for every holiday like no one else I know. She holds the record for owning the largest papier-mache pumpkin in the world. Their home was medicine the pharmacy couldn't provide. God blessed us so immensely through them. This provision benefited Ryan's physical health, and our psyches were healthier because of their generosity and hospitality. They loved us like family. They were a living example of Rex Hudler's "People will know you are a Christian by the way you love other people."

Back to the story, and for this part, I'm sharing the details more than usual because God's hand in the details matters on this one.

Back to September 2017: I was sitting in my car, about to get my hair cut, when Bethany calls. Bethany NE-VER calls. She always texts, and if she does, it is quick, as she is on her way to the next thing. That girl is on the move. No time for chitter-chatter! Of course, I answer because Bethany *never* calls.

I'm going to jump to the good part.

Bethany asked, "When are you coming back?"

I said, "We are waiting on one doctor. He specializes in MDS."

Bethany interrupts: "What's his name?" The new doctor has three names and none of them were familiar to me. I stumble through the first two, and in the middle of attempting the third, she finishes his name for me with a high-pitched question mark at the end. When I confirm that is the doctor, she replies in delight, "My son is friends with his son!" Bethany has just shifted from High to Turbo.

"I'm calling his wife." *Click.* The texts start to fly. "What is Ryan's birthdate?" And then, "He will see you on Tuesday."

There! You see why I had to tell you the details. God is so in the details. Sometimes we realize it, sometimes it's hidden from us, and sometimes He just plain shows off.

Ziplock Bag

In walks Dr. GGM. I have decided to forgo his full name from now on. "How do you know the McCanns?" I tell the story and think how crazy this must all sound. We went from being unknown to old friends in one appointment.

Ryan's bone marrow was failing; it wasn't producing enough red or white blood cells or platelets. To complicate matters, his DNA is making faulty chromosome 7s, which we would later learn makes MDS higher risk. The chemo used to kill Ewing's can damage or destroy any of your organs and can give you cancer. Ryan's bone marrow was damaged beyond repair, and his new cancer was MDS. The MDS median age is 76. I think of it like this; aging can require hip and knee replacements. Curing MDS requires a bone-marrow replacement called a "Stem-Cell-Transplant." The significant difference is Ryan is 22, not 76.

Most in their 70s take a low-dose chemo and opt out of a stem-cell transplant because it can be challenging just to survive the transplant. They live out their lives, often dying from something else, but that was not the scenario we faced. Without a successful stem-cell transplant, Ryan would not live beyond a year or maybe two. The disease would quickly progress to Acute Myeloid Leukemia. Because of the DNA malfunction, and secondary cancer caused by the first treatment, Ryan faced a much different prognosis. I couldn't believe we were back to life and death. My head dropped back against the wall. I tried to keep the tears from pooling over the edge, but there was a flood; they would not stay inside the banks.

As I recall GGM's words, we must rid his body of all the "bad 7s" (aka—monosomy 7s, a DNA abnormality). We will give him five shots of chemo in his stomach each month until the transplant. The shot will hopefully tell his body to put all the "bad 7s" in a Ziplock bag and get rid of them. We must eliminate them all, or the disease will return. Bad cells make more bad cells, and we must kill them all. I, of course, ask, "What are the chances we get rid of them all?" He replies, "Twenty-five percent."

We drove to Houston for the next five months so Ryan could receive the most painful shot in his stomach. A giant syringe filled with a thick, oily substance slowly entered his body for a few minutes, leaving a large mass in his stomach. I would pray in silence, pray for Ryan, pray for healing, pray for him to endure this pain. Ryan withdrew from college again. He couldn't manage to be out of school one week each month.

Ryan got his first chemo shot the very next day.

Two Years on Hold

Right there in our first appointment with Dr. GGM, he called the stem-cell transplant department head, considered to be one of the world's best Stem Cell Transplant doctors. God just moved the velvet stanchions and ushered us in like VIPs. Dr. GGM is no slouch; one of the top MDS doctors, flown worldwide to care for royalty in the middle east. God's provision was over the top.

Ryan would be receiving a stem-cell transplant within the next six months. If the MDS progressed to AML, Acute Myeloid Leukemia, they would move up the date. His Ewing's treatment protocol took ten months. Starting from his first "Ziplock" bag shot, the transplant, and recovery, would take a year and a half, and Ryan would not return to school for two full years. Once again, life skidded to a halt.

What about the wedding?

As hard as it was to hear, the wedding could not be next June. The first 100 days after a transplant are spent in Houston, and that's the minimum, if all goes well. Ryan's immunity would be fragile for an entire year following the transplant. The doctors said, "If you want to get married, you need to do it before the transplant." I couldn't believe

I was now not only begging to see Ryan and Jennifer get married, but I was also begging they'd have a life afterward.

Remember when I said we really love *that* Jennifer? From their personal journey, she and her family knew what it was like to deal with health problems that wreak havoc on life and have no regard for "plans." They also understood the seriousness of what Ryan would be going through. Ryan called his sweet bride-to-be to discuss their future options. I don't know what that call entailed and shouldn't, so I will jump to the good part.

After many tears and grieving the loss of her June dream wedding, Jennifer and her parents agreed that the wedding must go on. They came up with the date of December 16th, 2017. It was now October something, 2017. We had *60 days*. I cleared my throat when Ryan said, "They want to have the wedding on the 16th of December." I doubted getting any venue other than our barn to hold the wedding with this short notice. While we love, love, love Jennifer, I knew a barn wedding in December was out of the question.

I will never forget it because only God would write this story. Seriously, only God. Jennifer was attending graduate school in Kansas, and Ryan and I spent most of our days in the doctors' waiting rooms. We agreed to call everyone from the venue to the pastor and see if the 16th would work. (I told you I would be honest. I didn't think this was happening. I knew there would be a wedding—but on the *16th?* No way!) Ryan and I divided the list between us. I stood in one corner of the large waiting room, and he in another. We would look at each other across the room, and when we got a response, we'd give the thumbs up or thumbs down. We got *all thumbs up*, with exception of the wedding planner, and in the end, her replacement was better! The venue we had booked for June had a standing reservation by a local company's Christmas party each Saturday in mid-December for years, but the Friday before was open. When the venue called the company, explaining the situation, they gladly moved their Christmas party to Friday, a perfect wedding gift.

There was going to be a wedding on December 16, 2017!

Faulty 7s

There *were lots of ups and downs* before the transplant. Ryan was taking chemo, which doesn't go unnoticed, especially in a body whose bone marrow isn't working right. Jackson and Cooper were a 100% match to each other but 50% to Ryan, so they would not be the best donor. These results were hard to accept. Why wouldn't God have at least made the boys match Ryan? While searching for the perfect donor, we would get monthly updates on those faulty 7s. Ryan was such a trouper, but that statement doesn't cover it. Ryan was 22 and had to quit college twice to fight cancer. He was getting monthly bone-marrow extractions, which are very painful, receiving chemo again, requiring regular blood transfusions, and traveling to Houston one week a month with Mom. He was supposed to be living life, preparing for a wedding. It wasn't supposed to be like this. In November, his marrow revealed 19 of the 20 harvested cells had faulty 7s. The enemy was everywhere.

He Maketh No Mistake

My Father's way may twist and turn,
My heart may throb and ache,
But in my soul, I'm glad I know,
He maketh no mistake.
My cherished plans may go astray,
My hopes may fade away,
But still, I'll trust my Lord to lead
For He doth know the way.
Though night be dark and it may seem
That day will never break;

I'll pin my faith, my all in Him,
He maketh no mistake.
There's so much now I cannot see,
My eyesight's far too dim;
But come what may, I'll simply trust
And leave it all to Him.
For by and by the mist will lift
And plain it all He'll make,
Through all the way, though dark to me,
He made not one mistake.
— A.M. OVERTON

 Thank you to my childhood and lifetime friend Greg Edson, who encouraged me during Ryan's cancer battles. He sent this poem to me in 2016 and told me I was stronger than any of the combined high school football players or wrestlers he knew. Greg was a fierce competitor and friend. When he sent this poem to me, Greg did not have cancer. In late 2020 he was diagnosed with colon cancer. He is missed and loved by many. I hope you get a copy of this book in heaven, my good friend. Greg Edson 1966–2020

The Dance

 Before the wedding, Ryan was sitting on the couch, and I was in my chair. He couldn't see my face. "Mom, we need to choose a song to dance to for the wedding. You and me. I have some here to choose from."

He started listing the songs, and tears trickled down my face as I listened. The lump in my throat grew to a painful throb; this isn't how it was supposed to feel.

"The Dance" by Garth Brooks was on the list. I knew that song. *Everyone* knows that song. I talked about it earlier in the book. If you listened to it or read the words, you know that *no one* would be able to make it through that song if we chose it. Instead, we went with Louis Armstrong's "What a Wonderful World."

The first verse hangs in plain sight from my chair on my living room wall. Ryan and Jennifer bought the scripted sign for me for Christmas. I sit and think to myself, "What a wonderful world!"

The Wedding!

J*ennifer's family traditionally marries in June.* She had always pictured a warm wedding day. So, of course, that is what God provided. December 16, 2017, was a balmy 62 degrees! Why did we doubt it would be anything other than perfect?

I can't describe the reverberation of emotion in the sanctuary as we anticipated the bride coming down the aisle. Everyone there knew that this wasn't just any wedding; this was a miracle that everyone there had prayed for. The pastor's message was perfect. These two had been through so much, and their first year of marriage would be more daunting than the journey they had already endured.

When the pastor introduced "Mr. and Mrs. Ryan Ramshaw" for the first time, they grasped each other's hands and raised their arms above their heads like they had just crossed the finish line, and the crowd erupted. I love that memory.

2018

God's Got This

If you knew my Ryan, you would choose to save him. Donor #1 has chosen not to share his life-giving blood with Ryan. I got the call yesterday that the donor said, "No."

"If only he knew *my Ryan*," ripples through my veins. But the thing is, he is not *my* Ryan. He is His.

"God's Got This" is among the latest and more popular Christian sayings. Well, of course, He does. I certainly don't. I'm so far from "having this"! I can't imagine walking through this Valley of the Shadow of Death without Him. But what does "God's Got This" mean? Sometimes it's said with such flippancy, like we're saying, "Have a Coke and a Smile!"

"God's Got This!" *Do Do Do Do Dooooooo!*

(That's the catchy little tune that follows any advertising slogan.)

Does it mean God is going to do it My Way? No, because my way would not entail this much waiting and not even close to this much hurt. Cancer would never be part of the story I write. "His ways are not my ways . . . His thoughts are not my thoughts."

> *"For My thoughts are not your thoughts,*
> *neither are your ways My ways,"*
> *Declares the Lord.*
> *"As the heavens are higher than the earth,*
> *so are My ways higher than your ways*
> *And My thoughts than your thoughts.*
>
> — Is 55:8-9

Does saying, "God's Got This!" make it hurt less?

—No.

I lie in bed and cry, "God, I love Ryan so much. I don't want him to hurt." And I cry. And I cry. "God, I know You love him more than me, so I know it hurts You *even more* than it hurts me to watch Ryan in so much pain. Why?" I cry loud, long, and often.

I know God loves Ryan more than I love Ryan. I know this because He was willing to have His Son suffer for my son. Jesus said, "Yes" to the Father. He willingly became our donor and gave His life-giving blood.

For God so love the world that He sent His only Son that
whosoever believe in Him shall not perish but have everlasting life.
—Jn 3:16

So why doesn't He fix this? Why is He allowing so much hurt? A *second* cancer?

Is it sacrilege to ask?

No, God's a big boy, a really big boy, and it's OK to ask why. He can handle it.

These are the questions we ask God when life gets hard. I don't mean hard, like a *flat-tire hard,* the clothes washer breaking, or a long-line-in-the-grocery-store hard. I mean life-and-death hard, deep-painful-hurt-and-loss hard. We see tragedy and suffering play out on TV and social media daily in such volume it doesn't feel real anymore. We are numb to it, unable to absorb it.

We see tragedy and suffering play out on TV and social media daily in such volume it doesn't feel real anymore.

You will hear of wars and rumors of wars, but see to it that
you are not alarmed. Such things must happen, but the end
is still to come. Nation will rise against nation, and kingdom

against kingdom. There will be famines and earthquakes in
various places. All these are the beginning of birth pains.
— MATT 24:6-8

That saying, "God's Got This!" doesn't always feel real either because
it doesn't always look like He does. If you're still with me, you might be
thinking of your own suffering and thinking.

"Why God doesn't just fix this?" I don't know.

What I *do know* is this: "He will never leave me or forsake me"
(**Forsake** = abandon without protection) and the same goes for you.

And Jesus said, *"Yes."* He gave His blood, so I don't have to. My
blood wouldn't suffice, anyway.

Does it mean there won't be suffering? No.
Does it mean it won't hurt? No.
Does it mean He will do things my way? No.
It does mean,
"To all who did receive him, to those who believed in
His name, He gave the right to become children of God."
—JN 1:12

And *this* is how I know "God's Got This."

Smote the 7s

W*hat does an army of 1,000,000 men* look like? Ryan has an aerial shot
of the 2015 Royals World Series Parade in Kansas City. It is a *sea* of
blue. Some estimate 250,000, others say 800,000, but either way, if the
army against you looked like that, it would be hard to picture victory.
During the early 9th century BC, good King Asa of Judah had an army

of 300,000 men and *zero* chariots when he faced an army of 1,000,000 Cushite warriors (Ethiopians) and *300* chariots. It was the battle of Zephath. Asa's army was outnumbered almost 4 to 1.

Lately, life has felt like a game of numbers.

- On my 50th birthday, Ryan was diagnosed with MDS.
- His second cancer.
- The average age for an MDS patient is 76.
- Getting MDS at his age is 1 in a million.
- Ryan's MDS is high risk because his bone marrow is making faulty chromosome 7s.
- Ryan's MDS is high risk because it is a secondary cancer, caused by the chemo used to kill the 1st cancer.
- 200 of the 70 million children in the US will get Ewing's sarcoma this year, Ryan's first cancer.
- Because of the faulty chromosome 7, he will receive 5 painful shots in his stomach each month before his stem-cell transplant.
- We will travel 750 miles to Houston one way to receive the trial chemo and 750 miles back.
- 4-6 months of the trial chemo while waiting for the transplant.
- 60 days to plan a wedding of a lifetime.
- 86,400 minutes battling, not letting 1 second of joy be stolen as we prepare for the wedding.
- Blessings, too many to count!
- Waiting another 3 months to see if the trial chemo kills the faulty 7-cells.
- Praying for his donor, who is 29 years old and a perfect match.
- She matches because on chromosome 6, there are 12 proteins, and she and Ryan match all 12.
- Planning for a minimum of 114 days living in Houston for the transplant.
- Planning for 6 weeks in the hospital on the 18th floor.

- Day negative 12 Ryan gets 4 days of high-dose chemo to wipe out his immune system completely—every cell in his bone marrow.
- Day negative 7 seven starts 2 days of Natural killer cells taken from umbilical-cord blood. (I didn't even *know* those existed. God is *amazing*.)
- Day negative 9 to 12 wait for the chemo to leave his body.
- Day 0 is the day Ryan gets between 50 and 80 million donor stem cells and starts the countdown of 100 or more days in Houston.
- 4 weeks left on the 18th floor from day Zero.
- 1 year, no work or school from day Zero.
- 365 days from day zero for a "new normal" to return.

When we were told about Ryan's MDS, it was explained that his case is very high risk because it is a secondary cancer; the previous chemo caused MDS, and its seriousness was compounded by a chromosomal issue. Ewing's sarcoma, his first cancer, is also a chromosomal issue. Chromosomes 11 and 22 mistakenly connect, forming a tumor the body does not see as disease. That's a simple explanation of a very deadly cancer, but as you know, my fainting at the sight of blood ended my medical career early.

With his new cancer, it was explained that even if Ryan had a stem-cell transplant, that if we didn't rid his body of every *single one* of the faulty 7-cells, before the transplant, the chance for reoccurrence was high. Imminent! I don't know the number you assign to imminent, but I'm pretty sure it's 100%.

Ryan's bone-marrow test in November produced 20 cells for them to analyze, and 19 of the 20 had faulty 7s. That means, of the cells they collected, only one was healthy, and the other 19 had bad 7s. Walk that out, and Ryan was full of faulty cells.

How many days did Asa sit in anticipation, watching the Cushite army just keep coming? Could he even see any land the Cushite Army didn't cover?

Asa prepared his mighty warriors with shields and spears. In his preparation, Asa called to the Lord his God and said,

> *"Lord, there is no one like You to help the powerless against the mighty. Help us, Lord, our God, for we rely on You, and in Your name, we have come against this vast army. Lord, You are our God; do not let mere mortals prevail against You."*
> — 2 CHRON 14:11

This is the prayer I have been praying for Ryan. In November, the faulty cells surrounded and outnumbered the good 19 to 1. When Asa saw that he was outnumbered, he didn't lie down and say, "I am defeated, Lord. Why should I fight?" He got his army ready to fight, and he prayed. He called out to the Lord, proclaiming the truth. There is *none like You*. We are *powerless*, but *You* are our God, and in *Your name* we fight; do not let us be defeated.

And what happened next, both the Bible and history books agree on; The Cushites were crushed, defeated with too many casualties to count, and Asa's army was not. The *King James* translation says, "The Lord *smote* the Ethiopians before Asa and the army of Judah."

"Smote" means *to slay in combat or strike with passion*.

I would like to see how that happened or hear the conversation when the warriors returned home to explain what happened to their wives. How the land was covered in Cushites for as far as the eye could see. I imagine the story went something like, "There we sat, in the middle of this *sea* of enemy, and we still had to get ready to fight. We were *so scared*. We were outnumbered! And *then*. . . God just did it. God crushed the enemy."

"There we were, staring at more enemies than we ever imagined. We were all scared and thought for sure we would die. We ran into battle, and without our even raising a weapon, they just fell over dead." Well, that's what I imagined they said to their wives. I would still be the wife, saying, "But how did they die? What do you mean, *God did it*? Describe it to me!"

One commentary said the Spirit of the Lord crushed the Ethiopians. Was it a breeze that swept through each Ethiopian, causing them to fall one by one? Was it a giant domino chain reaction, or did they all fall at once? Did the Earth shake as the one million fell? I bet it shook!

As we have waited and, at the same time, done all we could to prepare for this battle, I've clung to this vision of Asa and the army of Judah entirely outnumbered. I am asking God, *Who is able* to crush the enemy—to rid Ryan's body of those faulty cells. I know his bad cells outnumber his good cells, 19 to 1, but I don't think about *that*. I picture Asa as he sat upon the hill, watching the one million Cushites march toward his army of 300,000, and *God just did it*. He smote the Cushites, and *that* is what I choose to see.

God is going to Smote the 7s. I can see it!

At the transplant, Lord, replace Ryan's marrow with Your marrow, fill him with Your blood, and defeat this cancer in Ryan once and for all. *Smote those 7s.*

Maybe you feel outnumbered. Perhaps you are looking around, and all you see is a vast ocean of the enemy, and defeat looks imminent. Cling to the vision of Asa and the army of Judah.

- Be ready to fight.
- Take up your weapons.
- Prepare.
- And cry out to the Lord, *who is able*, and ask Him to crush the enemy.

> *"Then Asa said, 'Lord, there is no one like You to help the powerless against the mighty.'"*
> — 2 CHRON 14:11 [PARTIAL]

To God be the Glory

I've Taken Up Knitting

I *decided to take up knitting.* I'm not the knitting type, but it's my effort to keep my hands and mind busy as I sit in the hospital. I had grand visions of what I would create. My expectations are *always* high.

My eyes envisioned a luxurious gray throw made from that oversized yarn. Seriously, how big are the knitting needles for that yarn? I even thought I could make *more than one.* You know, Christmas presents!

Instead, as I learned my new trade, my hands produced a pathetic attempt at a potholder, which might turn into a misshapen headband. I totally thought I could knit a throw! Several, in fact! I've torn out more stitches than I've kept, my expectations unmet. Three days of work, tearing out stitches, and this potholder-turned-headband wouldn't even circle a baby's melon.

My expectations of myself, life, and what it should be, have always set me up for disappointment. Ask anyone who lives with me: there is a pattern of grand visions colliding with less-than-enough talent, resources, or time to produce what exists in my sometimes-over-the-top imagination. It's not for lack of trying or planning. We all know by now I like a good plan,

My expectations of myself, life, and what it should be, have always set me up for disappointment.

but somehow my grandiose visions were always more than the reality that played out in life. As a kid, I would lie in bed, building houses in my head. My most extravagant had a *waterslide* in the hallways, and I envisioned riding the waves from room to room. Now, as a much wiser adult, I can see more than a few downfalls in that design. We all have a little of this inside our heads—visions of perfection, especially now that we have an electronic window into everyone else's images of the perfect world. It is so easy to compare our life to others'. With a click of a button, you can pull up the perfect house, perfect body, and perfect gray knitted throw. Honestly, the list is endless; pictures and videos abound. I wonder if those photos we fly through daily, fed to us by an unseen power, filling our mind with great expectations and even greater inadequacies, exist for much longer than it took to take the picture. With a bit of Photoshop to make it all look *so* perfect! How long does the kitchen counter stay clean, after all? How long does every hair stay in place?

Thinking I have God all figured out, and I don't, supports my theory of misconceived expectations, and the longer I live, the more obvious it is there is no predicting or figuring out God's next move.

> *The plans of the Lord stand firm forever, the*
> *purposes of His heart through all generations.*
> — Ps 33:11

Lately, I've been thinking a lot about Heaven. We're surrounded by sorrow, hurt, sickness, and loss. I can't help but have an increased longing for that mansion in the sky. Do you think there will be Pinterest in Heaven? Will we be able to redesign our home and what it looks like, where it sits from day to day? Think of how quickly God changes the sky, moving clouds in and out, changing the color as He pleases. Oh, and those sunsets He makes—what they must look like from Heaven. I know it's not just me longing for Heaven. I listen to sermons on Heaven and try to envision it. I have yet to hear anyone mention my idea about getting to redesign *my mansion* every day. I don't know what it will look like in heaven or what a day is like, how long it lasts, but we will see God and know Him fully, and everything around us will declare His glory, and our expectations will be blown away!

> *"For now, we see only a reflection as in a mirror; then*
> *we shall see face to face. Now I know in part; then*
> *I shall know fully, even as I am fully known.*
> — 1 Cor 13:12

So, what does this have to do with knitting? We envision this perfect Christian life; the vision is different for all of us, but we all have an expectation of what we think it is supposed to look like. That vision is based on all we have learned about or believe about God and what we think it takes to be a Christian, followed by a well-intentioned plan of action. Some may think you can be a good person. I've seen myself up close; my good-person routine won't cut it. Maybe you envision Morning Prayer Time, exercising to praise music, waking your spouse and kids with the joy of the Lord in the morning sunshine, and breakfast served in a bowl with a dollop of kindness on top, and, somewhere in the middle of that plan, *real life happens*. The plans made don't work out at all, and no one would describe you as joyful or kind before ten in the morning. Or maybe you gave up on what you think God wants, and there is no plan at all and no plan to make one.

When we don't meet our expectations or those of others, it can cause us to stop trying. People avoid failure and inadequacy for all sorts of reasons, in all kinds of ways. Unmet expectations can paralyze us or even cause us to walk away from a vision completely. It can cause us to distance ourselves from God out of guilt and shame. We stop talking to Him because we think He is disappointed in us, as if there is *anything we could do* to earn His love and approval in the first place.

So, what are God's expectations?

> *He has shown you, O mortal, what is good. And what*
> *does the LORD require of you? To act justly and to*
> *love mercy and to walk humbly with your God.*
> — Mic 6:8

Mortal. We aren't divine, but God is. This statement should lower our expectations of ourselves significantly.

Mercy is who God is. He *oozes* with mercy from every pore. Does God have pores? We mortals don't ooze with mercy. Suffering helps me *have* more mercy, but if I'm honest, there are days I would opt for less suffering, scrapping my deeper understanding of mercy altogether. But we can't love what we don't have, and suffering begets loving Mercy. You can't have one without the other. That silly song "Love and Marriage" plays in my head as I contemplate this thought. "Love and Marriage. Love and Marriage" Yep, suffering and mercy go together like a horse and carriage.

Walk humbly. Walk with Him each moment of the day. When I walk through my days and nights, there are a lot of "Please God's" even when He *has* already. He *has* done it already. It's won. The ending is written. This life we worry so much about is a vapor.

You do not know what tomorrow will bring, what your life will be!
For you are like vapor that appears for a little while, then vanishes.
—JAS 4:14

James goes on to say that what we should do instead of bragging about our plans is say,

"If it pleases the Lord, we will live and do this or that."
—JAS 4:15

We envision these grand plans, beautifully knitted throws, and such. Elaborate plans of how we will meet His expectations, which are well and good, but what God really wants is for us to choose to walk with Him through this vapor of a life.

Walk humbly with God, acknowledging *He* is divine, and *we* are mortal; that is *His plan.* Along the way, you might knit a headband or a potholder.

And God SMOTE the 7s!!!

W*e just got the call* that Ryan's bone marrow came back showing no sign of the faulty chromosome 7s! This is the best possible news we could have received.

He still requires a stem-cell transplant, and preparation for that will start in mid-March. Pray the donor commits, but I am confident she will. God is faithful!

We have prayed for Ryan that God would SMOTE the 7s, and God has done it. He smote the bad cells in Ryan's body until there were none.

God came to the rescue of King Asa and the army of Judah, as they were outnumbered by the Cushites, 1 million to 300,000. King Asa prayed to the Lord, "Lord, there is no one like you to help the powerless against the mighty. Help us, Lord our God, for we rely on you, and in your name, we have come against this vast army, Lord, you are our God; do not let mere mortals prevail against you."

It goes on to say in 2 Chronicles 14 that God SMOTE the Cushites with the power of his Spirit. He destroyed them all!

To God be the Glory!

He Stayed

T*onight, Ryan's sweetheart*, his bride, walked through the door, and her smile bounced across the room like sunshine, landing on him. Love.

Not everyone knows as much as I do about this sunshine named Jennifer; she was the friend I secretly stalked on Facebook months before Ryan mentioned her, thinking to myself there appears to be a pattern here. She's in a lot of his pictures. Despite multiple inquiries, Ryan always said, "Just friends."

And then, in the fall of 2015, dating officially began. None of us knew that, five weeks later, we would all meet at the hospital facing the unbelievable news of cancer. Earlier this week, as Ryan and I were preparing to go to the hospital, it sat on me hard and heavy, the weight of what we were getting ready for again: walking into a hospital for a procedure designed to give Ryan the maximum amount of chemo possible without killing him, with the hopes of replacing his broken immune system with that of a stranger. And it's not as if the thought had never occurred to me before, but at that moment, it was measured; she stayed.

Jennifer stayed, the first time after his Ewing's sarcoma diagnosis, after only five weeks of official dating. One of Richard's first conversations with her, just days after Ryan's diagnosis was, "If you're going to leave, it's best to leave now." But she stayed. After waiting a year post-treatment, Ryan's long-anticipated proposal of marriage came to be a reality. On August 26, 2017, he finally popped the question, and we all jumped for joy. There was going to be a celebration! A much-anticipated wedding! And on September 26, one month to the day later, a new cancer diagnosis; Again, she stayed.

She stayed with a love for Ryan, a joy for being with him, an acceptance of all the things that no longer looked like they imagined their life to be together. She stayed.

And tonight, she arrived with a smile and a joy to be there. On the 18th floor, the transplant floor, complete with masks, gloves, and a foam cushion for a bed. She stayed.

Life doesn't always end up like we imagined it would, and little girls spend a lot of time dreaming of their white gown, followed by an image of their forever Love, and not so much time imagining what it looks like to *stay* with that Love, for better or worse, in sickness and in health. But she stayed.

I've often wondered why we didn't find Ryan's cancer sooner. He had been in pain for a few months, was working with a physical therapist and taking steroids, the doctors thinking it was a bulging disk. I've laid awake nights critiquing my mothering skills, questioning why I didn't see it before. How could I let him down like this? Why didn't I do more *sooner?* Was I so all-consumed by Caelen that I couldn't see anything else? In hindsight, I see the purpose of the timing of Jennifer. Just like God ushers Spring into existence at the right time for flowers to bloom, God was waiting to move Jennifer into Ryan's life.

In Victor Frankl's book *Man's Search for Meaning*, Frankl, an Austrian Neurologist and Psychiatrist, writes of his time in the concentration camps of Nazi Germany. One of his main observations of the prisoners is that, if they had a reason to live, if they believed that their spouse or children were alive and waiting for them, they were able to fight through the suffering. "Those who have a *why* to live can bear with almost any *how*."—Victor Frankl

Ryan's "why" was Jennifer, a life with her, and he was willing to conquer any "how" to be with her.

Strangely the sacrifice of Christ's life reverses this philosophy of conquering the *how*. Christ's "why" for the cross, was to die for us, not to live. The "how," for enduring His suffering was so He could give *us* life. It is Good Friday, the ultimate day of celebrating that Christ stayed on the cross for us. He didn't have to; He chose to. We were His "why"!

He knows all the hurts and how staying doesn't always look or feel like what we imagined, but He promises to stay with us no matter what. And because He stayed, the Father will never turn away from us. He stayed.

And being found in human form, he humbled Himself by becoming obedient to the point of death, even death on a cross. Therefore, God has highly exalted Him and bestowed on Him the name that is above every name, so that at the name of Jesus every knee should bow, in heaven and on earth and under the earth, and every tongue confess that Jesus Christ is Lord, to the glory of God the Father.

— PHIL 2:8-11

A Crown of Beauty

M*y husband Richard is a Renaissance man.* He can fix anything around the house. He's a gardener, straight-as-an-arrow vegetable rows. He's an artisan rock layer, over-the-top talented, and gives a sharp haircut.

I would take my three little boys to get their hair cut, a redhead, a brunette, and a towhead. Boy's haircuts are "kind of *thang.*" There are no bows, braids, or barrettes. Your boy gets a *bad* haircut, and people will notice. Inevitably, I would bring them home freshly cut, their new trim far from meeting my expectations. Richard, who would often say about all sorts of things, "I can do that," only to be met with my doubting eyes, expressing, "I don't think so." Of course, he replied with his standard response, "I can cut their hair better than that!"

"Where did you learn to cut hair?" I chided. "People used to pay me to trim their cattle in 4-H. I was very good. It can't be that different." *Famous last words.* After casting a good share of doubt onto my confident coiffeur and multiple mall-salon botched buzz-cuts, I caved and allowed Richard to display his proudly proclaimed hair-trimming prowess.

It was the beginning of an every four-week shearing session at our house that still takes place today. Not only did we save a ton of cash, but Dad became the barber once a month and intimately combed and cut his son's hair as they chatted about life. Depending on the time of year, we might even hold the event outside, for old times' sake. After all, he did get his training at the acclaimed "Shawnee County 4-H Cattle Barn"; it's only appropriate. It used to be our joke, "You know you're a redneck when you cut your kid's hair while he sits on the trashcan outside and then have him run naked through the sprinkler in the backyard to wash off the remains." OK—*that* part of the ritual ended well over a decade ago. But, on my honor, we did that.

Hair is an intimate part of us, a beautiful design element, a crown framing our every expression, and the window to our souls laced with lashes. My boys never matched; the pile of hair on the floor looked like a calico cat. I loved how different they were. When Ryan lost his hair the first time, he had a group of about a dozen friends who all stood with him in solidarity; they shaved *their* heads, too. It was a very touching act of friendship, no matter how you look at it. Until Ryan explained to me, "I don't want to look at it. I know I'm sick. I don't want to be reminded every time I look at my friends." Perspective changes everything. I know he appreciated the loving gesture of his faithful friends who wanted to do *anything* they could to express, "We aren't leaving you now. We are right here with you!" Those young men are still his friends today.

Before the transplant, Ryan received four days of the highest dosage of Busulfan chemo his body could withstand. Chemo kills every rapidly dividing cell in the body. Hair has no chance of survival. During the transplant, it was, for the most part, just Ryan and me. Jennifer was finishing her master's in Speech Pathology in Kansas and could only come to visit a few times during his 34-day hospital stay. Truthfully, I don't think I could have been anywhere else but right there with Ryan. I didn't leave the hospital, not once.

The nurses know when the hair will fall out and bring you a pair of clippers. Hair on the pillow makes you itch, and while you wait as long as you can, at some point, it's time. It was time, he said. Connected to his transplant room, he had a large bathroom with a handicapped shower, large enough to hold a plastic chair. We arranged the chair, Ryan bravely positioned upright, eyes straight ahead. No words: his calm, firm resolve sat still. There would be no chatting about the day or life, as there would have been with Dad. I stood behind and held the small battery-operated clippers in my shaking hands. Hands that had never cut his hair. "I don't want to do this again! *I don't want to do this again!*" The words never left my lips; they were silent screams that only the heavens could hear. With all my might, I forced my sorrowful cries into the prison cell of my ribs. Silence! The tears fell as a steady stream, and I couldn't see. The trimmers skimmed his scalp, and the thin hair fell to his shoulders. It was happening. We were crossing the threshold again. What had been lost before he was losing again.

Ryan was born with red hair. Richard looked at me with questioning eyes, and I looked at him, and I said, "It's not me." It was Richard's Grandma Lizzie, who is now 107, who piped up with, "It was me!" Ryan's beautiful thick red hair has never grown back to its original color, texture, or thickness. Chemo kills so much beyond cancer. It often steals the color from the hair, like it steals the color from life. Richard would say, "That Ryan, he grows hair like a forest. It's so thick." That red forest never returned to what it had once been. It's hard to survive a fire and look the same.

The Spirit of the Sovereign Lord is on me,
because the Lord has anointed me
to proclaim good news to the poor.
He has sent me to bind up the brokenhearted,
to proclaim freedom for the captives
and release from darkness for the prisoners,
to proclaim the year of the Lord's favor
and the day of vengeance of our God,
to comfort all who mourn,
and provide for those who grieve in Zion—
to bestow on them a crown of beauty
instead of ashes,
the oil of joy
instead of mourning,
and a garment of praise
instead of a spirit of despair.
They will be called oaks of righteousness,
a planting of the Lord
for the display of his splendor.
— Is 61:1-3

Only God can bestow a crown of beauty, replacing the ashes of our life with *His* joy and praise. To Him be the Glory.

Natural Killer Cells

"It takes more faith to be an atheist than to believe in God."
— RUTH BELL GRAHAM

Science wasn't my best subject in school. I'm pretty sure I got a C in College Chemistry, and that was at a community college. But during the years, I've been with Caelen and Ryan, I have learned so much about the brain and the body and how God made us to survive the hardest of times. Caelen's brain had learned to turn off her pain receptors when she was young so that she could survive. One of her medications helps her feel pain by reducing the amount of adrenalin she produces, as she remains in a constant state of "Fight or Flight." still today.

We have met many gifted doctors with extraordinary minds during Ryan's journey. It is astounding to hear them say, "We don't know what causes the body to do that." At some point, they *all* say it about some miraculous act the body does to protect or regenerate. The words are spoken aloud, with puzzlement: "We don't know what makes that work." It's about that time, I think, this one *I know*. I may have only gotten a C in College Chemistry, but I know the answer to *this*.

God the Creator, He is beyond comprehension! Miracles are *His* thing: He likes to show up in places no one expects and do things people can't explain.

Today, Ryan is receiving Natural Killer cells, also known as, NKCs. The chemo kills all active and rapidly dividing cells, but they can't detect all the defective cells. God, in his all-knowing power, as our Creator, put an *exorbitant* amount of Natural Killer Cells in the umbilical cord to protect a newborn baby, a super-charge of immunity. NKC's are our body's first line of defense against any hurt, from a bruise to an infection, an army of cells rushing into combat ahead of all other cells. Our knowledgeable transplant doctor has developed a protocol that uses NKCs *after* the chemo. NKCs taken from an

God the Creator, He is beyond comprehension! Miracles are His thing: He likes to show up in places no one expects and do things people can't explain.

umbilical cord of a live birth have never seen any disease before. When they put the NKCs into Ryan, these superheroes can *read* cells, determining Healthy vs. Diseased. Since Ryan has no other infection or disease beyond cancer, the NKCs go in for "The Kill," targeting any enemy cells hidden away. The NKCSs destroy the diseased cells, which the chemo can't see and isn't able to kill! Go ahead and gasp. He is amazing! Miracles are His thing!

Isn't it interesting that the man-made chemo can't see what the God-made cells understand? The God-made cells can read, detect, and kill the diseased cells.

When you hear them sound a long blast on the trumpets, have the whole army give a loud shout; then the wall of the city will collapse, and the army will go up, everyone straight in.
—Josh 6:5

"Up to the walls of Jericho
With sword drawn in his hand
Go blow them horns like Joshua
The battle is in my hands
Joshua fit the battle of Jericho
Jericho Jericho
Joshua fit the battle of Jericho
And the walls came tumbling down"
— Lyrics from "Joshua Fit the Battle of Jericho"

I believe God is marching in the Natural Killer Cells to do what they were created to do. The battle is in His hands!

Suffer Well

We *are told he faces his most brutal week yet;* physical pain and fatigue. I listen to him breathe, labored, not his normal steady breath.

He coughs, and the insides of his esophagus slough off; the chemo has burned his entire digestive tract. I don't have eloquent words for this, taking his body to the brink, watching it break down and react to what seems like chemical warfare, not medicine.

Expecting a miracle. A *miracle.*

Waiting for someone else's cells, unknown and faceless, her defenses to move in, grow, multiply, and become part of him, those stem cells miraculously knowing where to go and what to do. But not yet. Ten more days, or 14 or 21.

No one knows but Him.

He quietly sits on the edge of his hospital bed, wills his 6-foot frame up, and pushes himself out of these four walls, dragging his IV companion as it fills him with nourishment, pain relief, and protection for what his body can no longer protect or produce.

Please protect him!

He never complains.

They don't complain. Ever!

They love each other through this, even when his young body is doing that of an old body. There is nothing glamorous or youthful about this deterioration. His quiet determination to be strong will never be celebrated on a field of sport, yet no match on those fields of green compares to the fight he fights.

What I witness is beyond strong, a drive to live. Live life.

A painful, grueling, long journey, and they love each other through it, *through* being the operative word.

And there is beauty in all of this—not that he hurts, but that he is so loved. Truly loved.

If you take these observations, I have learned from someone suffering well, here is what they boil down to.

- Face today.
- Breathe.
- Expect a miracle!
- Wait and remember; He knows the timing for everything.
- Will yourself up and out.
- Pray for protection.
- Don't complain.
- Be strong in the Lord.
- Live life.
- Love each other "through" hard, painful journeys.
- And there will be *beauty* in the love that is witnessed by our own eyes.

To God be the Glory!

When the Lord spoke, rejecting all of David's brothers for the opponent of Goliath the Giant, He said, "Do not consider his appearance or his height, for I have rejected him. The Lord does not look at the things people look at. People look at the outward appearance, but the Lord looks at the heart.

— 1 Sam 16:7

Engraftment

Engraftment *is not a word we use every day*. I'm not sure I ever used it before now. Roll back the clock a few thousand years, and the process of engrafting applied to olive trees, not stem cells. It's amazing how the basic idea used on olive trees is now a medical miracle called a *stem-cell transplant*.

It's hard to describe what it is like to live on a transplant floor, where everyone shares one goal: Engraftment! Engraftment of the transplanted cells is your ticket to the outside world. Engraftment means life. You get to live! Engraftment means your body has accepted someone else's cells, and they are now engrafting into your bone marrow and becoming your new immunity, changing you. Engraftment!

For an olive farmer, there are two kinds of olive trees, good ones that produce olives and wild ones that don't. Good olive trees produce juicy fruit—wait, that's a gum—and the wild olive trees don't. What's amazing is a cutting of a *good olive tree* can be engrafted into the trunk of a *wild olive tree*, and voila, your wild olive tree is making "Juicy Fruit." It's 4:00 a.m. as I write this, and my juicy-fruit pun is funny to me.

Engraftment is the process of "implanting." Each day you implant your prayers, your encouragement, and your support into our lives, and it gives us strength to bear this burden, to continue this harrowing journey. During "Ryan's Race," on the Facebook prayer page we set up, we have been blessed to hear from friends, strangers, acquaintances, and friends we never knew we had.

A friend from high school, one I've not seen in years, wrote me this note.

"I have read almost every post you have put on Facebook about Ryan's fight, and I am inspired by your words. I am normally not an emotional person, but I am almost in tears as I write this message. (I am sitting in the driver's license renewal office, by the way). Anyway, I just wanted you to know that I continue to think and pray for you, Ryan, and the rest of your family."

When a person sends you a note telling you he is praying for you, he has *engrafted* into your life, implanting encouragement, and the power of prayer. He has shared your burden.

Just today, Ryan got a text from a young man that had Ewing's sarcoma the same year he did. They have never met face to face. This is just a portion of the text . . .

"Your name is written at the top of my planner, so every time I open it, I remember to pray for strength in your fight." That's engraftment! That's implanting encouragement and prayer into someone else's life.

Another friend, whom I haven't seen in probably 30 years, sent me a note saying she reads our posts aloud to her family, so they can all pray. I never imagined our life, our struggle, playing out in someone else's kitchen and them praying for us. That's engraftment, implanting.

Galatians 6 says, *"Bear each other's burdens."* In this verse, "bear" comes from the Greek word *bastazo*. (I'm trying to make up for the Juicy Fruit joke. Do I sound smart?) In the New Testament, "bear" is used in conjunction with someone who is hurting, helpless, carrying a heavy load, burdened, and weak. When you're waiting for stem cells to engraft, your body is hurting, weak, and without protection from every imaginable virus, bacteria, or germ.

We are blessed with some very special friendships that would have never been part of our life outside of this difficult race. People, lots of people, have come alongside to help us carry this load and lessen the burden.

"I wouldn't wish this on my worst enemy! Thank you for the prayers. I'm sure it is hard to find words to say, but I know that we both know we have to consider it pure joy when we encounter trials. Your prayers and words of encouragement are a blessing to me."—Ryan Ramshaw

(Seriously, where did this child come from? I would have *never* been able to utter those words with the sincerity I know they are felt by Ryan, at age 23. Not a chance!)

Why share this burden with you? Why be honest about how hard this trial of suffering is? We share, hoping to help you carry your burden. If something we share implants encouragement to keep going, not to give up, and continue trusting God even when you can't understand why this is happening, that brings us joy! It gives purpose to all this suffering.

Engraftment! Life!

Truth: All of us are weak and in need of engraftment. Every single one of us needs a transplant! We are all the wild roots, the wild olive tree needing engraftment so we can produce juicy fruit.

> *. . . you, though a wild olive shoot, have been grafted in among the others and now share in the nourishing sap from the olive root . .*
> — ROM 11:17 [PARTIAL]

Engraftment: Christ's death is the ultimate gift of engraftment, where He transplants us into His family, and, ultimately, He bears every burden we have and gives us new life. *Everlasting life.*

Matthew 8:17 tells us, *Jesus "took on Himself our infirmities and to bear*—bastazo—*our sickness."*

> *Surely he took up our pain*
> *and bore our suffering,*
> *yet we considered Him punished by God,*
> *stricken by Him, and afflicted.*
> *But He was pierced for our transgressions,*
> *He was crushed for our iniquities;*
> *the punishment that brought us peace was on Him,*
> *and by His wounds we are healed.*
> — Is 53:4-5

Engraftment into Christ's family *is* eternal life. By his wounds we are healed. To God be the Glory!

Torn in Two

I *will tell you something I haven't told* anyone before because I am embarrassed and have been ashamed to ask anyone a question about it. I've gone to church my entire life, celebrating Easter, new dress, the basket, lunch after church, etc., but I don't think I ever had a deeply spiritual response to the event of the Crucifixion. Secretly, I thought I was supposed to *feel* more about Christ's death. I was missing something.

I knew to the best of my human ability that the pain and suffering of the cross was horrific. The Mel Gibson movie *The Passion of the Christ* forever changed my mental images of the beatings Christ endured before hanging on the cross. The graphic suffering was more than I could watch, but still, down deep, I kept thinking I was supposed to feel more about this act. Can you see why I am ashamed? There is this ever-so-slight fear that a bolt of lightning is about to strike me as I type this confession.

In this modern world, there is so much suffering, awful and evil acts, and, thanks to the Internet and R-rated movies, our minds can't stop seeing some horrific scenes we wish we hadn't. I wish I had never seen the movie *Silence of the Lambs*—pure evil on the big screen. When I considered Christ on the cross, I thought to myself, others have physically suffered worse tortures for more extended periods. People are enslaved and tortured for years without hope of rescue. What could be worse than being a child sex slave for years? Christ is not the only person in history crucified on a cross. I never thought the crucifixion was insignificant; I just secretly wondered how, if others suffer the same death or some more extensive suffering, what made Christ's crucifixion different?

At this point, I'm questioning if I should admit this. I know the crucifixion was a *big deal*. It is the only deal of the Christian faith. I know it was torture and horrific, and I don't have adequate adjectives to describe the suffering. I know Christ didn't have to do it or deserve it. But still, we have all heard stories of people giving their lives to save another, even strangers. Heroes who die on the battlefield, fighting for our freedoms, don't deserve to die. They do it to serve their country.

God, what is wrong with me that I don't get this? Of course, I am grateful that, because of Christ's death and the acceptance of Him being the sacrifice for my sin, that is how I am accepted into Heaven. But even that appreciation of the sacrificial act of the cross feels selfish. In my humanness, I can't help but value Christ's death, in part, because of what I get out of the deal. I can admit *that*. "Wow am I glad Christ died for my sins, so I don't have to go to Hell." It is an obvious perk. If you don't get that and you're a Christian, you're missing the Golden Ticket!

Christ endured all the ridicule and unwarranted judgment even after performing many miracles, saving and healing people, and living without sin. He was sentenced unjustly to death on a cross, never sinning and yet being hung next to thieves. "He could have called 10,000 angels!" The minute something is unfair, I yell, "Foul!" I'm all about what is fair! What is deserved! Jesus endured the "Not Fair" of all time! Think of what He could have done to the people spitting on him as He carried His cross. He could have yelled back at them so many things, like "You're going to regret you said that." Or that bolt of lightning I referred to, in a breath, a thought, He could have destroyed them all. Christ had the power to change it instantly, but He didn't.

Christ endured all the ridicule and unwarranted judgment even after performing many miracles, saving and healing people, and living without sin.

But it still felt like I was missing something more. What *piece* was I missing? What made this the ultimate act of love for all time?

If you have been to church, there is a good chance you have heard these words during communion, "This is my body broken for you, do this in remembrance of me" and "This is my blood, poured out for you, do this in remembrance of me." These are the words I've heard repeated over and over all my life, and yes, they are *meaningful*, but again, selfishly, it's because of the gift *I receive*, eternal life. It is a life-changing, eternity-giving gift. But what would this act of hanging on a cross mean if Heaven wasn't our destination? If there was no Golden Ticket?

Today is Ryan's 2-year birthday. Yes, his transplant was a success! He received new life with a stem-cell transplant, on April 11, 2018, and he is now two years post-transplant. God does some crazy things to make sure you know He is there with you, that He knows exactly where you are. Today on my Facebook, the video of us on TV in Houston popped up, "Your memory of April 11, 2016." Until today, I never noticed those happened on the same day, two years apart. Coincidence? No, He mercifully reminds me of His Ever-Present help and provision throughout this journey. The memories of his faithfulness are the gifts!

Fighting for life in a hospital is not what you might think. No, you don't knit beautiful throws. Remember my vision of knitting several Christmas gifts? No, you don't have deep, meaningful talks with your son. He is asleep or trying to fight off those painful thoughts that roll around in your head when you fight cancer. Not much from the outside world is funny or meaningful. You don't plan anything for the future. The future is on permanent hold. When you fight cancer, you do not think about where to go for dinner, the wedding next month, or anything outside of *getting through that day.*

God uses all sorts of ways to reach us and teach us, drawing us closer to Him. Life with cancer conjures up all sorts of questions about *why* God *allows* suffering. Is He really a good God? *All the time?* God's word is packed with Truth, but we still get stumped on things like *"The Lord will keep you from all harm—He will watch over your life."* (Ps 1:7)

You can spend a long time wrestling with that verse, as your son faces cancer. Twice! You can chew a long time on things, sitting alone next to your son on a transplant floor of a hospital. A lot of, "but I thought you said . . ."

I've shared honestly about all my wrestling and chewing on hard-to-understand things in life. "Unfair" is a biggie. God has used Ryan's two cancer battles to help me see my missing crucifixion piece.

"My God, My God, Why have you forsaken me?" was my missing piece. For all the days I spent alone sitting beside Ryan, watching him suffer, God never left me. *I* was never alone. *I* never faced being forsaken.

As Christ died, He *yelled*. It's the only time we hear Christ *yelling* in the Bible. I learned that from a Tim Keller sermon. It had not occurred to me that Christ was *not* a yeller. When Christ yelled, *"My God, My God, why have you forsaken me?"* the world went *dark*—and the Father turned away, separating Himself from His Son, as Christ entered Hell.

Hell. So, I read "Dante's Inferno" in college, and it gave me nightmares. I don't want to see the movie version. I don't want to imagine anyone going there.

If someone had told me in the hospital, "You have to leave Ryan now. You can't be here with him." The thought is too painful to consider. *The idea of that separation crushes me.* You would have had to drag me out kicking and screaming by my hair. I would have slept outside the door on the floor, in the lobby, but I could not leave him as he suffered.

That! That act of love, the ripping apart of the Father *from* the Son was my missing piece. Christ took the role of the sacrifice, and the Father willingly left Him, turning away from Him for the first time, forsaking Him during Christ's greatest suffering. People more intelligent than me could paint the cosmic picture of what that was like or the implications of it, Christ diving into the depths of Hell, all for the sake of children *who didn't deserve this gift.* I can only tell you what I know.

One night they tried to remove me from Ryan's room, and there was some yelling.

The Father left the Son; He turned away.
The Son willingly went, facing His only
separation from His Father.

The ripping and tearing apart of a union we can't comprehend. The Alpha and Omega, beginning and the end, never before separated. We speak about the broken body and the poured-out blood for our sake, our sin, the bread, and the cup. I am not arguing, nor am I in a position to argue anything theologically. I am only sharing an observation of the ripping apart of the Father and the Son, as it is not a coincidence that, at that moment when Christ gave up his spirit, the curtain of the temple was torn from top to bottom. This curtain measured 30 cubits by 30 cubits, (about 60 ft square) and had an estimated thickness of about 4 inches.

And when Jesus had cried out again in a loud voice,
He gave up His spirit. At that moment, the temple
curtain was torn in two from top to bottom. The earth
shook, the rocks split, and the tombs broke open.
— MATT 27:50-52 [PARTIAL]

God uses stories to teach us, creating pictures in our minds, so we can better understand what He is saying. The temple curtain, which was as thick as a wall, was torn in two. The hands of God reached down out of Heaven and ripped it apart like it was no more than a piece of paper. The earth shook. Rocks split open. I believe this represents the ripping apart of the Father and Son, not just an added visual effect for the sake of drama. Enduring the cross was a horrific physical torture and the sacrifice of all time. Remembering the ripping apart of the Father and Son, demonstrated by the torn curtain and the rocks splitting, helps me as I eat the bread and drink the cup. Christ's crucifixion, His life in exchange for mine, was the tearing of the veil and the pain felt by the separation of the Father from the Son, the gift of eternal life in Heaven.

Not a day goes by that I am not grateful that Heaven is waiting for me and for those I love most; without the promise of Heaven, I can't bear the thought of my loved ones dying. Because Christ was forsaken, I never have to face the despair of the Father leaving me. I will never yell, *"My God, My God, why have you forsaken me?"* because the Father, the Son, and the Holy Spirit will never leave me, only because Christ endured the Father leaving Him. When all was stripped away, I realized that they, the Father, the Son, and the Holy Spirit, being there with me, no matter what happens, *are my only hope and comfort.* It is an absolute truth that He is here with me. I'm thankful they are so patient with me as I wrestle, chew, and strive to understand their love for me.

May God use whatever He has to draw you close, whispering, *"I will never leave you. I will never forsake you."* May you always remember His *ever-present help* and His great love that came with their great sacrifice, the ripping and tearing apart of the Father and the Son.

To God Be the Glory

Tim Keller is one of my favorite teachers. It was often his voice I listened to in the middle of the night. I replaced my worry and fret with his teaching of truth. Funny, how you can't have two conversations in your mind at once. I lived most of my life before I understood this gift of never being forsaken by God, never separated from the Father. Tim Keller sums it up brilliantly:

> *"Jesus lost all His glory so that we could be clothed in it. He was shut out so we could get access. He was bound, nailed, so that we could be free. He was cast out so we could approach. And Jesus took away the only kind of suffering that can really destroy you: that is being cast away from God."*
> — TIM KELLER (1950–2023)

The Big Lessons

Surviving Suffering—On
a Sticky Note

The other day, a friend called and asked me if I could write down what I had learned during our time of great suffering. She had an anonymous friend who was asking for advice. I immediately pictured a sticky note on a mirror, filled with advice. What a ridiculous thought. A sticky note won't work. I asked if this unknown friend would like to meet to talk about what she was facing, and the answer was no. She did not want people to know about her struggle. That sounds normal for most of us. No one wants to hang out their dirty laundry for others to see or judge. But as days passed, and I was walking and thinking of that sticky note, I thought, *Could I do that? Could I write down how to get through suffering?*

In three years, Ryan had battled two life-threatening cancers, which included conversations about death and surgeries that could cripple him, and descriptions of chemo treatments followed by words of caution: "You will beg your parents to stop, but if you do, you will die." You never forget those kinds of words, ones you never *imagined* hearing in the first place. You don't forget the room, the plastic chair where you sat, or how hard it was to speak. In your lap is a spiral notebook you brought with you; with all the questions you could think to ask. The words go blurry as your eyes fill with tears. Your son sits on the exam table beside you, legs dangling over the edge; quiet—a grown man, but still your little boy. Your breath ceases to enter your lungs, and you tip your head back against the wall, trying to keep your tears from falling. You process words like "crippling surgery" and "death." The questions you prepared no longer matter because you never imagined it could be this bad. The lump in your throat stifles any sound you attempt. How do you survive that?

Sometimes knowing *what* to do is in part knowing what *not* to do. Social media provides a window into the world of millions of people's lives, some sharing details that just a decade ago would go unsaid, because, when you run into a friend at the store, and they ask how you are doing, your response usually includes the word, "Fine. Everything is fine."

One commonly shared statement spoken to those suffering or going through a difficult time is "good vibes." This popular phrase rubs me the wrong way for a few reasons, and I bring it up only because my reason for writing this book is to share what I learned going through "surviving suffering." I never would have chosen

> *Sometimes knowing what to do is in part knowing what not to do.*

to write a book on surviving suffering. I think we've established my plan was, *How can I avoid it?* That said, when I see people asking for *good vibes* or offering their *good vibes* as a viable solution, I cringe—because what can "good vibes" do? What can *my* good vibrations do for another living soul? And what are good vibes anyway, and how many does it take? Are they a modern substitution for prayer? Ryan's cancers put us dead center in front of life and death.

I could not imagine where we would be today if I had counted on "good vibes" to get Ryan or our family through this journey. When I prayed or asked others to pray, I put my faith in God's hands. I counted on Him, trusting Him—the "I am"—Creator of all. I stood on the foundation of faith in God. Some say that they can't believe in a god they can't see, and yet somehow, they can trust in the "good vibes" aka positive thoughts of other fallible humans. When I cried out to Jesus over and over, I knew He was there, and while He may not answer the way I wanted, He was the force I trusted.

> *The disciples woke Him, saying, "Lord, save us! We're going to drown!" He replied, "You of little faith, why are you so afraid?" Then He got up and rebuked the winds and waves, and it was completely calm. The men were amazed and asked, "What kind of man is this? Even the winds and waves obey Him!"*
> — MATT 8:25-27

When I prayed, it was Him, the one who calms the winds and waves. It wasn't my "good vibes," or anyone else's that got me through the fear that rippled through my body. It doesn't mean Ryan will never die or get sick again, but the "I am" is who *I am* trusting.

Cancer is one of those socially understood diseases, where people come running to help, casseroles in hand. But, before cancer, we had already survived what we thought would be our one "big trial of life." *We never imagined we would hear words like we aren't taking her home.* Those are words you never forget, either. While being one of the wildest and more unpredicted events of our life, her arrival was only the beginning of a journey so hard and long and full of loss that we could have never imagined or believed the description of it. We would have argued that it was not possible and that it simply couldn't be that hard. We learned early that diseases of the mind are not as socially acceptable or an understood condition. "Hidden Hurts" mean they don't exist in many people's eyes because they can't see them. I never expected God would allow two cancers after a decade of struggle and sorrow with a soul-injured child. How do you survive *that*?

Anyone who knows me knows it's a good thing I wasn't born in the time of outdoor plumbing. I would not have been a good Laura Ingalls, traveling across the country in a covered wagon. Nope, that's not me. However, Richard, my husband of 34 years, would have made quite a frontiersman. He's the guy you want on your team if you're on *Survivor*. When he thinks about our life since Caelen's arrival, he describes the years with her as the slow and constant uphill climb of the wagons headed west. Every day a slow plodding, a tiring subtle incline. Tall grasses so thick you wade through them like a strong river current pushing against you with all its might, a constant pressure that never lets up. The scenery changing so slowly that it is hard to tell if we are moving at all. There were days, weeks, months so hard; it was as if we left land to cross rivers and lost most of our valuables, but our fatigue was so great we just had to watch it float downstream. We watched our life float away piece by piece.

Exhaustion and defeat make you give up things you never thought you would. You can't hang on to it all. You hang on to what is most important and watch the rest float away. Ryan's battles, unlike Caelen's, were more like crossing the Rocky Mountains, a straight-up climb, where one wrong move could mean the difference between life and death, a fall to the bottom. On both journeys, we just had to survive.

Songs can speak so deeply to your soul. Some lyrics express exactly how you feel, like they are written for you, yet somehow resonate with thousands of other listeners. Rendering a song to hit the charts and be played for years and never lose the impact of the message means you've struck a chord with the masses. "Held," sung by Natalie Grant, is one of those songs, whose lyrics assure me I am not the only one trying to survive. The writer wrestles with the why's and the unfairness of life.

"Why? A thousand times, Why?" Followed by silence. We aren't promised answers. "It's not fair!" Yikes, that thought can consume an entire life. So many don't survive the "not fair" argument. I remember and believe the storybook version of life, that if we do what we ought, we can avoid nightmares altogether, but that isn't true. The promise is to be held by Him, not to be saved from all suffering.

Who shall separate us from the love of Christ? Shall trouble or hardship or persecution or famine or nakedness or danger or sword? As it is written:

> *"For your sake we face death all day long;*
> *We are considered as sheep to be slaughtered."*
> *No, in all these things we are more than conquerors through*
> *Him who loved us. For I am convinced that neither death*
> *nor life, neither angels nor demons, neither the present nor*
> *the future, nor any powers, neither height nor depth, nor*
> *anything else in all creation, will be able to separate us*
> *from the love of God that is in Christ Jesus our Lord.*
> — Rom 8:35-39

If you want a sticky-note version of how to survive suffering, you do it by standing on the promises of God.

> *"Standing on the promises of Christ my king,*
> *Through eternal ages let His praises ring;*
> *Glory in the highest, I will shout and sing,*
> *Standing on the promises of God."*
> *"Standing on the Promises"*
> — RUSSELL K. CARTER 1886

From a Distance

"From a Distance" *by Julie Gold*, sung by Bette Midler, is one of my favorite songs, and the story behind it makes it even more special. As the story is shared on performingsongwriter.com, detailing the life behind the lyrics, Gold was 30, discouraged after being in New York for eight years without any musical success. Her parents sent her a gift, her childhood piano. When it arrived at her tiny New York apartment, she was told she could not play it for 24 hours, as it needed time to settle. Like a good roommate, she doted on her old friend, polishing it and marveling at how well it fit in the corner. After the designated time passed, Gold sat down with her old friend, and "From a Distance" poured out. She is quoted as saying, "On one hand, it took me two hours to write. On the other hand, it took me 30 years. Pick whichever hand makes you happy. I love them both."

Cancer looks different from a distance, and suffering looks different when it's right in front of you and it's all you can see. Out of an airplane window, nothing looks like it does on the ground. The ocean can look like a solid mass of peaceful, still, blue waters, and yet when you're in it, the tiniest of waves just off the beach have the power to knock you off your feet. For our tenth anniversary, we took a vacation to Cancun. We were eating in a restaurant right on the beach. Looking out the windows, we watched this rather round woman, just at the water's edge, fall over in the waves. She got up and toppled over again. Well, she sort of got up, as the waves were dizzying her steps. The more she fell, the funnier it got. As we watched, the waves turned her into a drunken sailor stumbling across the deck of a ship being tossed by the waves of the sea.

Cancer looks different from a distance, and suffering looks different when it's right in front of you and it's all you can see.

The water's power grows just yards from the ocean's edge. Drift to where you can no longer touch, and you wonder where the still waters you saw from the airplane went. The blue mass, laced in white foam that you watched travel up the sandy beach, is now rhythmically crashing over your head; an endless supply of billowy waves blankets you, rolling your body like it weighed nothing at all.

From a distance, when I wake in the morning, I am no longer gasping for air, as if one of those ocean waves had just buried me under all its frothing power. When suffering was so close, it was all I could see; my very first thought in the morning was, "Dear Jesus, please help." Not spoken with audible words, but only a gasp for air, like the cancer itself had just punched me in the gut. Instantly my brain reacted, as it would in an ocean, seeing the next wave above your head about to crash over you. There is no time for thought or strategy. The waves rhythmically come crashing down, no matter what you do. My cry to Jesus wasn't said out of some disciplined habit. I wasn't following a step-by-step guide to walking with Jesus, requiring me to check a box. It was an innate reflex. A cry of "I need you, Jesus! I can't bear this moment alone." Those waking moments were the first time I could honestly say I felt the verse *"as the deer pants for water, so my soul pants for you."* Before suffering, I knew that verse. During suffering, I felt that thirst.

From a distance, the tears aren't as often. My memory and concentration gradually return as my brain slowly makes room for life, replacing survival tactics. It's shocking to be unable to remember something that once was part of your everyday life before cancer. Doctors' names replaced the names of people I worked with. New knowledge, medical terms, different people, and different places moved in. The new occupant was so large, everything else had to go. It is like my old life was put into storage somewhere else. I need to find the boxes where the memories are stored and open them up. I'm afraid the names of some people were permanently lost in the move.

From a distance, I can search my mind and formulate my thoughts for the big lessons that changed me and how I think and live.

When your nose is pressed so hard against an immovable object like suffering, your eyes can no longer see anything to the right or left. *Pride in my self-sufficiency* isn't exactly the thing I imagined God would reveal to me once I had some distance from it. There are many lessons learned from suffering, but I traveled a good distance before I could see the pride of my self-sufficiency that I wore as a medal of honor. My favorite greeting card was a black-and-white photo of a little girl holding up a boulder that I had planned to frame for my desk, before the waves rolled over me. (You might recognize it from the cover of this book.) She didn't just hold up one boulder but a *pile* of boulders on *top* of a boulder. Her body stiffened, arms straightened above her head, elbows and knees locked, she leans forward, hands firmly placed in position, ready to hold up a mountain of boulders for as long as everyone needed her to, for as long as God needed her to.

That was me! *That was how I saw me.* God, what do you need me to do for you today? I could organize and multi-task. Oh, and could I make one heck of a good plan!

"Don't Worry, God—I Got This."—until I didn't.

Until this one wave, a tsunami, hit and washed away my life and my plans. Everything I knew, who I was, swallowed by the frothy water. Nothing looked the same or ever would again.

The number-one response from others who hear that your child has cancer is, "I don't know what I would do if my kid got cancer." I've shared this story with you before but allow me to repeat it for the sake of this lesson. We went to the ER on a Saturday morning. There are some neon moments from that day burned into my eyes. I was at church the following day, meeting a friend who helped me set up "Ryan's Race," his Facebook prayer page. I was not adept at using Facebook back then. We were in the church office, and my head hurt, and all my thoughts were foggy. We sat in a cubicle inside the office, and no one knew we were there. In walked our pastor and another man we have known since before we started our families. Both men have three boys the same age as ours, friends of our sons. As they walked around the office, I heard the number-one response for the very first time. "I don't know what I would do if it was *my* son." The conversation ping-ponged back and forth, with no answers, just frothy turmoil, trying to imagine their response to a nightmare they hoped would never come.

The truth: the only fact about that statement is no one knows what they would do, not even a pastor. They think they do, but until it happens, it's just a plan. That's where our human pride and self-sufficiency appear. When people say, "'I don't know what I would do," the presumed assumption is that there is anything, any plan, you can do at all. Don't go too literal in your mind. Of course, you continue "to do," and the world continues to turn. It's not stopping, waiting to hear you give it the go-ahead. But that is where we go, or at least where I normally would go. *What is my plan?* Or here's a good one, "How will I fix this?"

For the first time, I had no plan, not even the beginning of one. I asked everyone to pray, and that was the end of my plan. Treatment plans were made. Appointments were scheduled, but there was no plan in which I could fix this or see how it would end. There was nothing I could control to change the circumstances. That little girl, so proud that she could hold up those boulders, collapsed to a puddle, no locked elbows, and knees, just a puddle and the *"conversations in the dark"* commenced. Just me and God and—*no plan.*

I've spoken of the moments and days immediately following the discovery of the tumor. So much happened in such a short period, it's hard to believe it was real. But from a distance, a long distance comparatively, I see I couldn't do anything. I couldn't even formulate prayers. I groaned and wept to God. For the first time in my life, I went to Him with *no plan.* Not even a "Could you do it this way?" Now, do you see the pride? I didn't, until I was up in that airplane seat, a long distance from the discovery of the tumor. I had no plan; even if I did, I had no power to change what was happening.

Do you know what follows the number-one statement, "I don't know what I would do if my kid got cancer."? It's "What did you do?" From 30,000 feet, from a great distance, I can honestly say my response was, "God, I have nothing, and I am nothing without You." Had I said those words before? Any respectable Christian has. But inside my head, a place God can clearly see every nook and cranny, I had this one little hidden thought that, well, "I'm not really nothing." I really can do some things without him." Of course, I meant the words, or I wanted to mean the words, "God, I have nothing, and I am nothing without you." All kinds of songs proclaim us to have nothing and be nothing without God; we sing them loudly on Sunday mornings or in our car. But do we really believe that, or are we just singing it because we know we are supposed to believe it?

I'm unsure of my rationale, thinking that God needed me to help execute His plan or to hear my ideas before He decided what to do next. I, of course, believed that God was 100% in control of everything. But somehow, in my mind, I thought I "helped" Him. I would ask for His will in my life, and I wanted it. I knew God's plan was better than mine. I mean, He is God, after all. But I still preferred that He agree with *my plan* or at least consult me. Now, when the following question is asked, "What did you do?" my response is, "I cried to God, because there was nothing I could do." I collapsed into a still puddle because I am nothing without Him.

"Be still and know that I am God."

Swingin' a Hammer

D*idn't I do what you told me to?* This book isn't a book about cancer or mental illness, or brain trauma. It's about how God spoke to me through my most profound and painful struggles, my suffering. I share the memories cautiously, and not nearly all of them; some things are just between you and God, and some are too ugly to repeat. I will say this here but will not elaborate further. About three years into our journey, and after a stout fight with the "system," we had access to documents explaining Caelen's history. The story is heartbreaking, and I hate what she went through, but it explains a lot. Unfortunately, the explanation doesn't change her or her fight to survive. It changes only what we know and how we see her. My hope, and yes, I see the irony in using *that* word, a word I previously struck from my Christian vocabulary, is that what I am sharing helps someone else continue their conversation with God, continue walking with Him, asking Him the hard questions. God changed me and is molding me into a vessel for Him to fill, and it is the hard times that painfully carve out my middle "making room for Him."

That I may know Him and the power of His resurrection,
and the fellowship of His sufferings, being conformed to His death.
— PHIL 3:10

Forgive me for making you jump from story to story and back and forth between time periods. In reflection, I have discovered overlapping lessons between the journeys, things I couldn't see then, things that became clear only by looking over my shoulder. Those verses about sharing in His sufferings didn't mean much to me before. Remember the "D" word—Discipline? Well, there is the "S" word, too—Suffering! Let's just skim over those verses with the *"S"* word. Looking back, I had much to learn before God sent me out to tell people how good He is, with any amount of "street cred." The daily grind of Caelen; that wagon train came long before the Rocky Mountains. It was *hard*. Hot, and freezing cold. I was dirty most of the time, and I hate being dirty, and I still can't see the end of the trail. How can I hope that things will ever change or improve when I see no sign of hope?

Remember "My Utmost for His Highest," January 24th, the day before Caelen arrived?

> *"The vision Paul had on the road to Damascus was not a passing emotional experience, but a vision that had very clear and emphatic directions for him." And Paul stated, "I was not disobedient to the heavenly vision" (Acts 26:19). Our Lord said to Paul, in effect, "Your whole life is to be overpowered or subdued by Me; you are to have no end, no aim, and no purpose but Mine."*

Yeah, there were *lots* of years I skipped reading that week in January. I struggled to reconcile our Jesus front-porch delivery with the reality I saw daily. I could not make sense of it. "Didn't I do what you told me to do?" "Why did you call me here, where I am clearly having no tangible success?" "I'm sacrificing time with my boys, all of my time, to care for her." "Why would you do this to me?" Yep, told ya: "I'm not real pretty in this story." Guess it's from all that dirt on the Oregon Trail!

I gotta believe that Noah building that ark for *one hundred years*, give or take a few, at least muttered something close to the same thing?

Didn't he at some point think *Why did you choose me?* And who makes pink and purple pictures depicting Noah's ark like it's a fairytale? That ridiculous giraffe head sticking out of the ark. Building that ark wasn't an easy ask! I don't think Noah saw anything around him shaded with pink and purple pastels. God said, *"He was pleased with Noah."* Yes, he was saving him, and his family, showing mercy, but *100 years* building an ark for the guy with whom you're pleased? Couldn't ya trick the guys you aren't pleased with into doing the work and then pull a "switcheroo" at the end? You're God. You can do anything!

I haven't even mentioned the ridicule Noah endured. "Rain?" "What's rain?" What's a *flood*?" Okay, the Bible doesn't ever actually say Noah was ridiculed, but if we take just a few moments and think about the state of the world, the depravity, God's plan was to destroy the population of the world with a flood, not because everyone was playing nice, but because of the evil He saw!

> *The Lord saw how great the wickedness of the human race had become on the earth, and that every inclination of the thoughts of the human heart was only evil all the time. The Lord regretted that He had made human beings on the Earth, and his heart was deeply troubled.*
> — GEN 6:5-6

I don't imagine Noah's neighbors came over to share in his labor. I doubt they patted Noah on the back and said, "Love what you're doing with the thing you're building in the backyard" as they all laughed and made the cuckoo motion with their fingers twirling beside their heads.

> *By faith Noah, when warned about things not yet seen, in holy fear built an ark to save his family. By his faith he condemned the world and became heir of the righteousness that is in keeping with faith.*
> — HEB 11:7

We don't really know—or, at least, *I* don't. I'm not a Bible scholar and wouldn't claim to be one, but that verse in Hebrews warning about "things not yet seen," a pretty strong case could be made for rain, a flood, and an ark! Noah had a whole lot more faith than I do or ever will, but in 100 years, don't you think he at least once every decade or so, snuck out back behind the ark and said, "God, did I get those measurements right? Is it really supposed to be this big? And could you repeat the part about the animals one more time? How will that work? That was like 30 years ago, and my memory is not what it used to be. And one more thing, money is kinda tight, and it would really cut down on the amount we're spending on marriage counseling if you could, I don't know, reassure her, send a raindrop or two, assuring her that I'm not crazy."

Preachers and theologians who get wind of my scenario may shout *heresy!* But thinking about what it might have been like for Noah every day swingin' that hammer, listening to the crowd, and his wife's doubting comments repeating in his head makes Noah real. He isn't a made-up character like "Woody" and "Buzz." He was a real man that God was pleased with, and yet He sent him somewhere hard for a long time, a really long time. He gave him a physical task that took a century of discipline to complete. I've never read a Bible verse that said the people in this book are fictitious characters who don't feel the same feelings you do or that they were *holier* back then. They weren't! They were real men and women, just like you and me. I think it helps to think about what it might have been like for them. It was Noah that went on that bender and the naked photos on the internet; those probably weren't in the baby Bible version of the story, but they happened. Okay, not the internet part, but I'm trying to take you to a place that's real. God doesn't call us to be perfect, and the stories in the Bible are full of real, very imperfect people.

And then an entire year living on the ark with all the animals! Did you ever notice that Noah's wife's and sons' wives' names aren't shared in the Bible. I think it's because those women used too many bad words. Four women on an ark for a year with all those animals—I bet they thought to themselves, *None of this was mentioned in the travel brochure that our husbands showed us.*

Yes, I joke, but it's important to remember that, just because it was a long time ago doesn't mean they weren't real people or that the ark magically didn't stink. There is a reason no one spent much time in front of the indoor hippo exhibit at our zoo. It stunk to high heaven! We don't like stinky things! What Noah did was hard. I tried to look to Noah's faithfulness to help me keep going, not to give up. What if Noah had given up? Ever thought of that?

What if I give up? What if you give up?

> *"In Holy fear Noah built the ark."*
> — Heb 11:7 [partial]

In Holy fear, we continue to walk this Oregon Trail, trusting that He has called us to this journey of faith.

You Did Choose Me for This, Right?

When *I quit reading hope verses* and that week in January in "My Utmost for His Highest," I wasn't mad at God—okay, maybe a *little*. I still read the Bible, prayed, went to church, but sang with a little less vigor on the "Here am I send me." I couldn't manage any additional mission trips. This one was lasting much longer than I thought it would. But I quit those things because I couldn't reconcile how God had sent me here. Why did my good God, whose plan is better than mine, do this? Why did you send me *here*?

I started to doubt the happenings of her arrival week. Maybe we heard God wrong. Maybe, this was all one great big misunderstanding, a mistake. I've repeatedly cried to Richard, "What if we get to heaven and God says, "You misunderstood. I never intended for her to land on *your* beach. I had another beach all ready for her with a mother who would have been much better than you." What if He says that? You think I'm joking? Nope, I'm not very pretty in this story. These are real thoughts and conversations, and the only reason I share them is that I think the world is over the perfect-Christian persona or the thought that, if life is hard, then there is no God. I think people need to know it's safe to go to God with everything, warts and all. He already knows your every thought, but He requires that you seek Him. You must invite Him into your life and all its ugliness.

> *Here I am! I stand at the door and knock. If anyone*
> *hears my voice and opens the door, I will come in*
> *and eat with that person, and they with me.*
> — REV 3:20

> *"The vision Paul had on the road to Damascus was*
> *not a passing emotional experience, but a vision that*
> *had very clear and emphatic directions for him."*
> — MY UTMOST FOR HIS HIGHEST, JANUARY 24TH.

What did that just say? *"The vision . . . was not a passing emotional experience."* *"But God had very clear and emphatic directions for him."* *That* is exactly what I asked God for, days before she was delivered. "Please don't let me get caught up in the emotion of this. I can't do this on emotion! This has to be from You. Billboard it for me! Write it in the sky, big and bold." That's pretty close to asking for *"clear and emphatic directions."* He didn't blind me like He did Paul, but I do think He blinded us from seeing what the future would hold, and then He spit her out, right on our beach.

"I was not disobedient to the heavenly vision" (Acts 26:19). Our Lord said to Paul, in effect, "Your whole life is to be overpowered or subdued by Me; you are to have no end, no aim, and no purpose but Mine." And the Lord also says to us, "You did not choose Me, but I chose you and appointed you that you should go . . ."
— JOHN 15:16–JANUARY 24, "MY UTMOST FOR HIS HIGHEST"

I wonder if Paul asked God, "I thought you were sending me to Rome? Wasn't this *Your* idea? Why the shipwreck?" Paul was living it all in real time. We get to study it *from a distance*, the reasons, the miracles, the view from the airplane seat, you know, the calm, solid blue mass of water. I'm sure God's plan, His purpose, became clear to Paul much quicker than it was becoming clear to me, but with all the detours and delays Paul endured, the snakebite, and jail time, did Paul ever ask, "That was *You* who blinded me on the road to Damascus, right? Did I hear you correctly? It was *me* You chose for this?"

I would never compare myself to the apostle Paul or my experiences to his, but those words *"Your whole life is to be overpowered or subdued by Me. You are to have no end, no aim and no purpose but Mine."* In college, I backpacked through Europe with a friend. There's a lot I forgot. But a memory that has never left me, was from a tour of the catacombs in Rome. You know the Roman Colosseum, where the Christians were fed to the lions for sport. We think our world is crazy! In the catacombs was a statue of a woman lying on her side, and the tour guide pointed out that her hand was positioned with three fingers held up in place. The guide explained that these three fingers represented the Father, the Son, and the Holy Ghost. Christian martyrs held their fingers in that position when they were being executed by the Romans, declaring that they would die before denouncing the Trinity. "No end, no aim, no purpose but Mine"—those are some heavy words. What does that look like in real life? In real time? Right now?

Who Is the Clay?

Yet, O Lord, you are our Father; we are the clay, and you
are our potter; we are all the work of Your hand.
— Is 64:8

I *still believe God doesn't want* to leave us broken. He is not an unmerciful God. I look forward to meeting Caelen in Heaven, the Caelen whose mind is not overpowered by trauma and the will to protect herself at any cost. So, all these years, I have read that verse for Caelen, Caelen being the clay. But the more I write and ponder "God sending me here," the more I get that I'm the clay in this story. God is changing me and molding me. I'm not fixing her.

The word which came to Jeremiah from the Lord, saying:

"Arise and go down to the potter's house, and there I will cause
you to hear My words." Then I went down to the potter's house, and
there he was, making something at the wheel. And the vessel that
he made of clay was marred in the hand of the potter; so he made it
again into another vessel, as it seemed good to the potter to make.
— Jer 18:3-4

I think God knew . . . (Well, of course, He did—it is me who's catching up on *His* plan.)

Remember my walks with God . . . In case you forgot, it went like this.

"I remember taking long walks on the dirt roads by our house and I would tell God, 'Give me a story so I can tell people about how good you are.' I wanted to tell how God's plan is always better than mine."

"Give me a story so I can tell people about how good you are."

- God knew that I didn't understand how good He is.
- God knew I would question His goodness if my life got hard.
- God knew I wasn't prepared to tell people how good He is, because, in my mind, His goodness depended on my performance and life's circumstances.

> *But we have this treasure in jars of clay to show that this all-surpassing power is from God and not from us. We are hard pressed on every side, but not crushed; perplexed, but not in despair; persecuted, but not abandoned; struck down, but not destroyed. We always carry around in our body the death of Jesus, so that the life of Jesus may also be revealed in our body. For we who are alive are always being given over to death for Jesus's sake, so that his life may also be revealed in our mortal body. So then, death is at work in us, but life is at work in you.*
> — 2 COR 4:7-12

The Potter knew He had to make me into a different vessel before I could tell His story.

> *"The root of all sin, and therefore our lostness, is grounded in our suspicions that God is not truly good."*
> — OSWALD CHAMBERS

Singing in Chains

When Paul and Silas were thrown into jail under false charges, first, they were stripped and beaten with rods. The jailer was commanded to guard them carefully, so he put their feet in the stocks. If it had been me, I'm sure that the pain from the beating would have been the worst part, but the false charges would have lit me up as well! I'm all about fair. Just sayin'. If it had been me, you can bet the other prisoners would have been saying, "Shut that girl up! We *all* don't belong in here!"

Later that night, Paul and Silas prayed and sang hymns to God as the other prisoners listened, and then there was an earthquake. The earthquake shook the prison's foundations, and the cell doors swung wide open. Despite the open doors, Paul, Silas, and the other prisoners did not escape.

When the jailer awoke and saw the conditions, he was about to kill himself. Paul shouted, *"Don't harm yourself! We are all here!"* In the end, God wrote another thriller. He wove a yarn that only God could. The jailer was saved, his family was saved, and Paul and Silas were freed by the magistrates that had ordered their beating and imprisonment. They escorted them out personally. It turns out magistrates are afraid of a God that can shake the foundation of their prison with an earthquake. Maybe they had heard about the plagues in Egypt of so long ago and didn't want to take their chances with frogs and locusts.

The part about Paul and Silas singing praise to God the Father while in chains is hard to imagine. Part of me has questioned that scene: *Who is this for? Why does God want us to praise Him when we are in chains? We have just been beaten, and* praise *is to roll off our tongues? I used to think this was all for God, and I couldn't reconcile who that God was.* But instead, I believe; God teaches us to praise Him in chains for our own good, for our own comfort. To take our thoughts captive, remind us of who He is and where He sits, and that nothing can separate us from His love.

If Caelen hadn't landed on our beach and Ryan had never gotten sick, I would've skipped over those D and S verses (Discipline and Suffering) and *hoped* God never called on me to wear the irons. I didn't want to have to wrestle with these questions. I was content not to talk about those questions that haunt our minds. Is God truly good? *All the time?*

If He is good, why is there so much evil and suffering in this world? Why doesn't He just fix it?

> *In all this, you greatly rejoice, though now for a little while*
> *you may have had to suffer grief in all kinds of trials. These*
> *have come so that the proven genuineness of your faith—of*
> *greater worth than gold, which perishes even though refined by*
> *fire—may result in praise, glory and honor when Jesus Christ*
> *is revealed. Though you have not seen him, you love him; and*
> *even though you do not see him now, you believe in him and*
> *are filled with an inexpressible and glorious joy, for you are*
> *receiving the end result of your faith, the salvation of your souls.*
> — 1 PET 1:6-9

And . . .

> *Who shall separate us from the love of Christ? Shall trouble*
> *or hardship or persecution or famine or nakedness or danger*
> *or sword? As it is written: "For your sake, we face death all*
> *day long, we are considered as sheep to be slaughtered." No,*
> *in all these things, we are more than conquerors through*
> *him who loved us. For I am convinced that neither death*
> *nor life, neither angels nor demons, neither the present nor*
> *the future, nor any powers, neither height nor depth, nor*
> *anything else in all creation, will be able to separate us*
> *from the love of God that is in Christ Jesus our Lord.*
> — ROM 8:35-39

Not even the lowest places, not even cancer, not even death, not even the ugliness staring back in the mirror, nothing can separate us from God's love. Singing in chains when our soul is beaten down by the struggles of this life, God shows us by the examples of Paul and Silas, that the praises we sing *aren't just for God*—they are to bring *us* comfort, as we face death all day long.

> *Let them give thanks to the Lord for his unfailing love*
> *and his wonderful deeds for mankind.*
> *Let them sacrifice thank offerings*
> *and tell of his works with songs of joy.*
> — Ps 107:21-22

But Mine Died

I*t's late as I begin this, or for some, it's early.* Time is a fluid abstract element that is part of our everyday life. Depending on where you are and what you are living through, life can sometimes feel unbearable, and at other times, you never want this time to end. When you are experiencing the joys of life, engagements, wedding celebrations, anticipating that baby on the way, watching a child hit a ball and make it to first base for the first time, time is something you hang onto when life is good. When life is good, you never want the good to end.

"LIFE IS GOOD." I bought one of those t-shirts sometime after my engagement and my wedding, probably a good few years after those early anniversaries. Honestly, those first few years of getting used to how incredibly different you are from your spouse and wondering how you missed all this before saying, "Yes to the dress," well, they can be rough. Maybe that's another book, but, for now, we'll stick with "LIFE IS GOOD." So sometime after the proposal, wedding gown, baby showers, and probably right around the time when Little League was in full swing, I bought my first and only "LIFE IS GOOD" shirt. I'm a pragmatist, and you need only one "LIFE IS GOOD" shirt. If you start wearing a "LIFE IS GOOD" shirt more than one day a week, I think there is a crowd out there that would like to punch you in the mouth until you tone down your happy-go-lucky mantra. I bought a hat, too. Hats somehow are more subtle. You can get away with wearing a "LIFE IS GOOD" hat more than once a week. I don't know where I rank the tire covers. Family stick-people stickers are more than I need to know about you as I sit at an intersection waiting for the light to change. So, I'd say decorating your car with a "LIFE IS GOOD" tire cover is a little much.

I am trying to remember if it was on the wagon trail or crossing the Rocky Mountains when I threw the t-shirt and the hat away. Donating is my normal repurposing of an unwanted or a no-longer-useful item, but the "LIFE IS GOOD" shirt and hat, in an act of defiance, they deserved to go straight to the garbage dump. I was condemning them to death. The hat had hung on a hook in my closet, taunting me. I wondered when I could ever wear it again and not feel like a liar. So, to the grave, they went!

Rick Warren (his wife is Kay) is the pastor who wrote *The Purpose Driven Life* in 2002; 50 million copies have been sold, and the book has been translated into 85 different languages! Do you think maybe people are looking for a purpose? In 2013, Rick and his wife Kay, lost their son, Matthew, who had struggled with depression and mental illness since early childhood, to suicide. I wrote down this quote somewhere on the second Rocky Mountain crossing. Kay Warren said, "She unabashedly pursued hope." And then he died. I wrote that down not because I could make the same claim but because I stood in awe of that statement. She went all the way to the wall, ran full speed toward *Hope,* and then he died. That's the part we pretend can't happen or don't talk about, death, or the ending we never imagined happening. It could be divorce, estrangement from family, or loss of self, due to addiction. It's an ending we wouldn't write for ourselves. Running toward Hope when you know in the back of your mind he could die, will die at some point. We all die eventually. Will my Hope die, too, if God doesn't do what I ask? It's the running toward Hope that requires Jesus. You can only "Unabashedly pursue hope" when you have Jesus. Without Him, you lose your nerve every time, because without Him, there is no real hope.

I've known I had to write this part of the story for some time now. It's not an easy part of the story, and without the Hope of Jesus, I couldn't write it with any honesty. It would be like wearing that "LIFE IS GOOD" hat and not believing it. I don't like to lie or pretend I'm something I'm not. I would be a horrible poker player. I've debated how to title this, because, in my head, the title that always comes to mind is *harsh*. It's like running full speed toward Hope and discovering Hope is a concrete wall disguised as something soft. It's called, "But mine died." Whether it's a parent, spouse, or child, death is a reality of life. It could be, "But mine divorced me"—the scenario of the ending is a harsh reality you can't fix, and you question surviving it. It could be, "mine isn't better," "mine is still sick," or "mine no longer speaks to me"—all unbearable.

When Ryan was first diagnosed with Ewing's, I joined a Facebook group for parents of kids who had Ewing's. It's such a rare cancer that it has parents from all over the world, and the group is still relatively small. It wasn't long before I asked the question all parents ask eventually, "Does everyone die? Does anyone survive this?" All but one child we "knew" when we started this battle has died; many fought it more than once and then died. Talk about hitting a concrete wall. The answers from my fellow Facebook group came back, "If your child survives, then the parent leaves the group. It's too painful to stay and continue to relive the memories even if your child lived." So, the impression to those in the group is that everyone dies. It is for that reason I've refused to leave. It has been seven years this month since Ryan received his last treatment for the first cancer, Ewing's sarcoma. I stay in the Facebook group so I can say, "Yes, my son survived. Don't lose hope. Life returns. It doesn't look the same, but it can return." Because I stay, I also see the farewells of the parents. It is the parent of the child who dies that says goodbye. In a sorrowful paragraph, the parent says farewell and exits a group they never wanted to be part of, only to enter a new group they never get to leave, the grieving-parent group.

Our home is covered in pictures. I hang only the images that bring me joy just by looking at them, a memory of a time gone by that I hope will never fade. It might be a professional shot, a picture of a cowboy, a baseball player, or an Easter-morning photoshoot on the front porch, but they are there. The photos on the walls, their faces staring back from all stages of life, evokes this plea to God, "Please don't make me look at these pictures without him." I *can't* write a chapter titled "but mine died" or "how I survived my child's death." I got as close to that edge as you can get. Twice. I got to the point both times when I said, "Don't keep him here for me. If he will suffer his whole life like this, don't do it for me." That is the closest I got to death.

Having children changes your life forever. Losing a child too soon changes you forever. I won't attempt to write and pretend to understand how a grieving parent feels, but I have gotten close enough to it to know that no matter what stage of grief you are in, you never, ever stop missing that child. You never look at those pictures on the wall the same. It's a safe bet that grieving parents are not a large portion of the "Life is good" customer base. I think there is a market for "Heaven will be awesome" t-shirts. Or maybe it's "Don't worry, Heaven rocks this earth." I think we'd all be better off if we talked more about Heaven and a little less about surviving life on Earth. Not that surviving on Earth is bad, or that I would wish my life or my children's lives to end, just having Heaven more in mind as the actual end game, the place we truly belong.

"Heaven Is for Real" is the story of 4-year-old Colton Burpo, who slips away to Heaven during an emergency surgery. When he returned to consciousness, he reported seeing what was happening in the operating room as his spirit hovered above, and he was no longer medically alive. Telling how he met his unborn sister, which he hadn't known about. He tells about his great grandpa, called Pop, whom he had never met. Like a man dying of thirst, the world consumed this story like a tall glass of water on a hot day. This $12-million low-budget film had a $3.7 million opening weekend, beating out "Captain America—The Winter

Soldier" and grossing $101 million worldwide. The book was a *New York Times* bestseller and sold 11 million copies in its first year. As appealing as Captain America is to so many, with a not-too-shabby gross of $74 million, it is still not as compelling as a little boy's account of Heaven, telling of things he could not have known unless Heaven was for real.

"Unabashedly pursuing hope"—I'm not sure I do that, even today. "Unabashedly pursuing" is a hard sprint toward something without caution or fear. I think I *jog* toward Hope *with my hands out*, fearful of a potential crash into a concrete wall, where my Hope might not survive. I still struggle with keeping my *Hope in God*, not how He does or doesn't answer my prayers. I still struggle to remember it's my Hope in God, not my ability to fix something or someone. While our circumstances with Caelen are not about facing the death of a child, they are very much about surviving a life here without a lot of Hope of her changing dramatically.

How do you keep hoping when nothing is changing? No amount of Hope will bring a child back to life. Finding Hope in these unchanging circumstances is a battle of wills. Will I be able to keep my eyes on Heaven, on Him? Will I keep my faith? Will my anger and grief consume me? Will I lose all Hope?

> *Brothers and sisters, I do not consider myself yet to have taken hold of it. But one thing I do: Forgetting what is behind and straining toward what is ahead, I press on toward the goal to win the prize for which God has called me heavenward in Christ Jesus.*
> — PHIL 3:13-14

"In this life you will have troubles" (Jn 16:33 [partial]). This is non-negotiable. Some survive unimaginable pain, the kind we write about and make movies about. Horatio G. Spafford is my go-to example for this. He was a wealthy Chicago businessman who lost his son to pneumonia in 1871 and much of his business the same year. Two years later, his wife and four daughters were traveling across the Atlantic to meet Horatio

in Europe, when their ship sank, and all four daughters were lost at sea. The stories behind the hymns that were written centuries before my birth have a much deeper meaning when I know why the author penned those words. "It Is Well with My Soul" becomes an entirely different act of worship when you know that Horatio wrote those words while traveling the same journey across the Atlantic. Some of the most profoundly touching words seem to be written in the most excruciating times.

> *"The things that hurt instruct."*
> — BENJAMIN FRANKLIN

Horatio Spafford had no idea how many fellow Christians would sing, "It is well, with my soul," weeping with him and with the Hope of Christ. I had never heard this quote before, but I think sharing it is critical. "Another of the ship's survivors, Pastor Weiss, later recalled Anna, Horatio's wife, saying, 'God gave me four daughters. Now they have been taken from me. Someday I will understand why.'"—St. Augustine.com

Just because Horatio was faithfully obedient to cling to his Savior during his deep suffering and pour out his soul in such a touching and honest verse does not mean that the days ahead of them on this Earth were without pain and doubt. Horatio and Anna clung to God and each other, pressing on toward the goal of Christ Jesus, clinging to their only Hope, but it is essential to realize that those days that they remained on this Earth did not pass without pain and sorrow.

"Christ in me" means something quite different from the weight of an impossible ideal, something far more glorious than the oppression of a pattern forever beyond all imitation. *"Christ in me"* means Christ bearing me along from within, Christ the motive-power that carries me on, Christ giving my whole life a wonderful poise and lift and turning every burden into wings. All this is in it when the apostle speaks of *"Christ in you, the hope of glory."* (Stewart, *A Man in Christ*, pg. 93)

Thank God Heaven is for real!

Prepare to Be Surprised

T*he day the doctor took out Ryan's port* for the first cancer, the verse from my daily devotional, "Jesus Calling," was the verse used on his Facebook Prayer page, "Ryan's Race." Ryan's favorite verse, *his life verse*, how fitting.

> *"Consider it pure joy, my brothers and sisters, whenever you face*
> *trials of many kinds, because you know that the testing of your*
> *faith produces perseverance. Let perseverance finish its work so*
> *that you may be mature and complete, not lacking anything."*
> —JAS 1: 2-4

"Whenever" means *every or any time*, and trials, as in *more than one*—many. The question *isn't* whether trials will come—it is what you will do *when* they come. My conversation with God continued, to

> *However, I consider my life worth nothing to me; **my only aim***
> *is to finish the race and complete the task the Lord Jesus has*
> *given me—the task of testifying to the good news of*
> *God's grace.*
> — ACTS 20:24

The words "my only aim" ring a bell? From January 24th, "My Utmost for His Highest." *"Our Lord said to Paul in effect,*

> *"Your whole life is to be overpowered or subdued by Me; you*
> *are to have no end, no aim, and no purpose but Mine."*
> *"We are inclined to look on our Lord as one who assists us*
> *in our endeavors for God. Yet our Lord places Himself as*
> *the absolute sovereign and supreme Lord over His disciples."*
> — MY UTMOST FOR HIS HIGHEST

Oh, yeah. Let that one sink in: So guilty of thinking of God as my personal assistant.

"Hey, God—I've got this great idea . . . could you help me out with it?" "I'd like to write a book about how good you are. Could you keep life perfect so I can do that?"

"My only aim" continues with,

> *"Go therefore and teach all nations" . . . He says,*
> *"Go on the revelation of My sovereignty, teach and*
> *preach out of a living experience of Me."*
> *"Teach and preach out of a living experience of Me."*

It has been my desire to be a speaker and author for more than two decades. The problem was I didn't know what I would write and talk about. *Slight problem.* I knew it would be about God, and I had all kinds of ideas (Well, of course, I did! You know that about me by now!), experiences, and lessons, even a few miracles, but the story never came. I started writing said "book" more times than I would like to admit. My computer is full of false starts, and I have yellow legal pads full of notes. I would sit down, write a page, maybe two, then . . . nothing . . . *crickets*. No story. I had a wonderful life, and God was the foundation of that life, but before I walked through my own trials, ones I had no solution for, it was only what I *thought I knew about God*, mixed in with more doubts than I realized. I could repeat what I knew about God from others, but I'm not smart enough to be a commentator on God's word, and I didn't want to be the Howard Cosell of the Christian life. In case this reference ages me, and you're thinking *"Howard Who?"* here's some context and a little humor from our story. When Ryan was an inpatient at MD Anderson for Cancer number one, the pediatric floor we stayed on was donated by George Foreman. One day Ryan was in the hall with a nurse, and Ryan commented on the placard displaying his name on the wall. The nurse replied, "Oh yeah, the grill guy." Ryan chuckled and said, "Or the two-time *Heavyweight Champion of the World.*" Well, Howard Cosell comes from the era when George was a boxer, not the grill-guy. Either way, Howard Cosell was a famous sports commentator; here is what *Wikipedia* says: "Cosell was widely known for his blustery, confident personality. Cosell said of himself, "I've been called arrogant, pompous, obnoxious, vain, cruel, verbose, a showoff. And, of course, I am." *This* isn't how I would describe myself, but writing a book on how *good* God is without experiencing trials in your life, well I can see how the reader *would think* I was arrogant, pompous, obnoxious, vain—well, you get the picture.

"*Go teach. Go preach. Out of your experiences with Me, the Sovereign God.*"

"The missionary is constantly tempted to overcomplicate the missionary task. We forget that the Great Commission is a call for the proclamation of the gospel—nothing less. This is more relevant than ever in our trying cultural setting."—Charles Spurgeon, 1861. Oh, my—what would Spurgeon say about 2023?!

> *What I tell you in the darkness, speak in the light; and what*
> *you hear whispered in your ear, proclaim upon the rooftops.*
> — MATT 10:27

I never wanted to write a book about our journey with Caelen. *I wasn't qualified; I wasn't pretty in the story,* nor did I have a viable solution to share. I didn't set out to write a book when Ryan got sick. I had no plan, no aim. My suffering poured out of me. *I couldn't keep it in.* It was too painful and a burden too heavy to carry alone. I simply wrote about what God was teaching me in the dark, what I heard Him whisper in my ear. I proclaim this because I want to share God's true goodness, even when life is really bad. I cannot keep it in! Proclaiming God's goodness is His gift to me in the middle of the worst suffering of my life. I never thought you'd send me here. I never knew what treasure I would find.

"Thus, writing requires a real act of trust. We have to say to ourselves: 'I do not yet know what I carry in my heart, but I trust that it will emerge as I write.' Writing is like giving away the few loaves and fishes one has, trusting that they will multiply in the giving. Once we dare to 'give away' on paper the few thoughts that come to us, we start discovering how much is hidden underneath these thoughts and gradually come in touch with our own riches."
— SEEDS OF HOPE, AUGUST 25

It was no surprise, to me anyway, that I was *not* one who would sing praises while in chains, and to be clear, I'm not bragging about my honed skills in the clinker still today. I've learned my lesson. I have never been a candidate for God's poster child on suffering well. I never even made the list of candidates. He knew I understood singing praises during suffering in theory only, and that was shaky, at best. I wanted to believe I could do it. I wanted to be "Prison Mike" singing in the middle of "prison-hard," (Thank you, again, Steve Carell, for making us laugh when I wasn't sure we ever would). I, of course, wanted to please Him, but I think we both knew there was this place where I doubted his goodness.

—Prison—Suffering—Sickness—Hard.

Before Cancer . . . Life had been moving along, not particularly joyfully. I repeated, *"This is the day the Lord has made, I will rejoice and be glad in it."* (Ps 118:24) I said it over and over again through clenched teeth. Coping with Caelen's struggles weighed me down. It had been a long, hard, dirty journey, and we had lost a lot along the way. We were alone, isolated in our disappointment and dismay, trudging down a path with no end in sight and no hope.

And then . . . *Cancer.* Ryan has cancer! *Equilibrium*, anyone?

Let's take a breath here . . . let that soak in. Your child suffering, fighting for life, soaks you to your bones. It seeps out at night, saturating you in fear.

Truth, I never imagined God would allow more struggle into our lives. The wagon trail was hard enough on its own. Isn't there some spreadsheet up in Heaven where some heavenly accountant—like maybe Matthew, a tax guy (he must love Excel), is keeping track of all of our struggles? Isn't somebody keeping track of the amount of suffering being deposited in my account? Shouldn't we be sharing the wealth? I did not see cancer coming. I don't think anyone saw cancer coming.

—January 25th "My Utmost for His Highest"

"No matter how well we may know God, the great lesson to learn is that He may break in at any minute. We tend to overlook this element of surprise, yet God never works in any other way. Suddenly—God meets our life ". . . when it pleased God. . . ."
"Keep your life so constantly in touch with God that His surprising power can break through at any point. Live in a constant state of expectancy and leave room for God to come in as He decides."

In addition to Caelen's surprise delivery, it was through Ryan's cancer battles that God broke in and overtook my life with an element of surprise when it pleased Him. God taught me the *Why?* of singing in chains, considering it *joy* when facing trials was for my *own* good, not His.

"Your whole life is to be overpowered or subdued by Me; you are to have no end, no aim, and no purpose but Mine."

Keeping my focus on Him, *praising* Him for what He has done, *dwelling* on His promises to me . . . *Proclaiming* them publicly—that was all God's *gift* to me. It was how He *saved* me from my thoughts of fear, sorrow, and hopelessness. Keeping our eyes on Him is how he saves us all from hopelessness.

"Leave room for God to come in as He decides" and prepare to be surprised!

Cling Tightly

Revelation—"a fact disclosed or revealed especially
in a dramatic or surprising way"
— DICTIONARY.COM

Y*ep*, dramatic, surprising; *that fit Caelen's delivery* and Ryan's cancers—
utter shock on both. We tried to answer the call on our life with Caelen
using much of our own strength and understanding, believing Christ
had given us this journey, and assuming it meant we could do it. Moses
felt a call to save his people from a life of slavery, but God didn't allow
that to happen until He sent him on a long journey.

"God allowed Moses to be driven into empty discouragement.
Sending him into the desert to feed sheep for forty years."
— MY UTMOST FOR HIS HIGHEST

Empty discouragement: Been there. Lived there. Still do sometimes.
Moses's 40-year desert walk was all *before* leading the Israelites out
of Egypt, through the wilderness, to the Promised Land for an additional 40 years.

"At the end of the first 40 years, God appeared to Moses and
said to him, '. . . bring My people . . . out of Egypt.' But
Moses said to God, 'Who am I that I should go . . . ?'"
— EX 3:10-11

"In the beginning Moses had realized that he was the
one to deliver the people, but he had to be trained and
disciplined by God first." (That doggone "D"word causes
lots of long walks!) *"He was right in his individual*

perspective, but he was not the person for the work until
he had learned true fellowship and oneness with God."
— My Utmost for His Highest

I never quit believing Jesus was the delivery man who carried Caelen up our front-porch steps, at least not completely, but I walked in the desert, and still do. I get emptied out and I ask Him, "Who am I that I should go?" Actually, I revert to "Why me? Why choose me? I'm just like her. I'm just like Caelen." He is still and always will be changing me for the work ahead. Lopping off chunks of clay and sending me on long walks in the desert.

"True fellowship and oneness with God" are clearly a priority to Him. Moses, one of God's greatest, the one *He* selected for the monumental job of leading His chosen people out of captivity, had to walk in the desert so he could *learn true fellowship* and oneness with God. A couple of things stand out about this detail, one, that it took Moses forty years before God determined that Moses *knew* Him, but even more important is how much God desires us to be as *one with* Him. It's a relationship with you that He desires. *"Look! I stand at the door and knock. If you hear my voice and open the door, I will come in, and we will share a meal together as friends."* (Rev 3:20) From the beginning to the end, God is desiring that fellowship with us.

"We may have the vision of God and a very clear understanding
of what God wants, and yet when we start to do it, there comes to
us something equivalent to Moses's forty years in the wilderness.
It's as if God had ignored the entire thing, and when we are
thoroughly discouraged, God comes back and revives His call
to us. And then we begin to tremble and say, 'Who am I that I
should go . . . ?' We must learn that God's great stride is summed
up in these words—'I AM WHO I AM . . . has sent me to you'
(Exodus 3:14). We must also learn that our individual effort for

God shows nothing but disrespect for Him—our individuality
is to be rendered radiant through a personal relationship
with God, so that He may be 'well pleased' (Matt 3:17)."
— MY UTMOST FOR HIS HIGHEST

Those words, "well pleased," make me think of Noah and the Ark, in whom God was "well pleased." I think of Job and how God said, "Have you considered my servant Job?" (Job 1:8), followed by unimaginable suffering we still talk about today. "Well pleased" meant something different in our home. As a mom, "Well pleased" meant *dessert* in our house, *not desert.* In case you mix those two up, I'd always opt for two desserts (2s's) vs one desert (1 s). God sends those He loves on long desert walks that empty us out of ourselves, our selfish ambition to please God on our own strength, holding up boulders and such, with one hand tied behind our back, proclaiming, "Don't Worry, God—I Got This." A long desert walk is different than what we expect from God when He is "well pleased." I expected dessert, maybe a nice double scoop of Baskin Robbins, Rocky Road, and Jamoca Almond Fudge, or a homemade chocolate cake with chocolate buttercream frosting, *not* the desert!

The direction given by Jesus in Matthew 28 is to teach
and preach, but it starts with "Go on the revelation
of. . . My sovereignty." "Go" simply means 'to live.'"
— MY UTMOST FOR HIS HIGHEST

I think what struck me was the revelation, the surprise, the dramatic shock of Ryan's cancer(s) that set me on the path, the journey to understanding the "Revelation of God's Sovereignty." We can all say, "God is sovereign" with confidence when "Life is Good," but do we believe it in the dead of night wrestling with fear and doubt, feeling helpless in our own strength, and hopeless that anything will ever change? Can I say it then? Can I say God is sovereign then?

God's absolute power controls our goings. He tells us to *Go. Preach. Teach.* Do this out of our *living experience.* We don't pick the locations or the events, *He does.*

> *"If you abide in Me, and My words abide in you . . ."*
> *(John 15:7)—that is the way to keep 'Going.' Where*
> *we are placed is then a matter of indifference to us,*
> *because God's sovereignty engineers our 'goings.'"*
> — My Utmost for His Highest

> *"And you shall be made witnesses to me in all these places."*
> — Acts 1:8 (partial)

These places, the places God chooses to send you. "Here I am, Send Me!"—MercyMe

Yes, God—make me a witness! Please let me sing backup!

"Can I get a witness? Yeah!"—Nicole C. Nordeman

"If you abide in me" sounds easier than it is . . .

Our humanness takes over, drowns Him out with all our great ideas and expectation for dessert, not desert, and the next thing you know, abiding isn't really what you're doing—it's more like you're just "hanging out" with your assistant, named God, hoping your plans work out. Anyone? Anyone?

Until . . .

Until God delivers you to a place you never imagined, a place you wouldn't tell your worst enemy to visit, a place so feared that there are simply two choices, "Believe and Abide in Him" or "Bail and Deny Him."

What delights God is clinging to Him, abiding in Him. I didn't do it out of a desire to perform, execute a "how-to-survive-suffering, strategy," or a striving out of my own will, hoping to avoid trials by following the "be good" rules I created in my head. In the end, I did it because where God had brought me, *clinging* to Him was the only thing that *could save me.* It's not more complicated than making that choice to *cling.*

We are to *"Go on the revelation of My sovereignty, teach and preach out of a living experience of me."* The story isn't *my* story, the story is *God's story* written on my life. *Your life, too.*

Singing praises in prison serves as a reminder to me of who He is, His power, His love, His presence in every part of my life, and that He has already won this war. Singing praises *is for me*, as it strengthens me with every word of His promises, and, at the same time, it pleases Him, as we cling tightly to our *only Hope.*

And while I was clinging to Him, He revealed His sovereignty, another big Bible word that I thought I understood but didn't. He is absolutely in charge of it all. All. I think we'd like to think somehow God was just distracted when something bad happens. When our kid gets sick, He must have been looking the other way? Bad things are happening, happening every second, and much of this life's suffering we will truly understand only once we are in Heaven, and thank God it is for real! Sometimes God sends you somewhere hard. Sometimes hard just happens. Either way, He is sovereign. He is still in charge.

> *"Difficulty is actually the atmosphere surrounding a miracle,*
> *or a miracle in its initial stage. Yet if it is to be a great miracle,*
> *the surrounding condition will be not simply a difficulty but*
> *an utter impossibility. And it is the clinging hand of His*
> *child that makes a desperate situation a delight to God."*
> — STREAMS IN THE DESERT

A Miracle: Something which leads to something out of and beyond themselves.

I never want to forget how hard this was or is. How utterly impossible this journey was! If I deny or forget it will only steal from His glory.

God delivered me to a place where I was completely dependent on Him; I was clinging to Him, in the middle of my desperate situation, clinging tight. I can't help but think of three-year-old Caelen pinching my pinky between her thumb and finger, *refusing* to grip my hand. How much I wanted her to trust me enough to cling to my hand tightly, to feel her whole hand firmly pressed in mine, trusting me, clinging to me.

"And it is the clinging hand of His child that makes a desperate situation a delight to God."

A delight to God, *my clinging hand in His hand,* in my desperate situation. How long had I been willing to only pinch His pinky versus cling tightly to the hand of God?

Choose to cling tightly, to believe and abide, and be ready for where He sends you.

To God be the Glory.

Epilogue

The Chapter We Never Imagined

A*s I write this epilogue,* I question, does anyone even read an epilogue? Isn't the story over?

When I submitted my transcript for professional editing, I never imagined what would happen next. Never. I thought our cancer journeys were over. I had cancer myself the summer before and didn't even consider adding it to the story. It seemed more like a case of the flu in comparison to Ryan's battles, how could I mention it? When I wrote the last chapter, "Cling Tightly" my book was done. Eight years of writing, editing, and an ocean of tears, it was a long labor and I begged God not to waste a single tear. I had major doubts about binding these words together and birthing them into the world, and then the unimaginable happened, four days after I submitted my transcript Ryan received his 3rd cancer diagnosis on August 1st, 2023. Acute Myeloid Leukemia. His MDS we battled before, returned with a vengeance manifesting itself in full-blown leukemia. We were crushed. No, that's not the word. I can't adequately describe the level of hurt we felt. In the entry titled "No Words" I shared about a mom telling me she had been in the hospital for a year with her baby, "For all the words in the English language, synonyms and antonyms, adjectives and adverbs, there is no version of "I'm sorry" or punctuation that will suffice." and there are no words in any language sufficient to describe our heartbreak.

Ryan was five years post-transplant and the doctors had said he was at the edge of the woods, almost out of them! He had completed college after having to quit twice, was accepted to the University of Kansas Medical School for their physical therapy program and graduated in May of 2023. Late July he started his first job as a Physical Therapist and Ryan and Jennifer bought their first house. I was showing Jennifer the ropes of painting a closet and we were finally living the life we weren't sure we'd live. I can't leave out that Caelen had also graduated high school. That was a herculean accomplishment! Cooper and Jackson had graduated college. We were breathing again, and I was handing over my book to a professional to have them tell me if my writings had any worth. The first half of 2023 we were living and then we were dying.

I canceled my book four days later. None of this matters anymore! I reinstated my book four days after that. It did matter.

Ryan didn't want to return to Houston, who would? I don't want to go to Houston to die. I thought those words that make time stand still were over and then I heard the worst words of all. Not a warning from a doctor, but fear spoke out of his mouth. Does he think he is going to die? Remember Dr. GGM? It took a phone call from him to get Ryan on a plane to Houston. Thanks to some generous people, a private jet flew us down. Ryan was too sick to fly commercially. Admitted immediately, the nightmare that had been so hard to put to bed was awake and screaming, "Look at me! Look at me!" The "Why's?" and disbelief, haunted me at all hours of the day and night smothering me in grief and despair. Again Lord? Again?

So of course, true to form, I commenced my mental wrestling matches with God. However, this time I had very little energy for a fight. This time, I just cried. This time, Jennifer was in the hospital full time, and they asked that I stay with them in Houston as a support. Most days it was just me and God. Once again, He cleared my calendar, and we went for a long walk.

"Prepare To Be Surprised," didn't I just say that a few pages ago? It was hard to find comfort in anything, I'm pretty sure I wrote about that. Peace was just as tough and the "Beef Jerky" of joy still didn't taste good. I was distraught in my sorrow. The loss this time, somehow was greater than before. Before, cancer just took our life away. This time, cancer took the life we had fought to have, away. It stole something we had learned was far more precious than we realized.

> *"Life is hard. It takes something harder than life*
> *to make you thankful you get to live it."*
> — CATHY RAMSHAW

(My friends call me Cathy; I'm assuming if you made it to the epilogue, we are friends by now.) That quote, I learned that wisdom through many tears.

So, what did I do? How did I survive? I read my own book.

After reading it, I am amazed at both the lessons and the wisdom, so much so I can only say to myself "I did not write this book." I am not that clever or capable of weaving the two incredibly complex stories of Ryan and Caelen together in such a way they could be comprehended. I also couldn't arrange the lessons together in the logical and progressive order they came. I wrote no outline. I wrote no main idea. I had no title. Truth, I wrote to survive. I couldn't have made it without seeking God's voice. So that leads me to conclude if I didn't write it that means God did. Between the two of us, my money is on God, as the author.

God whispered His words into my ears in the darkness and He said shout the lessons from the rooftops and that's what I did.

I can't write that the words of this book are the inspired words of God. The outrage spoken by the masses if I said that would be hard to endure and I'm not telling you I climbed Mount Sinai and walked back down with two tablets in hand, with my face glowing. But I am saying there is no way I wrote this book and artfully learned and communicated these lessons without a Teacher. How do I know? I went back through every verse, every sentence, and every word with the opportunity to change the letters on the page as I watched the unimaginable happen a third time. It was my chance to say this isn't true and I didn't change a thing. Once again, I would not write cancer into my life story, if I was the author. That mysterious verse, "And we know that in all things God works for the good of those who love Him, who have been called according to His purpose."—Romans 8:28 I don't think we will ever truly understand how this works, because we can't fathom the mind of the Lord.

Without suffering there is no darkness in life and God whispers His wisdom in my ear in the darkness, not in the light. Statistics say that faith in God is declining in America. People, consumed with access to instant information that they hold in their hand for a shocking number of hours in a day, are all too busy to seek God's wisdom. Some believe they are their own god or can be if they download this app. In cancer battle #3, the overreaching lesson was "Without faith, it is impossible to please God." How long had I stood under that boulder without the hope of my life circumstances changing, executing all the plans I could come up with, trying to make my life work out? Somehow in all this effort I had missed that without faith, it's impossible for me to please God. Can't I just be a good little Christian and follow the rules? Do I have to exercise my faith in You? I was trying to please Him, by doing it myself. My plans, my vision of "happily ever after" with Caelen, after happily ever after had long since evaporated, depleting me of that hope I had in God. Okay, hope in me.

> *"Now faith is the confidence in what we hope for*
> *and assurance about what we do not see. This is*
> *what the ancients were commended for."*
> — HEB 11:1-2.

David didn't fight the battle against Goliath because of his confidence in himself, he fought because of his confidence in the Lord.

"You come against me with a sword and a spear.
I come against you in the name of the Lord."
— I SAM 17:45 PARTIAL

How many times had I heard those words read to the boys at bedtime and missed it wasn't David's *good aim* at the giant's head that killed the Goliath? *It was the power of the Lord.*

"You'll remember, friends, that when I first came to you . . .
I was unsure of how to go about this and felt totally
inadequate—and so nothing I said could have impressed you
or anyone else. But the Message came through anyway. God's
Spirit and God's power did it, which made it clear that your
life of faith is a response to God's power, not to some fancy
mental or emotional footwork by me or anyone else."
— I COR 2:1-5 (THE MESSAGE, PARTIAL)

God's wisdom *"is not popular wisdom, the fashionable*
wisdom of high-priced experts that will be out-of-date
in a year or so. God's wisdom is something mysterious
that goes deep into the interior of his purposes."
— I COR 2:6-7 (THE MESSAGE, PARTIAL)

Those words, "mysterious—deep interior of His purposes." They are striking because after months of sorrow, a sequel to *transplant #1*, changing his blood type yet again. Pain. Suffering. I couldn't help but wonder if God was out of miracles. Would He allow this journey we thought was turning into life to end in death? It felt cruel. And then the deep interior of the cell revealed itself and God revealed His plan to us.

"Do you want to know why your first transplant failed," asked Dr. GGM. It was top on the list of my commonly asked questions. "Of course, we do!" Nothing beyond the beginning of this conversation presented to us on December 18th, 2023, will be in quotes and please remember, for good reason, I didn't pursue my medical career. With that in mind, brace yourself for the *"deep interior of His purposes."*

Medical advancements are in a transformative era and since Ryan's 2017 diagnosis with the help of new technology doctors are seeing into the molecular level, an even more microscopic genetic view of the cell. You might even call it the "mysterious deep interior." All this microscopic talk wasn't part of the conversation in 2017 because doctors couldn't see it, yet. But had they been able to see the "deep interior" of Ryan's cells they would have seen a genetic mutation, a cancer gene called the MECOM. The MECOM marker comes with some frightening statistics on the surface —*one, being a four to five-month survival expectancy.* At this point, I gasped, as the shocking failure of *transplant #1* became the shocking miracle that it worked at all and lasted five years and four months. (No, I didn't miss the obvious correlation of the MECOM survival numbers compared to Ryan's. God's power turned them on their head!) Had the eyes been able to see the deep interior of the cell in 2017, the treatment protocol and timeline would have sped up to try to keep up with what the doctors knew about the MECOM. Instead, we had a celebration, a wedding. Ryan walked the hard journey to recovery and didn't look back for five years and four months. The timing of cancer diagnosis #3 felt nothing short of cruel. He worked six days in a profession that took ten years to get to. The house they never slept in would sit empty as we faced what felt like a Giant we couldn't defeat.

Ryan reached remission with one seven-day-round of chemo and sixty days after arriving in Houston a new donor with a new blood type was ready and the battle commenced. His body worn from two cancer battles was not recovering or responding the same. It was harder and longer before Ryan emerged on the other side. His first biopsy after *transplant #2* revealed 100% engraftment of the new donor, something they said had a 25% chance of working.

Because in August of 2023, the new technology could see into the molecular level of the cell, they compared the sample to the cells of 2017 revealing the presence of the MECOM marker in both samples. The chemotherapy given to Ryan before *transplant #2* targeted the MECOM and the Giant took a deathly fall to the ground.

Because there is no more MECOM marker in your latest biopsy, I would expect a 95–98% chance this disease never returns.

The chapter we never imagined revealed a battle the Lord had been fighting in the "mysterious deep interior" that man could not see.

> *"No, we declare God's wisdom, a mystery that has been hidden*
> *and that God destined for our glory before time began. None of*
> *the rulers of this age understood it, for if they had, they would*
> *not have crucified the Lord of glory. However, as it is written:*
> *"What no eye has seen,*
> *what no ear has heard,*
> *and what no human mind has conceived"—*
> *the things God has prepared for those who love him—*
> *These are the things God has revealed to us by his Spirit.*
> *The Spirit searches all things, even the deep things of God.*
> — I COR 2:7-10

Choose to cling tightly, to believe and abide, and be ready for where He sends you.

To God be the Glory.

About the Author

Catherine Ramshaw dreamed of writing a book about how good God is and how His plan is always better than hers, but it wasn't until her life's journeys took her to places she never thought God would allow, that she learned how truly good He is and how mysterious His plan is. Catherine shares the conversations she had in the dark with God when life skidded to a halt, no longer looked like life at all and when God's plan no longer looked better than what she had envisioned. Learn what treasures were found as she intimately shares the questions she asked when her good God no longer looked like the God she thought she knew.

This 52-week journal provides additional scripture and questions to ask God in your own darkness, as you seek to draw closer to Him and feel the strength of the Holy Spirit.

Go to CatherineRamshaw.com for more details on where to order the companion journal.

Notes

He Shelters Our Eyes

1. Cowman L.B., "Streams in the Desert", 1996, Cowman Publications, Inc., and Copyright @ 1996 by Zondervan, Grand Rapids Michigan

I Can't Feel Your Peace

2. Smith, Michael W. & Strasser, David. "Step by Step." *Worship Again*, Universal Music Brentwood Publishing, 2002.

Hurricane

3. Crowder, David & McMillan, John Mark. "How He Loves," *Church Music*, Sixsteps, 2005.

4. JR Macduff—August 28th. Cowman L.B., Streams in the Desert, 1996, Cowman Publications, Inc., and Copyright @1996 by Zondervan, Grand Rapids, Michigan

Give Me a Story

5. Millard, Bart, Mercy Me. "I Can Only Imagine." *Almost There*, Pete Kipley, 2001.

6.   *I Can Only Imagine.* Directed by Erwin Brothers and written by Alex Cramer, starring Michael J. Finley and Dennis Quaid, Lionsgate and Roadside Attractions, 2018.

7.   Millard, Bart, Mercy Me. "Here I Am Send Me." *Almost There*, Pete Kipley, 2001.

Ever Pleasant Help

8.   Cowman L.B., "Streams in the Desert," 1996, Cowman Publications, Inc., and Copyright @ 1996 by Zondervan, Grand Rapids, Michigan

9.   Cowman L.B., "Streams in the Desert," 1996, Cowman Publications, Inc., and Copyright @ 1996 by Zondervan, Grand Rapids, Michigan

10.   Cowman L.B., "Streams in the Desert," 1996, Cowman Publications, Inc., and Copyright @ 1996 by Zondervan, Grand Rapids, Michigan

11.   McDonald, George, "Man's Difficulty with Prayer," *The Works of George McDonald, 1824–1905*

Your Hands Made Us All

12.   Lucado, Max, Grace for the Moment, 2000 J. Countryman, a division of Thomas Nelson, Inc., Nashville, Tennessee

13.   Chambers, Oswald, "My Utmost for His Highest, an Updated Edition in Today's Language, 1992 Oswald Chambers Publications Association. Ltd original copyright 1935 by Dodd, Mead & Company, Inc.

Our Beach

14. Chambers, Oswald, My Utmost for His Highest, an Updated Edition in Today's Language, 1992 Oswald Chambers Publications Association. Ltd original copyright 1935 by Dodd, Mead & Company, Inc.

Adopted by God

15. Lucado, Max, Grace for the Moment, 2000 J. Countryman, a division of Thomas Nelson, Inc., Nashville, Tennessee

And they lived happily ever after

16. Cleveland Clinic, Reactive Attachment Disorder (RAD), 2022. My.clevelandclinic.org

I do it!

17. Van Der Kolk, Bessel, M.D., *The Body Keeps Score*, 2014, Viking Press.

18. Young, Sarah, *Jesus Calling, Enjoying Peace in His Presence*, 2004 Thomas Nelson Inc., Nashville, Tennessee

I Thought You Told Us to Go Here

19. Hillsong United, Houston, Joel, Crocker, Matt, Lighthelm, Solomon. "Oceans, Where My Feet May Fail." *Zion*, Hillsong Capitol CMG, 2013.

Life Is Good?

20. Young, Sarah, *Jesus Calling, Enjoying Peace in His Presence*, 2004 Thomas Nelson Inc., Nashville, Tennessee

Is Everything Going to Be Okay?

21.   Casting, Crowns, Herms, Bernie, Hall, Mark, West, Matthew. "Just Be Held." *Thrive*, Beach Street and Reunion Records, 2014.

Peace Out of a Drive-through Window

22.   Howarth Lemmel, Helen. "Turn Your Eyes Upon Jesus." Glad Songs 1918, Gospel Truth in Song, Clarke, Harry, 1924.

Suffering Was the Plan

23.   Brooks, Garth, Arata, Tony. "The Dance." *Garth Brooks*, Capitol Nashville, 1989.

24.   Hackett, Vernell 2020, "soundslikenashville.com Citing "Playboy" magazine interview, 1994

Thou Shut the Door Upon Me

25.   Cowman L.B., "Streams in the Desert", 1996, Cowman Publications, Inc., and Copyright @ 1996 by Zondervan, Grand Rapids, Michigan (April 4th and 5th)

Singing Backup

26.   Battistelli, Francesca. "If We're Honest." *Write Your Story*, Word Entertainment and Fervant Records, Eskelin, Ian, 2014.

27.   Mullen, Nicole C. "Can I Get a Witness." *Talk About It*, Mulle, David, Niebank, Justin, Mullen, Nicole C., Word, 2001.

God Showing Off

28.   Hudler, Rex, 2008, "*Splinters*" Rex Hudler 2008

Whisper the Name of Jesus

29. Gaither, Bill & Gloria. "There's Just Something About That Name." Gaither, Bill, 1970.

What Do You See?

30. Payne, Keith, 2013, "Your Hidden Censor: What Your Mind Will Not Let You See," *Scientific American*. June 11, 2013

31. Zinczenko, David, 2011, "Eat This, Not That!" Galvanized Media, 2011

Shekinah Glory

32. Crosby, Fanny. "He Hideth My Soul." 1890.

You Don't Wear Mascara to a War Zone

33. Stead, Louisa M.R., Kirkpatrick, William J. 1882 "Tis So Sweet to Trust in Jesus," Steads Song of Triumph

Natural Killer Cells

34. It is believed that the lyrics of "Joshua Fit the Battle of Jericho" was or were written by slaves but copyright by Jay Roberts in 1865.

Surviving Suffering on a Sticky Note

35. Carter, Russel K. "Standing on the Promises." 1886.

From a Distance

36. Gold, Julie. "From a Distance." 1985 performingsongwriter .com June 16, 2015

Swingin' a Hammer

37.   Chambers, Oswald, My Utmost for His Highest, an Updated Edition in Today's Language, 1992 Oswald Chambers Publications Association. Ltd original copyright 1935 by Dodd, Mead & Company, Inc. January 24th Devotional

You Did Choose Me for This, Right?

38.   Chambers, Oswald, My Utmost for His Highest, an Updated Edition in Today's Language, 1992 Oswald Chambers Publications Association. Ltd original copyright 1935 by Dodd, Mead & Company, Inc.

39.   Millard, Bart, Mercy Me. "Here I Am Send Me." *Almost There*, Pete Kipley, 2001.

But Mine Died

40.   Warren, Rick, "The Purpose Driven Life", 2002, Zondervan.

41.   Burpo, Todd, Vincent, Lynn, 2010, Sony Pictures, 2012, *Heaven Is for Real*

42.   Spafford, Horatio, 1873, "It is Well with My Soul," St. Augustine. com, October 16, 2014

43.   Stewart, Stuart, James, 1935, Regent College Publishing, "A Man in Christ," 1935

Prepare to Be Surprised

44.   Young, Sarah, *Jesus Calling, Enjoying Peace in His Presence*, 2004 Thomas Nelson Inc., Nashville, Tennessee

45.   Chambers, Oswald, My Utmost for His Highest, an Updated Edition in Today's Language, 1992 Oswald Chambers

Publications Association. Ltd original copyright 1935 by Dodd, Mead & Company, Inc.

46.   Holloway, Terese, 2010, "Seeds of Hope," Creation House 2010

47.   Carrell, Steve, Gervais, Ricky, and Stephen Merchant, "The Office" Season 3 episode 9. November 30, 2006

48.   Chambers, Oswald, My Utmost for His Highest, an Updated Edition in Today's Language, 1992 Oswald Chambers Publications Association. Ltd original copyright 1935 by Dodd, Mead & Company, Inc.

Cling Tightly

49.   Chambers, Oswald, My Utmost for His Highest, an Updated Edition in Today's Language, 1992 Oswald Chambers Publications Association. Ltd original copyright 1935 by Dodd, Mead & Company, Inc.

50.   Cowman L.B., "Streams in the Desert," 1996, Cowman Publications, Inc., and Copyright @ 1996 by Zondervan, Grand Rapids, Michigan

Bible Versions and Translations Used Throughout the Book

1. New International Version
2. New Heart English Bible
3. New Living Translation
4. New Revised Standard Version
5. Modern English Version
6. The Voice
7. God's Word
8. New American Standard
9. King James Version
10. Amplified Bible
11. Legacy Standard Bible
12. Major Standard Bible
13. Christian Standard Bible
14. New International Readers Version
15. BibleGateway.com. Created by: Nick Hengeveld 1993. Owned by: Gospel Communications (1995-2008). Zondervan (2008-present)
16. Quest Study Bible June 1978. New International Version, Colorado Springs, Colorado

17. YouVersion Bible.com app. Created by Bobby Gruenewald and Life.Church 2008. Sponsored by David Green